# ADAM MICKIEWICZ

# FOREFATHERS' EVE

TRANSLATED BY
CHARLES
S. KRASZEWSKI

This book was published with the support
of the Hanna and Zdzislaw Broncel Charitable Trust

**GLAGOSLAV PUBLICATIONS**

# FOREFATHERS' EVE
by Adam Mickiewicz

Translated by Charles S. Kraszewski

This book was published with the support
of the Hanna and Zdzislaw Broncel Charitable Trust

This book has been published with the support
of the ©POLAND Translation Program

Cover art features a keystone from
the Wawel Castle in Kraków carved about 1390

Publishers
Maxim Hodak & Max Mendor

© 2016, Charles S. Kraszewski

© 2016, Glagoslav Publications, United Kingdom

Glagoslav Publications Ltd
88-90 Hatton Garden
EC1N 8PN London
United Kingdom

www.glagoslav.com

ISBN: 978-1-91141-400-1

A catalogue record for this book is available from the British Library.

This book is in copyright. No part of this publication may be
reproduced, stored in a retrieval system or transmitted in any form or by
any means without the prior permission in writing of the publisher, nor
be otherwise circulated in any form of binding
or cover other than that in which it is published without a similar
condition, including this condition, being imposed
on the subsequent purchaser.

# ADAM MICKIEWICZ

# FOREFATHERS' EVE

ADAM MICKIEWICZ

1798 – 1855

## Introduction

Adam Mickiewicz (1798-1855) is the national poet of Poland. He was a born writer, successful in each and every genre he attempted. His lyric poems, collected in *Ballady i romanse* [*Ballads and Romances*, 1822] ushered the Romantic movement into Polish literature with the same élan as Wordsworth/Coleridge's *Lyrical Ballads* in the British Isles. His *Sonety miłosne* and *Sonety krymskie* [*Erotic* and *Crimean Sonnets*, 1826] form one of the most accomplished cycles in that demanding form since Petrarch. The great Italian is palpably present in many of the former, while the latter, short, descriptive works of jewel-like perfection, are matched only by DuBellay's Roman sonnets. One must wait until the twentieth century — the poems of Robinson Jeffers, and Albert Camus' *Noces* come to mind — for similarly evocative renderings of nature and history.

His narrative poems, *Konrad Wallenrod* (1828) and *Grażyna* (1823) reveal his sustained mastery of longer poetic genres, and his epic in twelve cantos, *Pan Tadeusz* (1834) is universally recognised as Poland's national epic, as well as the last Vergilian epic written in Europe. His quasi-Biblical *Księgi narodu i pielgrzymstwa polskiego* [*Books of the Polish Nation and Polish Pilgrimage*, 1832] put the anglophone reader in mind of a more practicable William Blake. With their socially and politically-applied Christianity, Mickiewicz had an appreciable influence on the thought of his friend, Lammenais. Finally, his *Cours de littérature slave professé au Collége de France*, delivered during his exile in Paris, and published posthumously in 1860, is one of the first balanced and comprehensive accounts of the Slavic traditions in literature and culture to meet Western eyes.

Greatest of all his works, however, is *Dziady* [*Forefathers' Eve*], the monumental four-part drama begun in the early 1820s, and brought to a conclusion some ten years later. While based on contemporary Polish history — especially the oppression of Poles in the Russian Partition of the country — the work rises above national particularism to address general human themes, such as the interpenetration of the worlds of spirit and matter, the imperative of free will and the responsibilities enjoined thereby upon the individual, and the role of the individual in both the human collective and the Communion of the Saints. Influenced by both Johann Wolfgang von Goethe and Dante Alighieri, in *Forefathers' Eve* Mickiewicz succeeded in creating a truly universal work of literature that appeals to men and women of all nations, traditions, and times.

"Literature is news that STAYS news,"* said Ezra Pound. It is *Forefathers' Eve* that assures Mickiewicz a place in the ranks of the "great Europeans" like Goethe and Dante, Shakespeare and Eliot, among those described by Pound in *The Spirit of Romance*:

> All ages are contemporaneous. It is B.C., let us say, in Morocco. The Middle Ages are in Russia. The future stirs already in the minds of the few. This is especially true of literature, where the real time is independent of the apparent, and where many dead men are our grandchildren's contemporaries, while many of our contemporaries have been already gathered into Abraham's bosom, or some more fitting receptacle.**

To paraphrase George Steiner, the greatness of a book can also be measured by how often a mature culture returns to it, re-reads it, reinterprets it, and itself, in its light. The character of Gustaw/Konrad enjoys in Polish theatre the mythic stature of Hamlet in the English world. When an actor is cast in this role, he knows that he has "made it." But it's not just about aesthetics. Throughout its troubled history, Poland has looked to Mickiewicz and *Forefathers' Eve* to give expression to its yearnings and sorrow. The play was staged, and banned, under Soviet pressure, as late as 1968 for its perceived anti-Russian commentary, and the great anti-epic of the Solidarity movement, Stanisław Barańczak's *Sztuczne oddychanie* [*Artificial Respiration*, 1979] is a palpably bitter inversion of its great-souled hero.

Indeed, although as we shall see *Forefathers' Eve* is addressed to and appreciable by men and women of all times, the play springs from a very concrete time and place: the Lithuanian marches of the old Polish Republic, which in 1795 had been completely swallowed by the Russian Empire. It is only right that we shall concern ourselves first with Polish readings, and

---

\* Ezra Pound, *ABC of Reading* (New York: New Directions, 1960), p. 29.
\*\* Ezra Pound, *The Spirit of Romance* (New York: New Directions, 2005), p. 6.

re-readings, of the play. Still, it must be borne in mind what Albert Camus said about particularism and universalism in the context of the French-Algerian crisis of the mid-twentieth century:

> Some prefer the universal, to the detriment of the particular. Others, the particular to the detriment of the universal. But the two of them go together. In order to discover human society, it is necessary to go by way of national society. In order to preserve the national society, it must be considered from a universal perspective.[*]

And so we begin.

### THE NATIONAL CONTEXT

Adam Mickiewicz's *Forefathers' Eve* is the most important text of Polish Romanticism. Seen through the prism of what the Romantic period — indeed the entirety of the nineteenth century — means to Poland, it is not too much to say that *Forefathers' Eve* is the most important text of Polish literature, period. Part III — that segment of the four part dramatic epic that most speaks of, and to, the political and ontological aspirations of Poland — was composed in the early 1830s, a period known in Polish history as the Partitions. For various reasons, including the rather widespread and anarchic republicanism of the old Polish Kingdom, Poland, which during the Renaissance had been the largest territorial entity in Europe, had been whittled down progressively by three surrounding empires — Russia, Prussia, and Austria — until in 1795, it disappeared completely from the political map of the world.

It was not always thus. Since its baptism in 965, Poland had been a significant player in the politics that shaped the modern European continent. It cooperated with the eastern politics of the Holy Roman Empire, while never being subsumed into it, and constituted what some even now fondly refer to as the "bulwark of Christianity" in the east. It played a major role in the expansion of Christendom into the northeast (converting the last pagan people of the continent, the Lithuanians, in the late Middle Ages), and consistently beat back the territorial pretensions of

---

[*]   Albert Camus, *Actuelles III: chroniques algériennes 1939-1958* (Paris: Gallimard, 1994), p. 20.

the Islamic Ottoman Empire in the south-east. In 1683, it was a Polish army, under King Jan III Sobieski, that turned the tide at the siege of Vienna, and defeated a Turkish army whose threat to Christian Europe was the most serious since that overcome eight centuries earlier by Charles Martel at Poitiers. Gustaw, in Part IV, reminisces about reenacting this battle with his childhood friends. The Polish kingdom successfully addressed challenges from Christians as well: subduing the German Teutonic Knights in Pomerania, and keeping the rising power of Muscovy in check. At one point, Poland occupied Moscow and imposed its own candidate upon the Tsarist throne. (The national Russian holiday of November 4, "Unity Day," celebrates the expulsion of the Polish troops from Moscow in 1612, which brought the "Time of Troubles" to an end).

Whether, or how much of the blame for Poland's shipwreck may be lain on the Poles themselves, the subjugation of this once fairly powerful nation to the Germans and Russians was a shock to the national consciousness. Germanisation and Russification, of varying insistence and intensity, added to the humiliation, and stiffened the national resolve to remain Polish, in spite of it all. At a time when the nation was deprived of political autonomy, the role of the poet took on a special eloquence. Paraphrasing Percy Bysshe Shelley, in the Poland of the Partitions, the poet became the acknowledged legislator of the people. Poles of all three partitions looked to Adam Mickiewicz (especially) and his colleagues Juliusz Słowacki and Zygmunt Krasiński — the so-called *trzech wieszczy* ["three bards"] for aid, not only in the perpetuation of the national language and literary traditions, but also for guidance in political and metaphysical matters.

The Partitions would last over a century: from 1795 until the reestablishment of the Republic of Poland following World War I in 1918. During that time, a number of writers, such as the historical novelists Józef Ignacy Kraszewski and Henryk Sienkiewicz, painters like Jan Matejko and Artur Grottger, musicians like Frédéric Chopin and Henryk Moniuszko, would keep the national traditions alive in times that otherwise did not bode well for the continuing viability of the Polish consciousness. To understand the seriousness of the threat one need only glance across the southern border into Bohemia. Germanisation had progressed so far in the Czech lands since the battle of Bilá Hora (1620), that knowledge of Czech had well-nigh completely disappeared from the educated classes by the time of the *národní obrození* [national revival] of the Romantic Age. Three hundred years on from their national catastrophe, the Czech romantic poets had to reconstruct their national tongue from the speech of the peasantry, with a heavy infusion of Polish and Russian loan-words.

Yet although all of the above-mentioned Polish artists were respected and heeded by their compatriots, none of them approached the authority of Mickiewicz, and among Mickiewicz's writings, none was more important in this context than *Forefathers' Eve*. No work of literature or art was more readily acknowledged as an outpouring of the suffering, patriotic Polish soul than Scene II of Act III, the so-called Great Improvisation. As we shall see when we come to discuss Part III, the Great Improvisation is the epitome of the nationalist strain of Polish Romanticism. The shaman-like hero, Konrad, imprisoned by the Russians, launches into an inspired accusation of God Himself for the situation in which innocent Poland finds herself. Half Job, half Manfred, Konrad's great soliloquy is the touchstone against which all thoughts of independence and political autonomy are proven.

As is the case with all foundational texts, the manner in which *Forefathers' Eve* in general, and the Improvisation* in particular, are understood, coopted, and exploited, is directly relatable to the character of the period in question, or the temper of the group or individual receptor. This was already noted, with perspicacity, in 1905 by Stanisław Tarnowski, rector of the University of Kraków:

> What is this? "Blasphemy, impiety, challenging God," said these; "The sense of one's power, the consciousness of one's genius, extended to the very last boundaries of boldness and pride," said others, who adored the openness and limitless daring of greatness; still others saw in the Improvisation its patriotic side alone, and in the poet, such an avenger of the fatherland as fears not even God Almighty, and calls Him before his own judgment bench [...] Everyone made of the Improvisation something of their own; they stretched it to cover their own impressions and thoughts,

---

\*       The soliloquy is called an Improvisation, because Mickiewicz was modelling it on the popularity of improvised poetic performances popular in XVIIIth-XIXth century Europe. As Wacław Borowski points out, even the varied metre of the Great Improvisation, as well as its tone, which alternates between tight, inspired poetry and looser, more prosaic lines, indicates the conscious shaping of the soliloquy on that model. Cf Borowski, *O poezji Mickiewicza* (Lublin: Towarzystwo Naukowe KUL, 1958), vol. II, p. 113.

suggesting, imposing their own ideas upon it; everyone saw in it what they wanted to see; everyone had his own Improvisation.*

Thus Tarnowski, writing with the *sang-froid* and objectivism of a conservative in the generally calm Austro-Hungarian city of Kraków, in that Partition which accorded Poles the most autonomy. It is worthwhile to note Tarnowski's even-handed assessment of the reception history of *Forefathers' Eve*. What he writes of Poles in the nineteenth century, can also be applied to Poles of the twentieth, whose political situation, until 1989, was not dissimilar to that of their ancestors during the Partitions. For after the short-lived honeymoon of virtual peace, stretching from the end of the First World War in 1918 until the outbreak of the Second (on Polish territory) in 1939, Poland was once more to be partitioned: this time, on September 17, 1939, between Nazi Germany and Soviet Russia. Following the war and the Yalta Agreement, so fatal to Eastern and Central Europe, Poland was to be submerged once more into the Russian sphere of influence, her autonomy strongly curtailed, subjected to the imposition of a foreign political system — atheistic communism — which differed from that of the Tsar in both quality and intensity.

Yet *Forefathers' Eve* continued to be used, and abused, by Poles of all political stripes eager to "impose their own ideas upon it." Like the Bible, which, as the common saying goes, can be used to prove anything, so Mickiewicz and his *Dziady* were invoked, now by communists, as a "progressive" work, foreseeing the triumph of the proletariat, and now by anti-communists, rallying around Mickiewicz and his work as proto-dissidentism.

The former tendency can be illustrated by a 1947 essay by Julian Przyboś who, besides being a talented avant-garde poet in his own right, was by turns anarchist, socialist, and communist:

> No, the third part of *Forefathers' Eve* has never been a normal read for me. It is a mad, hectic work — rebellious, revolutionary, striking at the foundations of the world of tyranny and crime — it will never be for me a mere aesthetic experience. The cries of pain and anger, and vengeance, mix in with, and drown out, the harmonious

---

\* Stanisław Tarnowski, *Historya literatury polskiej*.(Kraków: Spółka wydawnicza polska, 1905), Tom V: Wiek XIX, 1831-1850, pp. 18-19.

angelic choirs. From beneath the clouds of religious decoration, from beneath the angelic flowers, emerge and flash again and again the stiletto and battle-axe of the avenger.*

Thus a Pole writing in the darker days of Stalinism, which, like many others, he actively supported, whether out of conviction, or fear — a member of a college of "bards" enunciating a message of liberty quite different from that underwritten by the *trzech wieszczy*, Mickiewicz, Słowacki, Krasiński.

Communist, state-supported readings of Mickiewicz and *Forefathers' Eve* continued in Poland as long as Soviet bayonets propped up the unpopular system of "popular democracy." As late as the early eighties of the last century, this is how the work was presented to high school students, via the officially sanctioned textbook on Romanticism:

> Mickiewicz created a work in which he expressed both the state of his own personal feelings and the drama of his oppressed nation [...] The spiritual transformation of Gustaw into Konrad constitutes as it were the key to understanding the chief idea of the play. It possesses the eloquence of a symbol. For it signifies the overcoming of a personal crisis in the name of the fatherland, to which Part III of *Forefathers' Eve* is dedicated [...] Konrad [...] becomes the representative of his oppressed nation and the spokesman of its deepest desires [...] *Forefathers' Eve* Part III initiates a new chapter in the development of literature following the 1830 Insurrection. It introduces us into the sphere of the most significant problems of the contemporary life of the nation. Although it refers to happenings from before the November Uprising [of 1830], it forces one to meditate on the contemporary situation and on the tasks which confront modern generations of Poles. In a different way, and on different levels, the images of martyrdom it presents remind us of our duty to our fatherland.**

---

\*    Julian Przyboś, "Około *Dziadów*," in *Czytając Mickiewicza* (Warszawa: Rytm, 1998), p. 131.

\*\*    Helena Starzec, ed., et al. *Romantyzm: Literatura polska dla klasy II liceum ogólnokształcącego oraz techników i liceów zawodowych* (Warszawa: WSP, 1974), pp. 97, 99-102.

In this way, *Forefathers' Eve* becomes a paedagogical tool for "meditating" on what one owes to the state — in this case, the communist Polish People's Republic.

Yet just a few short years before this, in the year of revolution that was 1968, Mickiewicz and *Forefathers' Eve* introduced a different set of problems into the contemporary life of the nation. That was the year in which the theatrical director Kazimierz Dejmek realised *Forefathers' Eve* on stage in Warsaw in a way that — whether it was intended or not<sup>*</sup> — was seen to challenge the continued Russian dominance of Polish political life, and, by extension, the communist system then in place, and the Party which ruled Poland on behalf of Moscow. As Kinga Olszewska writes:

> The authorities saw Dejmek's *Dziady* as a provocation, since it deals with the issue of Russian imperialism and the colonization of Poland during the partitions of the eighteenth century. The authorities recognized that the staging of *Dziady* would have a negative impact on relations between Poland and the USSR. The intellectuals saw the withdrawal of *Dziady,* one of the most significant works of Polish Romanticism, as an attack on the essence of national tradition and a negation of historical circumstances, in which Russia was an aggressor.<sup>**</sup>

Under Soviet pressure, the government ordered the production shut down only two months after its November premiere, and this led to even greater unrest among students, who took to the streets, until repressed by the government police forces, and "spontaneous" anti-demonstrations of workers carrying signs reading "Students, Back to your Books!"<sup>***</sup>

---

\*       Dejmek was a member of the Polish Communist Party (PZPR). Supposedly, the production was to be in honour of the fiftieth anniversary of the Soviet Revolution. He was subsequently drummed out of the Party, and lost his job at the National Theatre in Warsaw.

\*\*       Kinga Olszcwska, *Wanderers Across Language: Exile in Irish and Polish Literature of the Twentieth Century.* (Oxford: Legenda, 2007), p. 29.

\*\*\*       And "Zionists to Israel!" The fracas surrounding *Forefathers' Eve* provided the government with an opportunity to purge its ranks of "Zionists." Deprived of their Polish citizenship, many Polish Jews emigrated to Israel in forced successive waves that depopulated the traditional Jewish population of Poland even more, following the systematic Nazi ethnic cleansing of the war years.

Here we certainly come into contact with the universal eloquence of *Forefathers' Eve*. Mark Kurlansky is perfectly correct when he states, "to stage *Dziady* in Warsaw was no more controversial than a production of *Hamlet* in London or Molière in Paris."\* Whether or not the play can be read, or manipulated, into a propaganda piece for or against communism, the thing that should concern all of us is the ability of a government to oppress the free speech of the stage, out of its panic about what it might mean."As Adam Michnik comments: "The decision to close the play was proof that the government was stupid and did not understand Poles. Mickiewicz is our Whitman, our Victor Hugo... It was an outburst of communist barbarism to attack Mickiewicz."\*\*\*

In the same year that the above-cited high school textbook was printed, Stanisław Barańczak began work on *Sztuczne oddychanie* [*Artificial Respiration*], an anti-epic describing the impossibilities of individual action, even in a quest to save oneself, in a totalitarian society like the Polish People's Republic. That poetic cycle is somewhat of an intentionally negative image of *Forefathers' Eve*. It too was repressed by the government.\*\*\*\* Barbaric or not, it is the fate of great works of literature to stir people so deeply, as to be adopted by them, and used as cudgels against the opposition, as if their creators had been members of the organisation in question *avant le mot*. It is testimony to the greatness

---

\*  Mark Kurlansky, *1968: The Year that Rocked the World* (New York: Random House, 2005), p. 73.

\*\*  There are different ways in which texts are controlled. Concerning the London that Kurlansky refers to, the *London Evening Standard* of 23 February 2015 ran a story about Mark Rylance, who reports that "he has had to remove parts of Shakespeare's plays because they are 'anti-Semitic.'" In the un-bylined article, he continues:"I don't think there's pressure (to remove) the bawdy jokes. He's bawdier a lot more times than people realise. The pressures I feel are more for times where he will say something very antisemitic. I have to make the decision, do I include that or not. There are some very unfortunate antisemitic things that characters say.If a character says it, it doesn't mean the author means it but since the holocaust ... these statements have a lot more resonance now than they did at that time." He does not say whether he is self-censoring the unnamed passages in plays he directs, or whether the "pressure" he felt he was under was applied from an outside source.

\*\*\*  Kurlansky, p. 76,

\*\*\*\*  It was passed around in Poland, in typescript. It was eventually published by the Polish emigré press Aneks in London, in 1978.

of the greatest literary works that they can be adopted and brandished by folks of mutually inimical political camps. That is certainly the case of Mickiewicz's *Dziady*. The communist Przyboś asserts that the "revolutionary" nature of Part III is a rallying cry for the progressive, marxist camp. Anti-communists have used the same text as a hammer against Russian hegemony which, in its Soviet guise no less than its Tsarist, exerted a stifling influence on Polish autonomy, culture, and free expression. No matter what the card-carrying Party member Kazimierz Dejmek intended with his fateful production of *Dziady*, perhaps the Party members who over-reacted in pulling it from the stage felt a real, and not imagined, threat to their vicarious rule of the country? For how eloquent, in the context of the imposed, foreign rule from Moscow, in the context of 1969 and 1989, are the words with which Mickiewicz begins his introduction to Part III:

> For half a century now, Poland has been the scene of such ceaseless, unflagging, inexorable cruelty at the hands of the tyrants who oppress Her, and such illimitable devotion and endurance on the part of Her suffering peoples as the world has not seen since the days of the persecuted Christians.

It matters nothing that Mickiewicz wrote those words in 1832; no one can stop the twentieth century reader from smiling wryly, and making appropriate connections with his or her own situation.

Indeed, the communists got as good as they gave, as far as Mickiewicz is concerned. In 1989, Tadeusz Konwicki produced his cinematic adaptation entitled *Lawa* [*Lava*], from a key scene in Part III. As Małgorzata Terlecka-Reksnis points out, there is no doubt about Konwicki's intention in filming this work in the dying days of Polish communism: "[Konwicki's *Lawa* is], for us masses of common people, a certain type of artistic *summa*, a consideration, through the matrix of *Forefathers' Eve*, of our experiences of war and communism."* Writing in the *Kwartalnik filmowy* in 2002, Barbara Głębicka-Giza concurs:

---

\*       Aleksandr Fiut, et. al. *Kompleks Konwicki: materiały z sesji naukowej zorganizowanej w dniach 27-29 października 2009 roku przez Wydział Zarządzania i Komunikacji Społecznej UJ oraz Wydział Polonistyki UJ* (Krakow: Universitas, 2010), p. 318.

In his adaptation, Konwicki intended to illustrate his conviction concerning the contemporaneity of *Forefathers' Eve*. Through his introduction of the character of the old Poet, who it seems was to symbolize the writer himself, he obtained the effect of a universalization of the play.*

To speak more precisely, in the case of Konwicki — as in that of so many others — we have an author/interpreter taking conscious advantage of the universal appeal of Mickiewicz's play, which is pre-extant to his artistic machinations. It is the universal nature of *Forefathers' Eve* which allows artists like Konwicki to exploit the text for the particular statements, political and otherwise, which they wish to make. The somewhat iconoclastic Jan Walc puts the matter in an interesting, if not altogether sympathetic, context when he writes thus of how subsequent generations have understood *Forefathers' Eve* in a manner consistent with their own beliefs and world views:

> Part III of *Forefathers' Eve* is a work from the crossroads. It was written in mid-road between Vilnius and Paris, worked up from contradictory lines and scenes, without beginning or end; it is as difficult and unclear as the Polish situation itself; it constructs a true, archly Polish synthesis from a great variety of false details. It is a work that prompts the strangest interpretations. It is at bottom incomprehensible, and yet still vibrant after one hundred and fifty years.**

Most people familiar with *Forefathers' Eve* would take issue with much of what Walc asserts in this passage; I certainly do. What he sees as contradiction and unclarity is the — at times clumsy — breadth of vision and Romantic openness to the inexplicable that gave rise, ultimately, to a new form of drama: Polish Monumental Drama, which unapologetically confounds time with eternity, but always tends to a moral order which is far from incomprehensible. It is this openness and breadth, which we also

---

\*      Barbara Głębicka-Giza "'DOLINA ISSY', 'LAWA' i 'KRONIKA WYPADKÓW MIŁOSNYCH'. O autorskiej twórczości TADEUSZA KONWICKIEGO" in *Kwartalnik Filmowy* 44 (2002), p. 203.
\*\*      Jan Walc, *Architekt Arki* (Chotomów: Verba, 1991), p. 142.

have referred to as universality, which has guaranteed the continued vitality of the work, and its contemporary relevance, for now little less than two hundred years since its composition. I believe that I am not alone in my conviction that *Forefathers' Eve* will continue to be read, understood, and exploited for as long as the Polish language continues to exist.

As far as Walc's charges of the drama being "without beginning or end" (part and parcel of his somewhat bemused assertion of the contradictory structure of the cycle), we shall now move on to address this in our overview of the publication history and ordering of sequences.

### PUBLICATION HISTORY; THE FOUR PARTS

*Forefathers' Eve* can best be described as a dramatic sequence in verse, divided into four parts, with a lyric cycle — the *Ustęp* — appended to Part III. It is tempting to call it a closet drama, but that would be misleading. Wacław Borowy speaks of its operatic qualities, and likens Part II to cantata form.* Stanisław Pigoń compares its structure to that of an oratorium.** Portions of it — especially Part III — have been staged successfully, beginning with Stanisław Wyspiański's seminal production in Kraków, more than one hundred years ago (1901). In 2015, the Teatr Polski of Wrocław undertook the mammoth task of staging the entire cycle — for the first time in history.

Whether or not Mickiewicz intended his work for stage production, a comparison of *Forefathers' Eve* with another contemporary Monumental Drama, Zygmunt Krasiński's *Nieboska komedia* [*Undivine Comedy*, 1833], proves that Mickiewicz created a work more convenable to the traditional stage than that of his fellow "bard." Of course, *Forefathers' Eve* presents us with some jarring scene shifts. The action takes place now a prison cell, now at a ball, and at the conclusion of Part III, we find ourselves outside, beholding the rushing penal carriages as they are whipped along the road to interior exile in the depths of Russia. However, these shifting scenes are no more difficult to arrange on stage than Brecht... or Shakespeare, who also played fast and loose with the unity of space and time. All of Part IV plays out in the very conventional settings of the Priest's study. And even

---

\*   Wacław Borowy, *O poezji Mickiewicza* (Lublin: Towarzystwo naukowe Katolickiego Uniwersytetu Lubelskiego, 1958), Vol. I, pp. 112-113 *ff.*

\*\*   Stanisław Pigoń, *Formowanie* Dziadów części drugiej (Warszawa: Państwowy Instytut Wydawniczy, 1967, p. 5.

those less than naturalistic touches — the floating spirit of the Maiden from Part II, for example — are contextualised in a believable theatrical space (the nighttime chapel) that creates no great difficulty for the spectator's necessary suspension of disbelief. In comparison with this, the didascalia of Krasiński's imaginary world, full of flying spirits who lead the main character to an abyss into which he is tempted to hurl himself; in among revolutionary hosts at the siege of the last aristocratic outpost in the Holy Cross Mountains; and, finally, to the Second Coming of Christ, present the director and scenographer with challenges that can only be described, as well-nigh insurmountable.

So much for the generic description of Mickiewicz's greatest work. Whether it is witnessed on stage, or read silently, as the train hurtles along and the book is jostled by our neighbour's elbow, it is a comprehensible narrative, with beginning, middle, and end — despite what Walc suggests to the contrary. The only question is, what is the order in which the segments ought to be presented?

As far as the publication history of *Forefathers' Eve* is concerned, Parts II and IV were the first sections to see print, in the 1823 collection of the poet's works entitled *Poezye Tom II* [*Poetry: Volume II*]. These are known as the *Dziady Wileńsko-Kowieńskie*, because of the place of their composition. Mickiewicz began the work as a student in Vilnius, and brought it to a close in Kowno (Kaunas), where for a short time he taught school. Part III, the *Dziady drezdeńskie*, were written while the poet was living in Dresden (1832). In that same year, Part III was published in Paris. The *Ustęp* [*Fragment*, or, as we choose to translate the word, *Passages*] date from the same period, and are a lyric continuation of the action described in Part III. Part I, *Widowisko* [*The Spectacle*] is dated from the early 1820s. It is considered to be the first part of the work, abandoned by the poet for reasons unknown. It never saw print during the poet's lifetime, appearing in 1860 in a posthumous collection of his poetry published in Paris.

Each of the parts is built around the character of an enigmatic hero, who is now jilted lover, now poetic shaman, now "pilgrim" banished (as was Mickiewicz himself) from the Polish-Lithuanian provinces of the Russian Empire to an internal exile. Sometimes, he is a revenant spirit. These seemingly different characters are one and the same protagonist, whose various metamorphoses describe a process of emotional and spiritual growth. In the broadest terms, as our above-cited textbook states, this growth is a progression from self-absorption to other-centredness, first in relation to his fatherland, and then, in relation to all of humanity. The question is again, in what order are we to witness these transformations? As Borowy states, even the first readers of the cycle were perplexed.*

The usual sequencing of *Forefathers' Eve* respects the order of publication established during the poet's life. Thus, the order of sections in a modern volume of Mickiewicz's works, such as the one we used for this translation,** proceeds from Part II to Part IV, thence to Part III (with the *Passages*) and, finally, to Part I, as a sort of appendix which is often overlooked in critical considerations of the dramatic cycle. This scheme, with Part III coming after Part IV, is followed even by those editors, such as "P.W.", who brought out an 1864 version of the complete *Dziady* beginning the cycle with Part I.*** The logic of this order is that it makes clear the progression of the hero dear to the hearts of all patriotically-motivated readers. Part II and Part IV are both concerned with the tragic, unrequited love of Gustaw, a Wertherian character who has done away with himself out of despair. In Part III, we come across Gustaw in prison for nationalistic activities frowned upon by the Tsarist authorities. At an early moment in Part III, we witness him dramatically re-Christen himself Konrad. This change of names signifies the great inner transformation of the character from a self-absorbed disappointed lover, pleading for the rights of the heart in a cold world of marriages arranged like business propositions, to a politically aware, nationalist revolutionary, who embraces his whole nation — "all of its generations" — in a selfless quest to free it from oppression.

The progression which we propose in this translation of *Forefathers' Eve* — and I am not aware of any other edition which does so — is the logical numerical progression of Part I being followed by Part II, which then proceeds to Part III (with the *Passages*), and concludes with Part IV. We do so for the following reasons. Firstly, even if it be true that the

---

\*        Borowy, I, 103.

\*\*       The four-volume *Dzieła poetyckie* [*Poetic Works*], edited by Stanisław Pigoń (Warszawa: Cyztelnik, 1983).

\*\*\*      Adam Mickiewicz, *Dziady. Nowe wydanie zupełne* (Wrocław: H. Skutsch, 1864). In his note to the table of contents, P.W. writes: *Cześć Czwarta poprzedza Część Trzecią, według układu zachowanego przez Autora w ostatnim wydaniu* ["Part Four precedes part Three, according to the order preserved by the Author in the last edition"]. It is unclear what last edition is being referred to. However, the implication seems to be that this is the order preserved by Mickiewicz in all complete editions published during his lifetime.

final segment of *Forefathers' Eve* composed by Mickiewicz was Part III, it remains a curious thing that he should give it a numerical designation that places it between the two earlier published sections II and IV. Why, after all, did Mickiewicz choose to entitle the 1823 segments Part II and Part IV? Was this simply calculated, Romantic mystification on his part? The desire to suggest the "magnificent torso" genre popular during the Romantic period, the literary equivalent of the artificial ruins sprinkled about the grounds of romantically-inclined lords? Wacław Borowy seems to think so:

> This was an age that had just witnessed a wave of great philological discoveries, as well as great philological-literary forgeries and *pastiches*. Contemporary philological discoveries taught the public to value ancient works, even if they were only preserved in fragments; in the forgeries and *pastiches* fragmentary composition was often utilised to foster the illusion of authenticity. (Already in 1760, James MacPherson's publication of the first volume of the so-called Ossian bore the title *Fragments of Ancient Poetry*). And so other literary works too began to appear in fragments. The example of Goethe, who entitled the first version of his *Faust* (1790) *Faust, ein Fragment*, especially encouraged others to adopt this stratagem.*

Yet if that were the case with Mickiewicz, why should he not entitle the 1832 segment "Part V"? In that way, he could have had his cake and eaten it too: the progression from Gustaw (II,IV) to Konrad (III) would have been retained, and with it the teasing lacuna: II... IV,V. The designation "Part III" is too suggestive for us not to think that the poet intended for it to be inserted between II and IV. In further defence of this supposition, we would also ask why Mickiewicz began the published portions of *Forefathers' Eve* with Part "II." If he had given up on Part I, *Widowisko*, why not retitle what was truly the first published segment, "Part I," especially if *Widowisko* had been surpassed, abandoned, and was never to see the light of day? Borowy at least entertains the possibility that a more traditional ordering of the sequence might have been intended by the poet himself:

> Nine years later, Mickiewicz was to write and publish one more segment of *Forefathers' Eve* [Part III], compositionally linked, in a

---

\*        Borowy, I, 103.

certain manner, to the earlier parts. Twelve years later still, while preparing for publication the final collected edition of his poetry to see the light of day during his lifetime, the poet allowed himself to mention the existence of still another part (namely, Part I) to be found "among the author's manuscripts." He also announced that, upon its publication, he intended to change the "order" of the already published sections. Should we take these statements *à la lettre,* or as just another compositional fiction? It is improbable that we shall ever know the answer to that question.\*

That said, if "P.W." feels himself entitled to reestablish Part I at the beginning of his 1864 edition of *Dziady*, and we have no quarrel with that whatsoever, we feel ourselves justified too in suggesting that Part I was never really abandoned, that perhaps it is reasonable to take Mickiewicz at his word here; i.e., that he kept Part II as Part II because he intended one day to return to *The Spectacle* and reposition it at the head of the work. And thus, it is at least arguable that Part III was entitled Part III because the poet felt that this was the proper place for that part of his hero's story.

Looking at the transformation of the main character according to the scheme adopted for this translation, we also see a satisfying progression, indeed, an opening out of the individual toward others that is even broader than that achieved in the usual order. In Part I, the unnamed Young Man is completely self-centred, by which we mean that, while yearning, just like the Maiden at the start of the segment, for his Platonic "other half," he has not yet made contact with her. If the Young Man is Gustaw, and the Maiden is Maryla, the story of their love is recounted here in all of its innocence. *Ab ovo*, certainly, yet this is not a bad thing: we have the two individuals sketched out for us, as longing lovers, dimly aware of each other, tending towards one other, but never having been in physical proximity to each other. They are blissful in their ignorance of the pain that is due to crash down upon them, when they finally do meet.

In Part II, their love has played out, albeit off-stage. We do not witness its growth, its raptures or its heartbreak. What we do know, is that it is over. The folkloristic element of the semi-pagan ritual, enacted in Lithuania around All Souls' Day, in which the souls of the recently departed are

---

\*   Borowy, I, 104.

conjured forth so that the living can come to know how they can help them navigate the suffering of Purgatory and finally enter into their heavenly reward, is introduced. Whether or not Gustaw — still unnamed — is among the living, or is himself one of the dead, is none too clear. What we have in Part II is a very romantic plea, incarnated by the Young Wife (Maryla) separated from Gustaw by her unwelcome marriage to an unloved spouse, and the Young Man (Gustaw), both as a silent, reproachful revenant, and an eloquent spokesperson for romantic love, as the narrator of the poem that fronts the piece, "Upiór" ["The Walking Dead"].

The segment ends with the spirit of the Young Man ignoring the urgent spells of the *guślarz*, or wizard, who presides at the rites. Perhaps it is because he is still alive; his still living soul was attracted to the *Forefathers' Eve* gathering along with those of the departed — more by the workings of the reciprocal yearning between himself and Maryla, than the prayers and charms of the *guślarz* and chorus. When Part III begins, we come across the Young Man in jail. He is sleeping — his soul is, in short, elsewhere — but when he awakens, he takes the dramatic step of inscribing on the wall "Gustaw is Dead, Konrad is Born," and the date on which the odd transformation took place. And thus begins the metamorphosis from the self-absorbed unrequited lover, to the "great soul," the Byronic poet who will even challenge God on behalf of his nation.

The shift is abrupt and unsettling. It is not often that a character changes his name in the middle of his story. And if that were to be the case, one would expect a bit of a push-back from the other characters who, acting as our representatives on stage, might be expected to confront "the character formerly referred to as Gustaw" with astonished incomprehension. "Konrad? Who's Konrad? What? You want to be called Konrad now? Why?" In Mickiewicz's play, this does not happen. Characters are introduced to the stage, fellow prisoners of Gustaw/Konrad, and — although the renaming has just, in fact, taken place — they refer to him as Konrad, as if that's all they've ever known him by.

That he is the same character as Gustaw of Part II will be made patent at the end of Part III. Maryla, upset at not being able to contact him at a subsequent Forefathers' Eve rite, is comforted by the *guślarz,* who explains to her that, if he cannot be conjured forth, perhaps he has changed the faith of his fathers or (what we now know to be the actual case), he has changed his name. Part III ends with the *guślarz* and girl watching the string of penal wagons rush into internal exile in the depths of Russia.

And there she recognises him, at last, sitting on his wagon, proud and disdainful, with a wound on his chest, and a mark on his forehead.

As we have noted, Part III is the most patriotic, nationally-oriented segment of the drama, and as such, it has received the most commentary since its first composition. The *Ustęp* [*Passages*], a lyrical collection of seven narrative poems, continues the story of the exile, introduced at the conclusion of the dramatic portion of Part III. It should be pointed out that Konrad undergoes two transformations in Part III. First of all, as noted, he shifts from introspection (Gustaw) into dedication to a greater cause, that of national liberation (Konrad). Second, he shifts from egoism to self-abnegation. The desire to recreate a better Poland than that made by the hands of God, as he puts it in the Great Improvisation, proves to be unrealisable. As in Pushkin's *Evgeny Onegin*, here we witness one more "death of Byronism;" there are no "great souls;" one cannot achieve superhuman feats, because there are no supermen. After his fevered soliloquy — and subsequent exorcism — Konrad falls into the background of the story, only to emerge at the end, where he replaces his unrealistic desires to move heaven and earth with an act of small, though real, charity, such as the weakest among us may perform, effecting thereby some real good.

This shrinking of Konrad's character continues in the *Passages*. Whereas the protagonist of the *Passages* is Russia herself — Mickiewicz casts a jaundiced, though marvellously descriptive, eye on the Tsarist Empire — there is one recurring character in them, known only as "the pilgrim." This is Konrad again, his overweening personality shrunk even further, to human dimensions, and indeed to anonymity. We will consider what the term "pilgrim" might man in the context of this journey later on. What is important here, is that the pilgrim, although no longer an agent, is nonetheless a witness; his pilgrimage is a learning process that will redound to the benefit of his people. The theme of an opening out, from individual concerns to wider, national concerns, which is the entirety of Part III, is continued in the *Passages*.

We mentioned that when he is seen by the girl hiding in he hollow tree with the *guślarz* at the conclusion of Part III, Konrad has wounds on his breast and forehead. These wounds are sacramental rather than literal: outward signs of an inner reality. They are the scars of spiritual struggles, visible only to the eye of the spiritually initiated: the shaman-like *guślarz*, and the Maiden whom he guides to that spiritual knowledge.

In Part IV, the long interview between Gustaw and the Priest — his boyhood teacher — we are given to understand at the very start of the segment that there is something odd about this midnight visitor. Although he seems a bit off his rocker, the pure-hearted children wonder immediately: is this a ghost? Is this a dead man returned from the grave? And toward the end of the segment we realise that, indeed, here Gustaw is a revenant.

This, that now he is really one of the "walking dead," is as good a reason as any to place Part IV after Part III, as the segment that brings *Forefathers' Eve* to a close. But there is an even better, philosophical reason for doing so. Gustaw, in his final incarnation, is still smarting because of the heartbreak hinted at in Part II — but that is something irrelevant now, he tells us, as he and Maryla are destined to be reunited in heaven anyway. More importantly, he has moved past not only individual, erotic love, but patriotic love, for his fatherland, as well. The final plea he makes returns us full cycle to the Dantean atmosphere of the midnight rites of Part II: it is a plea on behalf of the suffering souls of Purgatory, for succour from the living. Thus, it is a further broadening out of the soul of the character towards a love of all humanity.

It is on the basis of the transformation of the main character of Mickiewicz's play that we suggest the order of segments as printed in this book. In Part I, the Young Man is alone, yearning towards erotic fulfilment with a female he senses, but has not yet come to know. In Part II, the love has come and gone; blasted, it still torments him. In Part III, erotic love is superseded by a love of country, while in Part IV, now that he has passed over to the other side, even this love is seen as too particular, and his concern implicitly embraces the millions of men and women, of all colours and nationalities, who are suffering hopefully in Purgatory. In short, the story of Gustaw/Konrad is not that of a man who learns to love more than one mere woman, it is the story of the Christian soul, who learns to love everyone.

I cannot say whether Mickiewicz would approve of this re-ordering. Nor is there any obstacle presented to the reader who wishes to follow the traditional scheme: II-IV-III-I. Because each of these segments, though linked, constitutes an integral story in its own right, a smooth progression through the book in that manner will cost the reader nothing more than a little back-and-forth shuffling, as she or he moves through this greatest monument of Polish literature.

## PART I, *THE SPECTACLE*

We now move on to a consideration of the cycle, part by part.

The fact that Mickiewicz never published the so-called *Widowisko* ["Spectacle"] suggests that the text is unfinished. That said, the fact that he neither destroyed the manuscript, nor renumbered the polished segments of the drama, suggests at least that he did not reject out of hand a final reconstitution of the entire drama, with the addition of a freshly redacted, and perhaps broadened, Part I at the head.

Although Part I is most frequently treated as a sort of appendix to *Dziady*, it belongs, as its numerical designation intimates, at the very beginning of the entire cycle. The posthumous 1864 edition, referred to above, places it there. It is not only the numbering of the segments that suggests this; it is also apparent from a consideration of the one recurring male character: Gustaw.

The Gustaw that we come across in Part I is an as-yet unspoiled youth. He is an embryonic character. Not only has he not yet begun to trouble himself with the plight of his partitioned nation, but he has not even had his heart broken by Maryla. We meet him, at the very tail-end of Part I, as a budding poet, a dreamer who would like to be a carefree earthling like his hunting companions, but is predisposed, not to say doomed, to leave the broad highway trod by happy youths and wander lost among the wonders of nature, losing track of clearly marked paths by chasing chimeras in the clouds. He is a man of feeling — perhaps of too much feeling — whose eyes will suddenly well with tears without, it seems, rhyme or reason. And while, true to the basic tenet of Polish Monumental drama (that the worlds of spirit and flesh intersect and overlap), the "spiritual" intimations that tease his super-sensitive antennae arise, not from Dantean spirits, ghosts, or angels, but from a "kindred soul," a *donna ideale*, whom he senses about him, but with whom he cannot seem to make contact. When he does brush up against a numinous form — that of the very curious Black Huntsman in the final scene of the drama — he displays none of the boldness we shall have come to expect of him from his behaviour in Parts II, III and IV. He is positively terrified by this odd creature, seeks to flee him, and when treated to a display of the latter's clairvoyance (or cold reading?), he literally squeals in fright.

Now, if Gustaw, in Part I, is a demonstrably weak protagonist, does this make the young Mickiewicz who created him a weak poet? The answer to that question is a resounding No. Whether or not the beauties of the

Polish verse are mirrored in my English translation is not for me to say. We can, however, comment upon the poet's dramatic sense, which is apparent in any language. Insofar as that is the question before us, we must remark that this early work is much more than a loosely-bound collection of lyric poems revolving around an otherworldly theme. On the contrary, the construction of *Forefathers' Eve*, Part I shows a mature feeling for dramatic narrative.

Were we to divide the Part into scenes, we would find the following eleven:
1. Girl Alone
2. Guślarz, Villagers
3. Young Men and Widow
4. Young Men and Old Man
5. Guślarz' invocation
6. Child and Old Man
7. Child's song ("The Enchanted Youth")
8. Young Men
9. Song of the Huntsman (sung by the Young Men)
10. Gustaw Alone
11. Gustaw and Huntsman

The very manner in which scene 1 segues into scene 2 is a masterstroke of stagecraft. Part I begins in a very naturalistic manner. The didascalia, so different from those found in the other parts, are Ibsenian in their description of the box stage. A very conventional drama begins in scene 1, in which the young Girl, foiled by a guttering candle in her desire to finish reading the epistolary novel *Valérie* (with its hero "Gustave") sets off into an elaborate soliloquy in which she both complains of her loneliness and expresses her desire to finally contact the "kindred soul" she imagines must be destined her. No sooner has she finished her long aside than the chorus of villagers, led by the Old Man (the "guślarz," or wizard, who conducts the Forefathers' Eve rites) crosses the stage on their way to the place where the rites are to be celebrated.

We are stunned and disoriented by this sudden shift: they enter and progress through her bedroom? Of course not; without warning, the scene has shifted outside, where we will remain for the rest of the short play. The fact that there is nothing to signal this shift of scenery might seem, at first, to indicate a compositional flaw. However, nothing can be further from the truth. With this brusque shift of scenes, Adam Mickiewicz inaugurates the defining characteristic of Polish Monumental Drama: the interpenetration of the worlds of temporality and eternity, of this life and that beyond the grave. We exist, as it were, in the shaded area of the Venn diagram, where time and eternity, eroding matter and indestructible spirit, intersect. As the Girl puts it during the opening soliloquy, when she determines to turn from the unsatisfying world to hold converse with "shades:"

> Life among the shades of an imagined earth?
> The real, tedious one, has not half its worth.
> Shades only? In this world where we draw breath
> Walk there no souls hid from our eyes by death?

This characteristic — the consciousness of the existence of that "shaded area" — which can only be compared to the manner in which the ancient epics are played out on two levels, that of the gods and that of men, will dominate the latter portions of *Forefathers' Eve*. It will be found in the works of the Polish Romantic dramatists who come after Mickiewicz and learn from him: such as Juliusz Słowacki's *Kordian*, Zygmunt Krasiński's *Undivine Comedy*, Cyprian Kamil Norwid's *Krakus*, and continue to define the Polish Monumental Theatre well into the twentieth century. We find it, for example, at the beginning of the century, in Stanisław Wyspiański's *Wesele* [*The Wedding Feast*], and near its end, in the "theatrical spectacula" of Tadeusz Kantor.\* As Małgorzata Dziewulska puts it,

> Beginning with Mickiewicz "one might establish the beginnings of [...] a purely Polish variant of theatrical thought," the especial characteristic of which is its passing beyond [mere theatre], immutably moving towards para-religious activity.\*\*

---

\*     For two recent studies of the persistent influence of Mickiewicz's *Forefathers' Eve* on Polish avant-garde drama, see Magda Romańska's 2012 book *The Post-traumatic Theatre of Grotowski and Kantor: History and Holocaust in Akropolis and The Dead Class*, and Kris Salata's 2012 article "O Homem Interior e sua Ação: Jerzy Grotowski e a herança de Adam Mickiewicz e do romantismo polonês."

\*\*    Małgorzata Dziewulska, *Artyści i pielgrzymi* (Wrocław: Wydawnictwo Dolnośląskie, 1995), p. 140. Cited in Dariusz Kosiński and Mieczysław Limanowski, *Polski teatr przemiany* (Wrocław: Instytut im. Jerzego Grotowskiego, 2007), p. 8.

We are all part of one continuum. Life declines to death, from the loam of death arises new life, and the dead are present now, not only in the spiritual realm, but also in the succeeding generations they engendered. As the Chorus of Young Men sing, chiding the gloomy *guślarz*:

> Not all your kin lie in the grave;
> Consider all the joys you have!
> Take some from us, our happy throng,
> And seek your dead among the young.

And the old grandfather too, after his Nestor-like lament on the passing away of love, and the generation he held so dear ("Your faces, voices, hands, which now surround / Me — What are they worth?") takes comfort in sensing the presence of his departed daughter in the voice of his living grandson:

> Only your voice, my grandchild, yet remains —
> A childish echo of dear, long-dead strains;
> Through it there bubbles your late mother's laugh!

What a gloomy prayer he "blesses" his grandson with: "Lord, let him die young!" It is flippant in its bitterness; it suggests too close an association of this life with that beyond the great divide, such as might misprise the gift of bodily existence, however troubled, however brief.

For neither death nor life is to be taken lightly. Mickiewicz may have his characters plead for tolerance in relation to the semi-pagan rites, at which the Catholic Church looked askance, but this festival, with its "white necromancy," is an exception, not the rule. Once a year,\* it ought to be

---

\*     Or perhaps "once a season." In his meticulously researched study of the genesis of Part II, Stanisław Pigoń suggests that *Forefathers' Eve* ceremonies were held "at least four times a year: at the beginning of spring, at the end of autumn, in midsummer, and in midwinter." Mickiewicz plays fast and loose with these seasonal rites, as the temporal setting of the action seems to comprise them all. However, he seems to concentrate on the Springtime *Dziady*, which was "inclusive […] a collective celebration taking place beyond the individual hearthside, in the graveyard of an Orthodox or Uniate church, or among ancient grave mounds (*mogiły*) out in the fields. Not just one family, but the entire parish community, took part." Pigoń, p. 13.

indulged in, for the benefit of the purgatorial souls, and for the solace of those who remain behind. However, life is not to be despised. The festive night over, we must leave the graveyard and return for twelve months of normal life in the sunshine.

The general burden of the Young Men's choruses, whether they are directed at the young Widow or the Old Man, is a celebration of youth and life. There is something noble, and fresh, in the almost expressionistic calm with which the Young Men state their satisfaction in taking their stand in mid-road, between cradle and grave, "beneath the pristine skies."

> The sun has set, the children run,
> The old folk weep and moan.
> But soon enough breaks the new dawn
> When all are coming home.
>
> Before those kids grow grey,
> Or bell for oldsters toll,
> More than one moment gay
> Will yet delight their soul.

Like their fresh, healthy attachment to robust life, the love they celebrate in song and argument is a healthy, normal, erotic and human love. They beg the young Widow — a character the didascalia allude to as identical with, or equivalent to, the mourning girl in Mickiewicz's programmatic ballad "Romantyczność" [Romanticism]* — not to forget

---

\*      "Romantyczność," from Mickiewicz's first collection of verse, *Ballady i Romanse* [*Ballads and Romanses*], has been called the Marseillaise of Polish Romanticism — just as the volume in which it first appears has been described as influencing the course of Polish literature in much the same way that Wordsworth and Coleridge's *Lyrical Ballads* did for English. It describes a young girl, in the daylight, suddenly caught up into a trance, during which she converses with the revenant spirit of her dead lover. The village divides into two camps: the simple folk cross themselves and begin to pray for her, understanding the ecstasy as a spiritual experience. Then, along comes a rationalist scientist, who proclaims the girl "mad," because with his "microscopes and lenses" he can't discern anything out of the ordinary there, let alone a ghost. The narrator then takes voice. Although he doesn't aver to have seen the spirit himself (but then again, no one, besides the girl, has), he takes the side of the common people, because there are "higher truths" than those of science, to arrive at which one must turn one's eye inward, and "look

her first husband ("buy him a Mass," they suggest), but to let her mourning run its course already, for her own good, and get on with the business of life in choosing a new mate.

Here, as in Parts II and IV, erotic love is a terrible mistress, the *kythera deina* invoked with trembling lips by poets stretching from Sappho to Ezra Pound. It is Love that ruins the life of the knight Poraj in the ballad sung by the young Boy at the urging of his grandfather; it is love — "the voice that shot me through" — the passing of which that same grandfather mourns in his expressive lament on the fleetness of time.

Its daemonic character is also evident in the carefully bookended soliloquies of the Girl at the beginning and Gustaw at the end of the segment. Here the matter takes on a Petrarchan, or Neoplatonic eloquence. The Girl — we might as well call her Maryla already, although she is not named in Part I — sighs for just a glimpse of her Platonic "other half," who surely must be waiting for her somewhere, since every atom of creation, she insists, finds its destined pairing. The Platonism of her yearning, not so much toward an earthly love, as to the Ideal, is patent toward the conclusion of her soliloquy:

> Oh, if we but with yearning wings might push
> Apart the clouds, and feel the passing rush
> Of pennons — share one word, exchange one glance —
> Oh, that would be enough of a romance:
> To know, for sure, that both of us exist!
> Then would the soul, whose flagging joys desist
> Almost to feel, so tightly are they wound
> About by torturous pain, unchained, rebound,
> Their shackles shed, toward the skies,
> And this deaf cave become a paradise!

Gustaw fairly repeats her sentiments during his anabasis through the woods. Not only that, but his sense that some spiritual presence actually

---

into the heart." Mickiewicz disdainfully refers to the rationalist as a *mędrzec* — a "wiseman." In the Choral dialogues of Part I, the guślarz invites all penitent souls to turn away from "wisemen" and to the "white necromancy" — the *guśle* — of the mystical rites leading to a higher knowledge. For a serviceable English version of "Romantyczność," see W.H. Auden's translation entitled "The Romantic."

does visit him from time to time, "breathing my breath, heart keeping time with mine," which would otherwise sound like Romantic cant, takes on a believability when seen as a conscious pairing with Maryla's earlier words.

Where are you? Lonely daughter of mystery?

O, let your soul take on, at least
The vain and passing stuff of flesh;
Cover yourself but with a crease
Of rainbow, or a spring's bright flash!

O, let your myriad glories
Long, long into my parched eyes sink!
O, your lips' subtle melodies,
Long, long my thirsty ears would drink!

Shine unto me, dear Sun! I long
With your image to scald my eyes!
Sing, Siren! At your thrilling song
I'll slumber, dreaming of the skies!

As far as the story of Maryla and Gustaw is concerned, the tragic love, of which we learn only after its shipwreck, in Parts II and IV, is a fresh thing in Part I, unsullied, undamaged, unthreatened, because, as yet, uncommenced, in a physical sense at least. Maryla and Gustaw yearn for one another, cannot yet contact one another, and yet they are happy. They know each other not, except in the most teasing fashion; Gustaw is both pained at the fact that he can catch no more than a glimpse of his ideal lover, and yet enraptured all the same by her ephemeral visits.

Here lies the crux of their incipient tragedy. On the one hand, this demonstrable "elective affinity" of Maryla's soul for Gustaw's (and vice-versa) suggests that what Gustaw will say in Part IV about their literally being destined one for another by God is true. They are, in the most real sense of the tired phrase, "soul mates." Yet Mickiewicz, who knew the work of Dante, must also have known the great truth of Neoplatonic love that informs the troubadours, Petrarch, and the Florentine himself: that the *donna ideale* can be worshipped, but never possessed. The tragedy of Gustaw's love is not so much that Maryla will become the wife of someone else. After all, neither Dante nor Petrarch physically possessed Beatrice or Laura. Rather, Gustaw's tragedy is that, unsatisfied with the future glory he was promised to share with Maryla, he sought — almost blasphemously, as it were — to precipitate it, corporeally, here and now.

Hence the frisson with which Part I comes to an end, in the eerie interview of Gustaw with the Black Huntsman. A creepy bloke he, who introduces himself as:

> A huntsman, like you... With a bit more might,
> Though just as eager. But while you cover
> The woods by day, I'm out hunting at night.
> You skulk for beasts, while I ambush... lovers.

This may be mere jocularity; a witticism playing on the fact of his having "chased down" the helpless "quarry" that was the lost young man. Yet he is a "black" huntsman — an adjective that can both refer to his swarthy appearance, and his mysterious nature. For he presents himself as spiritually prescient; if Gustaw "feels around him" the lover who — somehow — races to him on the wings of the spirit, something that might be explained by the antennae of the heart, the fact that the Black Huntsman recognises this too is quite odd indeed:

> Know first, that someone watches over you —
> A certain being, everywhere you stray,
> Who'd like to take form that you might see,
> And visit — If you're steadfast in what you say...

Has he second sight? Or is he still playing with Gustaw, having overheard his romantic soliloquy? We don't know. Gustaw, however, opts for the former, and his hair veritably stands on end. He has not yet grown into the shaman of Part III who will assert his spiritual dominance over all things, except God — with whom he will, however, claim equal power. Here, rather than being cheered by the Huntsman's metaphysical confirmation of the "being" that ranges about him at all times, aching to take form and "visit" him, Gustaw feels his hackles rise, and seeks to flee the Huntsman in terror. Again, Mickiewicz reminds us that his Halloween story need not necessarily have a happy ending.

In short, Part I, far from being inchoate or rough, is a well-crafted introduction to the entirety of *Forefathers' Eve*. Persons and themes and even verbal refrains ("All is darkness, all is quiet") are introduced here, to be developed and expanded upon in the other three parts. It is, also, Gustaw's introduction to the searing pains which must accompany the great delights of his love for Maryla. Is it this which becomes suddenly apparent to the sensitive poet, in a flash of epiphany, and has him nearly jump out of his skin in terror?

## PART II

Revenant spirits form their own subgroup of the literature of the Romantic Age. Most often, they are associated with an unhappy love story. In Gottfried August Bürger's *Lenore* (1773) and Karol Jaromír Erben's *Svatební košile* [*The Wedding Shirts*, 1853], the longed-for lover, whether he be truly the soul of the heroine's love or a demonic spirit, lures the human on to destruction. In Bürger's ballad, Lenore is lost; in Erben's Biedermeyer retelling, she repents of her tempting of heaven and, through the intercession of the Blessed Virgin Mary, the bloodthirsty ghost is laid, and the Czech maiden escapes unscathed.

Not all revenant tales are finger-wagging and catechetical, like Erben's, or ghost stories, like *Lenore*. Revenant tales figure largely in the folk poetry of the Slovaks, and there, more often than not, the returning spirit seeks not the destruction of his former, earthly love, but returns to impart some wisdom to her, from beyond the grave, to teach her.* This is also characteristic of Part II of *Forefathers' Eve*. On the one hand, in it, Mickiewicz continues his story of the fated lovers parted by man and death; on the other, the holistic, Catholic view of life characteristic of the "sturdy folk," which sees creation, and life, as an endless continuum, and death, not as a wall, but a permeable membrane, is underscored in a manner which recalls Dante's *Divine Comedy.*** In Part I of *Forefathers' Eve*,

---

\*     For a more detailed discussion of this, see my "Revenant Spirits in Slovak Folk Narrative Poems," *Kosmas*, XX (2007) 2:1-27. I discuss Erben's poem, and Mickiewicz's "Ucieczka" ["The Escape,"] mentioned below, in my *Romantic Hero and Contemporary Anti-Hero in Polish and Czech Literature: Great Souls and Grey Men*. Lewiston/Queenston/Lampeter: The Edwin Mellen Press, 1997.

\*\*    Katarzyna Lukas explores the Catholic underpinnings of Part IV of Mickiewicz's drama in her "Der romantische Protagonist als Träger des

we accompanied the people to the graveyard, but did not witness the rites. In Part II, the entirety of the segment is played out in the deserted chapel, during the "Mass" on behalf of the departed souls; the aim of the ritual is hinged on that idea of the permeable "membrane" of the grave. The spirits are called forth so that the living, who still care for them, may learn "what they need" in the species of prayer or offering, to ease their transition from Purgatory to Paradise.

If Stanisław Pigoń is correct in assuming that the *Dziady* ritual that Mickiewicz is basing his work on is that celebrated in the Springtime, we see that it was a very fitting choice made by the poet:

> The [Springtime *Dziady*] were celebrated right after Easter, around the time of the first Sunday after the holiday; the exact dates varied by location, but generally: from Saturday until Tuesday. According to the Church calendar, that Sunday, known as Leading Sunday [*Niedziela przewodnia*] is especially set aside in remembrance of Christ's descent into Hell and his leading out therefrom the souls of the patriarchs and Old Testament prophets into the spheres of Heaven. By its very nature then, it is a very fitting time for prayers on behalf of the dead, to lead the penitent souls out of the depths of Purgatory.*

Wacław Borowy, after the German translator of *Forefathers' Eve* Siegfried Lipiner, states that "the three scenes with these spirits constitute a development of a certain thought, of authentic and full humanity."** That is certainly the case, as even the appearance of the bloodthirsty local tyrant elicits in the congregation a remarkable response of generosity. Yet we are in timeless Catholicity here, rather than the eighteenth century Enlightenment (which Borowy is so fond of referring us to); if there is a didacticism here, it takes place not so much directly between poet and reader as it does indirectly, through the lessons imparted by the dead to the living. The latter wish to aid the former, of course, through their ritual

---

katholischen Weltbildes. Über den IV. Teil des dramatischen Fragments Dziady von Adam Mickiewicz in deutschsprachigen Übersetzungen" *Studia Germanica Posnaniensia* XXX (2006): 5-33.

\*  Pigoń, pp. 13-14.
\*\*  Borowy, I, 112.

offerings. But transfer also occurs "from there, to here," as the stories told by the revenant spirits — like the *racconti* of the souls encountered by Dante on his journey — contain a moral for the living, by the aid of which they can better themselves, and avoid the pains of Purgation once they cross through that inevitable portal. While delineating the distinctions between the Catholic doctrine of Purgatory, and the Eastern, Orthodox belief of the soul's penumbral existence after the death of the body, Stanisław Pigoń underlines this two-way transfer in his book on the structural development of Part II:

> The state of expectation can at the same time be a state of perfecting, but not through satisfaction or posthumous suffering. The only road to that [perfection] may be the help of the living, not even so much through their particular intention, as above all through the practice of mercy, alms, and prayers, and through such actions especially performed by the elderly and the poor; sometimes also by way of the consumption of sanctified meals. In this way the "communion of the saints" comes into being. For, reciprocally, the living also draw strength and inspiration from the realm of the afterlife. [...] In a word, on just such a base of religious faith and direct intimacy do the world of time and the world of eternity bring aid to one another, and that aid of the most effective sort.\*

It is the wise, and stirringly written, Dantean passages of Part II, which illustrate that circle of charity which is the Communion of the Saints, that first raise Mickiewicz's *Forefathers' Eve* past local interest and make of it a universal work appealing to all human beings. The lessons told, in turn, by the two departed Children, the (damned) Landowner and the flighty Maiden, and internalised by the chanting Chorus, set the poet in the company of Goethe and Dante. Forerunning Joseph Campbell and Karl Jung by more than a century, in his introduction to the segment, Mickiewicz suggests that we tell such stories, not because we are Lithuanian or of a Romantic bent, but because we are human. It is an archetypical tale, encoded, as Jung might say, in our very spines:

---

\*    Pigoń, with reference to P. Evdokimov's *Prawosławie* (Warszawa, 1964). p. 16.

The beginnings of this ritual stretch back to pagan times, and it was once known as the *uczta kozła* or "goat's feast." The celebrant was called the *Koźlarz, Huslar* or *Guślarz*, a person both priest and bard. [...] It is noteworthy that the custom of banqueting the dead seems to be common to all pagan peoples, whether we be speaking of Homeric Greece, the Scandinavian countries, the Orient, or the far-off islands of the New World. Our Dziady are exceptional in that the pagan ceremonies are now intermixed with notions borrowed from the Christian religion, especially as the feast of All Souls falls roughly at the same time that Dziady are celebrated.

However, the Leitmotiv of love, which binds the entire dramatic cycle together — the frustrated love of the Young Man (Gustaw, though unnamed) and the Young Girl (Maryla, likewise anonymous) is introduced at the beginning of Part II, and brings it to a dramatic conclusion.

Part II is fronted by the lyric poem "Upiór" ["The Walking Dead"].\* While unsure whether or not the walking dead of this poem is intended to be identified with the revenant Hermit of Part IV, Wacław Borowy calls it "an introduction, a sort of overture that sets the mood for the entire cycle."\*\* Quite Romantic in a Bürgeresque fashion, it tells the story, in unabashed technicolor, of a very palpable zombie:

> The breast swells, yet cold is that breast,
> His lips and eyelids wide are spread,
> He's here again, yet somewhere else:
> Who is this man? The living dead.
>
> Those who live nearby his grave
> Know that each year his tomb is riven:

---

\*     "Upiór," the Polish form of a common Slavic word, is etymologically connected with the English "vampire" (itself a borrowing from Hungarian, and perhaps originally Turkish, in which tongue *ubir* means "witch"). While there are vampiric overtones in a song from Part III, *upiór* can mean "phantom" as well as any sort of evil spirit. It seems to us that "walking dead" most suits the ambiguous nature of Mickiewicz's hero, who shifts not only between personalities, but also between states of life, and death; indeed, his status, which side of the "membrane" he finds himself on, is never altogether clear.

\*\*     Borowy, I, 106.

> He wakes each year on All Souls' Eve,
> And makes his way toward the living.
>
> But when four Sundays' bells will fade,
> Then he returns, his strength expired.
> Breast bathed in blood from wounds fresh made,
> He sleeps again in churchyard mire.

The anonymous writer of the obituary of Adam Mickiewicz printed in the May, 1856 edition of *The Gentleman's Magazine,* in an otherwise perceptive overview of the stature of the Polish poet, finds in this play grounds for disgust. He calls *Forefathers' Eve* "a wild and irregular drama," and describes it thus:

> Entitled Dziady, a word in Polish denoting "Ancestors," [it is] applied by the Lithuanians to an annual festival, in which the dead are believed to rise from their graves to be fed by the living. On this wretched superstition, and on that of the vampire, both too horrible for poetic use, Mickiewicz wastes some pages of powerful but revolting poetry.*

True, we have a "vampire" here, or some sort of walking dead, or revenant spirit. Each November he is harried out of the quiet of his grave to walk among the living. The motif will be repeated in Part III, where Konrad, the patriotic incarnation of Gustaw (more on that later) sings a bloodcurdling song of vengeance at a gathering of his imprisoned friends:

> And my Song says: I shall go out tonight
> > Upon my countrymen to chew —
> Whomever with these fangs I bite
> > Perforce becomes a vengeful vampire, too!
> > Yes! vengeance, vengeance,
> > > vengeance on our enemies!
> > With or without God's sanction,
> > > as the Lord shall please!

---

\*      Anonymous, "Obituary — Adam Mickiewicz," in *The Gentleman's Review* (May, 1856), 45:537-540, p. 538a.

Similar to the writer of the obituary, Lautréamont (Isidore-Lucien Ducasse) also understood Mickiewicz's revenant a tad too literally. Mario Praz quotes a letter from the author of *Les Chants de Maldoror* in which he speaks of having written "Something along the lines of Byron's Manfred and Mickiewicz's Konrad, but, all the same, quite a bit more terrible." By that he seems to mean that Maldoror will take blasphemy to a level at which both Manfred — who in his interview with Arimanes explicitly professes faith in a Creator God — and Konrad (who falls unconscious before he can spit out the last blasphemous word of his tirade, that God is a "Tsar") — retreat. But in another letter, also quoted by Praz, he writes:

> I have sung evil just as have Mickiewicz, Byron, Milton, Southey, A. de Musset, Baudelaire, etc. Naturally, I have exaggerated the diapason a bit in order to achieve something new in the sense of that sublime literature, which does not sing despair for any other reason than to oppress the reader, and make him desire the good as a remedy.*

Is it that we, inheritors of a culture fascinated with the morbid, a culture that Lautréamont himself helped conjure into being, have been so desensitised by slasher movies and the like that the rather tame "vampires" we come across in Mickiewicz seem quaint? Or, how is it that Lautréamont even conceived of Mickiewicz as a "singer of evil" to the extent of including him in the same group as Baudelaire? One can only reckon that he has misread the text, and the writer. Mickiewicz's "walking dead" is a metaphor, not a ghoul; Konrad's later blasphemy is far from heroic: it is the same sort of human frustration, albeit much greater in degree, as that experienced by any person who has ever shaken his fist at the heavens. Konrad's song in Part III cannot, obviously, be taken literally; it is an attempt at sympathetic magic, a metaphorical expression of revolutionary yearnings felt by the generation his protagonist represents:

> Then shall we go as one our thirst to slake
>     Upon the foes who us enslave,
> And through their hearts we'll drive a stake

---

\*       Mario Praz, *The Romantic Agony* (Oxford: Oxford Univeristy Press, 1970), p. 165.

> That they might never rise from out the grave.
> Yes! vengeance, vengeance,
> > vengeance on our enemies!
> With or without God's sanction,
> > as the Lord shall please!

Slyly, he reverses the roles here: the final punishment inflicted upon the tsarist oppressors of his slain country will be that reserved in folklore for the walking dead — a stake through the heart, so that once dead, they will remain in the ground.

These citations come from Part III. Yet even here, in the case of the Wertherian Gustaw, the poet's purpose is not to terrify. Mickiewicz is not looking for cheap thrills, revolting or otherwise. His *upiór*, also according to the laws of purgation, is undergoing a penance of "four Sundays'" duration, at the end of which the (self-inflicted) wound that cut him off, prematurely, from the community he must visit, is newly administered:

> Tales of this man who walks the gloom
> Are many — he was young, and still
> Live those who wept on his fresh tomb —
> They say he died of his own will.

The Catholic Church that Mickiewicz knew looked askance at suicide. God, to quote the play from which the poet took the motto for Part II, "set his canon 'gainst self-slaughter." Suicides were not laid to rest in consecrated ground, no Requiem could be sung for them, and — it was assumed — they sank straight to Hell, fall where they may, as Dante puts it. In *Forefathers' Eve*, Mickiewicz shows himself ahead of his times by alleging extenuating circumstances for the unholy act which, though it must be punished, and severely at that, need not result in damnation. The one great extenuating circumstance is love. The "walking dead" in Part II, and Gustaw in Part IV, will both implicitly, and explicitly, argue that the greater sin is on the part of those who interposed themselves between the Man and Woman that God destined for each other, for all time. God's will simply cannot be overridden by man's. In an interesting take on "what God hath joined, let no man sunder," even the otherwise unforgivable act of suicide cannot be allowed to impede the eternal union of the two souls, which will take place — we learn in Part IV — once Maryla's life has run its course. At that moment,

Gustaw's trials of purgation will come to an end, and God's will — stymied here below by man — will at last be done, for all time.

This exculpatory nature of love — or at least its value as mitigation — is expressed by that most Catholic of poets, Dante, as well. Sins of the flesh, the sins of misguided love, are declared to be the "sins that God hates least," and, accordingly, even those who are damned for perverted love, such as the famous pair of adulterers Paolo and Francesca, are tormented less severely than the icy, conniving hearts, the fraudulent (and fraud, we are told, is the sin that God most abhors).

The mitigating value of love is also a characteristic of the healthy, commonsensical wisdom of the folk. And that very aspect of the folkloric fabric of *Forefathers' Eve* is what Mickiewicz chooses to emphasise in his prose introduction to Part II:

> The so-pious intent of this feast, as well as the lonely places where the ceremonies are held, the late hour, and the fantastic rituals at one time spoke strongly to my imagination; I listened to the legends, stories and songs of deceased persons returning to the living with requests or warnings, and in all of the monstrous inventions one could yet discover certain moral tendencies and teachings set forth in a sensual, folkish manner.

The way in which Mickiewicz speaks of discovering "certain moral tendencies and teachings set forth in a sensual, folkish manner" seems condescending; as if the refined, philosophe-educated elite were in possession of a civilised code, only dimly apparent to the "folk" and clumsily expressed by them. Of course, that would be to completely ignore the moral primacy he accords the simple people, in "Romantyczność" for example, where it is they who are aware of "higher truths" unknown to the wisemen of the world, who gather their empirical evidence on all hands, yet never look into their own heart. Interestingly enough, Mickiewicz's presentation of the Dziady rituals is more than mere Romantic colourisation. According to Stanisław Stankiewicz, ethnographic studies in Belarus underscore the veracity of much of Mickiewicz's statements:

> The observance of Dziady is held among the Belarusan people twice a year. The rituals are celebrated in cottage or cemetery (not, however, in a chapel and not in secret, and the clergy, whether

Orthodox or Uniate, at times also take part). The ritual in the cottage is presided over by the man of the house or the eldest family member, who intones the prayers, casts the spells, and evokes the forefathers, setting aside for them food and drink. At the cemetery, sometimes a wandering beggar (a *starec*) officiates; at times the same person leads the ritual in both places.[*]

In his vivid introduction, then, Mickiewicz is speaking on behalf of the folk, encouraging that elite not to disdain the ancient rites and simple beliefs of the common people, as does the man who was to speak so harshly of *Dziady* in *The Gentleman's Magazine*. Civilisation tends to isolate; the primitive community of the village is a community of support, where the imperative of reciprocal aid and charity extends even beyond the grave:

> Purgatory's suffering souls!
> Wherever in the world you be:
> If in flaming tar you roll,
> Or in an icy river freeze,
> Or if, for greater punishment,
> Within a blazing log you're pent
> That cries and whistles as the flames
> Gnaw at its slow-consuming frame,
> Come, hurry to our company!

So chants the Guślarz, opening the rites in the dark chapel. Whereas many of the more enlightened Christians, even of Mickiewicz's own time, were doubtful, not only of the existence of Purgatory and the efficacy of prayers for the dead, but even of the idea of a caring, personal God who intervenes in human history, the simple folk of Mickiewicz's drama not only uphold an ancient faith, but they feel the presence of those spirits about them, here and now. For them (and this is not necessarily a primitive thought) Purgatory is not a particular place, as Dante describes it, allegorically; it is a state into which the saved soul, still bearing the burden

---

[*] Cited by Borowy, I, 107-108. A recent monograph (2009) by Piotr Grochowski is devoted to such beggars, and their poetic role as wandering folk-minstrels in the old Polish countryside: *Dziady. Rzecz o wędrownych żebrakach i ich pieśniach*.

of unpractised penitence, enters, upon the death of the body. As a state, it is merely a different level of this our reality; the suffering souls of the dead are about us, here and now: locked in the ice of the river over which our children skate, paying back the penalty for more serious sins in the whistling log burning right now in the hearth at which we warm them, when they return from play.

The sense of unbroken community is underscored by the arrival of the first two souls attracted to the rite: Józia and Rózia: children who passed away prematurely, and whose mother is among the villagers in the chapel. The little boy addresses his mother as naturally as if he were standing before her in the kitchen:

> What's wrong, Mama? Look — it's Józia—
> Don't you know me? Your little bunny!
> And here with me's my sister Rózia.
> We fly through Heaven, Mama, now —
> It's more fun than with you, and how!
> Look at the sunny crowns we wear!
>                               [...]
> Heaven's fun! Everything's here —
> And every day's a new surprise.
> But even though everything's here,
> We're bored sometimes ... we're scared — a lot ...
> O, Mummy, your two little dears
> Can't find their way to God!

Perhaps nowhere else is the permeable membrane of death shown to better advantage than here. First, like any other Purgatorial spirits, the two children come with a request. The living can shorten their period of penitence and help them "find God" in this way:

> So sweet a life on earth we had,
> Too sweet, and this is why we're sad.
> Our life was just one long caress;
> We've never tasted bitterness.
>                               [...]
> We've come here to your Dziady feast
> Not for prayers or for treats;

> We don't need any Masses said,
> We don't need cakes, or milk, or bread,
> But rather wormwood. Please, two grains,
> And for your taking such small pains
> Our penance will be completed.
> For listen now to our bequest:
> According to God's just command,
> He who's not tasted bitterness
> Will take no sweets from Jesus' hand.

Second, their appearance at the ceremony is also to the benefit of the living. Obviously, one can only imagine what a comfort it would be to their mourning mother, to see them, hear them, and fill her heart with the assurance that they are in a better place, comforted, rejoicing, and beyond all harm. But it is not only she who is benefited by their words. Like the other souls conjured forth on Forefathers' Eve, the children come bearing a message for the living, which is dutifully repeated, internalised, by the Chorus:[*]

> Listen, listen to their bequest:
> According to God's just command,
> He who's not tasted bitterness
> Will take no sweets from Jesus' hand.

In other words, be patient under suffering; those who offer up their sufferings here below, who accept them as a good thing, endured for the love of God, will have so much of an easier road once past the gates of death. We have, in short, a passage from the Sermon on the Mount, boiled down to its common-sense essentials.

Not all of the dead who are conjured are saved, though penitential, souls in Purgatory.[**] The next soul to appear is that of a local landowner,

---

[*] The message is internalised, but the repetition of the words suggests antiphonal prayer. Interestingly, Pigoń speaks of the structure of Part II, with the ritual back-and-forth between *guślarz* and Chorus, as a structural imitation of the Angelus prayer. This is particularly important, in that the Angelus is not merely a Marian devotion, but is especially related to petitions for the eternal rest of the departed. See Pigoń, pp. 19-20.

[**] The children and the maiden are saved, purgatorial souls; the landowner is hopelessly damned. Still, Jan Walc sets forth an interesting theory which links

damned for his cruelty to his serfs. When queried by the Guślarz what would help him reach heaven, he replies:

> Heaven? O, you blaspheme in vain.
> I don't want Heaven! Not at all —
> Only a loss would be my gain —
> I only wish my soul would crawl
> A little faster out of me.
> A hundred times I'd rather be
> Pinned to the very floor of Hell
> Than wandering here about my woods —
> I'd bear each type of torture well,
> Yet I can't bear to see the goods
> I once enjoyed, and every station
> Of late-beloved abomination!
> [...]
>
> [...] such is the Judge's will
> That I must house my damned soul
> Within this tattered corpse until
> One of you pity my hard dole —
> One of you, of my former serfs
> Should feed my hunger, slake my thirst.

Non-Catholics may find this passage a bit confusing. First of all, Purgatory, although a place of suffering, is a place of joy, as well. It is not a testing ground suspended between Heaven and Hell, from which the souls there imprisoned will migrate, up or down, depending on their actions or the prayers of others. There is no downward movement from Purgatory. Purgatory is filled with souls destined for heaven, whose sins have been absolved in confession, but who did not complete the penitence required of them during life. Thus, such souls must pass some time in suffering in this place of "purgation," until their debt to

---

them together: "And yet there is something that binds all of the sinners, whose souls have arrived at the Forefathers' Eve ceremony — their introspection, their living for themselves alone, without a care for others." p. 36. Which really is to say that all of them have sinned, for sin is the reckless decision to selfishly follow one's own inclinations, maugre others, maugre God Himself. The distinction is: the maiden and the children have atoned for their sins, the landowner has not.

God — to put it most simplistically — is paid back, either through their patient suffering, or with the help of the prayers offered up by the living on their behalf, which shorten their punitive stay. Every soul in Purgatory is saved; their next destination is one and the same: Paradise.

The landowner, or "lord," who appears now is not among their number. He is damned, and nothing that the living might do would be capable of overturning that verdict. Still, he is condemned by God to wander the nights in his old, sensitive flesh, at which the "nocturnal birds" — the souls of those of his serfs he starved and tormented during life — tear and torment in their turn. Only if he were able, in his state, to receive one crumb, one drop, from his former serfs, in a sign of forgiveness, would this physical torment end, and he would be cast into the Hell for which he perversely longs. Small comfort, that! But he seems to think it would be better than having to wander his woods, which have now passed on to someone else. Despite the best will of the living villagers, however, his request will go unfulfilled:

> CHORUS OF NOCTURNAL BIRDS.
> In vain he begs, in vain he prays:
> For we night-fliers, crows, eagles, owls,
> His sable train, were once his slaves;
> He starved us, now we feed his howls!
> We'll eat the food and quaff the drink
> That's offered him, with beak and claw
> We'll tear it, be it on the brink
> Of his parched, blistered, hungry maw,
> Be it within his gripping mouth,
> With my talons I'll rip it out!
> I'll reach down to his very bowels!
> You had no mercy on us, lord,
> Nor shall we best you on that score!

Mickiewicz is no more a theologian than Dante; he is a poet, writing a drama. Certainly, there is nothing in Christian theology — Catholic or otherwise — that suggests this sort of anti-Purgatory, this state in which a condemned soul is made to undergo a foretaste of his eternal sufferings, before he "merits" a release to the infernal lake. Likewise, the fact that his tormentors are the souls of those people he treated so horribly during life is problematic. One of them speaks:

> They chased me like a wolf through all
> The garden — to the garden wall.
> Thence was I hauled in front of you
> (Them snapping, snarling all the while) —
> They hauled me off to face a trial
> And over what? Some apples, pears …
> Fruits of the field, like water, fire,
> Which God intended Man to share!
> And yet my lord cried out in ire
> "Make an example out of him!"

Is this part of the eternal reward of that poor soul? That he is now the torturer of the man who tortured him? If so, that's a fairly sick conception of the repose of heaven, where "every tear will be wiped away." But again: we are not reading theology here, we are reading poetry. And this table-turning scene fits in well with the simplistic concepts of folk justice — like Dante's *contrapassi* — that the common-sense metaphysics of the village present.*

When this lot disappear, we are treated to one more interview with a Purgatorial soul. This is that of:

> […] Zosia, born and raised
> Among you, and my beauty's praise
> Was ever on your lips, with spite,
> For I held marriage in despite —
> My beauty lost to everyone.

---

\*      Who says that the tormenting "Nocturnal Birds" are *saved* souls? Just because they were victimised during life, doesn't mean that they too did not come up short at the individual judgement and, like their lord, are themselves damned to Hell. This may be an echo, conscious or not, of Dante's *contrapasso* of the thieves in Hell, who pursue one another in the guise of reptiles, stealing the human form of their "victims" only to be pursued by them in turn, once the odd metamorphosis takes place. Even in the more theologically traditional world of the *Divine Comedy* we come across instances of sinners constituting the punishment of other sinners, which we may be seeing here.

It is interesting that Mickiewicz should introduce, as his last conjured spirit, that of a beautiful girl (so beautiful, that the Guślarz at first mistakes her for the Virgin Mary) whose one sin was that she disdained wedlock. She is held out of heaven, not by the pride with which she undoubtedly was afflicted, but because she did not share her beauty with another. Mickiewicz is not one to accept the Catholic idea, certainly still prevalent in his day, that virginity was a higher calling than matrimony. No, man was made for woman, and vice-versa; the natural destiny of our kind is love: erotic, lifelong, creative union. "To what serves mortal beauty?" G.M. Hopkins was to ask, a few decades later, referring to erotic charm as "dangerous." Well, it serves to the natural attraction of man to woman, woman to man, Mickiewicz would answer, and from thence to matrimony. Almost as if he were taking a page from Dante's concept of Neoplatonic love; i.e. that erotic love between men and women here below serves the purpose of teaching us of the higher love that God has for our soul, the teaching that Zosia provides, internalised by the Chorus, reads:

> Consider well the fate she's found;
> According to God's just command:
> Whose feet have never touched the ground
> Will never tread His promised land.

The fact that God intends, in general, that man find woman and woman man, returns us to the particular of: God intended Gustaw for Maryla, and Maryla for Gustaw — the constant, erotic thread that binds together all of the parts of *Forefathers' Eve*. And, sure enough, although the dawn is about to break, and the Guślarz starts to wind down the ceremony, one more "spirit" appears: that of a young man, conjured, not so much by his words, as by the presence of the girl for whom he was destined, although their union was impeded by men:

> His hand he lays upon his chest,
> Upon the blackened cavity
> And none but her he deigns to see.

The fact that man's will is puny in comparison to destiny — which is just another way of saying the will of God — is underscored by the fact that the Guślarz cannot manage this unexpected spirit. Throughout all the preceding scenes, he was in perfect control of the revenants. He directed the sacramentals of the rites, he ordered about both living and dead, he even determined the order of the visitants. Now, not only did he not call forth the equivocal spirit of the young man with the bloody breast, but neither by word, gesture, curse or spell can he command the spirit to action, or speech.

GUŚLARZ.
Spirit blessed or sprite accursed,
Be off from this our sacred rite.
You see the floor gapes open wide —
Go in again, from whence you burst —
Beware! —
    He stands there, just the same!
— Before I curse you in God's name!
/pause/
Be gone through wood! Be gone through river!
Be gone and perish, cursed forever!
— I've never seen the likes before.
He stands there, dumbly, and ignores!

He's "never seen the likes of this before?" He's never known the power of love? The Guślarz, perhaps, is just as conservative in this regard as the elites. The toffs round about arrange marriages with one eye on the dowry, calculating the advantages that will accrue to the family from this match or that. The common folk can be just as crafty. One is reminded of that scene in *Evgeny Onegin*, by Mickiewicz's friend Aleksandr Pushkin, when Tatyana confides to her aged nurse the fascination she feels for her Byronic neighbour. At the question, "Were you ever in love?" the old woman crosses herself, and jumps back as if she had been asked "Have you ever had yellow fever?" As the story continues, we learn that the old woman indeed had been in love, with her late husband, but love is not what drew them together. Their marriage was arranged by other people, from considerations other than the erotic; only later did they learn to "love" each other. Tatyana there, and Gustaw/Maryla here, represent that rather new idea of Romantic love, based on mutual attraction. We are so used, these days, to the rights of the heart, and the importance that sympathetic attraction has for lasting marriages, that it is difficult to appreciate how revolutionary a thought this was in the days when Pushkin and Mickiewicz were writing.

At any rate, that is what is going on here. From the mute spectre, the Guślarz turns to the girl who, just like the spirit, stands there numb, entranced, a living mirror image of the dead young man:

> This defies all human reason!
> Shepherdess! You know this person?
> Something horrid's here, or worse —
> For whom have you got mourning weeds on?
> Your husband and your folk are well?
> What? Silent too? Nothing to tell?
> Look here, and say something, my child!
> Hey! Are you dead? Why do you smile?
> What does this mean, this smile, this grin?
> What do you find so gay in him?

She is wearing "mourning weeds," which surprises the Guślarz. He knows her, he knows her family: there have been no deaths among her kin. Obviously, she has them on for the very person whose spiritual part now stands in front of her. Again, the permeable membrane: she came here, no less than the mother of the dead children did, prepared for, hoping to be comforted by, the appearance of the person she so longs for, who is separated from her by death. She is satisfied: she smiles.

None of this means anything to the Guślarz. Husband alive, family well — the fact that she is wearing black, in this regard, emphasises the anti-conventional nature of her love. Those, like the Guślarz, who respect the conventions of society, are nonplussed, if not appalled, by her emotional preference for this man who is not her husband. Yet that is all grist to Mickiewicz's mill. Parent and priest and kinsmen do what they will, the fact remains: Gustaw and Maryla were destined for one another by God Himself, and this union trumps all others.

We have been referring to the Young Man in Part I, and the Spectre here in Part II, as Gustaw; we have been calling the Young Girl in Part I, and the Shepherdess in Part II, Maryla. In actual fact, these names are not used by the poet in reference to his hero and heroine until Part IV. In this dramatic sequence of shifting identities (Gustaw explicitly "becomes" Konrad in Part III; the Young Man is now a revenant spirit, now a man of flesh and blood), we are not wrong to do so. As we said, one of the strands that links the four parts of *Forefathers' Eve* together is the Leitmotiv of divinely predestined love, thwarted by men, but eventually triumphant. Whenever the Leitmotiv is introduced, it is one and the same: the woman has been induced to forsake her true love in favour of a more lucrative match; the young man despairs (quite literally), but remains faithful to her, in life, and beyond the grave. It is thus obvious that in this way, the four segments of Mickiewicz's masterpiece revolve around one and the same pair of star-crossed lovers.

More problematic, and much more frequently repeated, is the sort of identification that our anonymous writer in *The Gentleman's Magazine* makes via biographical criticism:

> The Childe Harold of Byron is not more transparently Byron than the maniac of the Dziady is Mickiewicz himself. It is well known to his friends that while a student at Wilna he had become enamoured of a lady bearing the name of Maria Wereszczakówna, the sister of a fellow-student; and that she, after apparently encouraging his attentions, had rejected him in favour of a suitor of higher position. Many of the minor incidents referred to by the maniac are known to have occurred to the poet; but it is not known that Mickiewicz had ever actually been out of his senses. Strange indeed are the confessions of genius.*

As with most biographical criticism, the truth behind this is not so cut and dried. In letters to his friends from this period, Mickiewicz speaks of leaving the Nowogrodek area, and Maria behind him, in a "peaceful enough" mood, and even though he was no doubt strongly attracted to her:

> Wiedziałem, ze jej uczucia nie tej natury co moje, że ją straciłem, wiem, co się z nią i co ze mną stanie, i nie uważam jej za bardzo nieszczęśliwą. Mylisz [się] kiedy myślisz, że jej wesołość mnie smuci, a smutek pochlebia. [...] Życzę jej wszelkiego szczęścia najszczerzej, ale nie wszelkie może, mnie tyle ile ją pocieszać i dlatego nie o wszystkim chcę wiedzieć.**

---

\*      Anonymous, "Obituary — Adam Mickiewicz," p.538a.
\*\*     Adam Mickiewicz, Letter to Onufry Pietraszkiewicz dated 13 IX 1821 [25 IX 1821 *new style*], cited in Grzegorz Szelwach, *Listy Adama Mickiewicza (Lata 1817-1833)* (New York: PIASA Books, 2006), pp. 72-73.

[I knew that her feelings were not of the same nature as mine, that I had lost her; I know what will become of her and what of me, and I do not think her very unhappy. You are mistaken when you assume that I am saddened by her happiness, and that sadness becomes me [...] I wish her all the happiness in the world, sincerely, well, perhaps not *all* happiness; I wish myself enough so that she would be happy, and for this reason I don't want to find out about everything.]

Do these sound like the words of an obsessive young man, in the throes of love's despair who, even from beyond the grave, will not leave her side?

>     Good Lord, the sprite is going too!
>     Wherever she, he's at her side.
>     What else will happen here tonight?

The poet and critic Jarosław Marek Rymkiewicz perhaps leans too far in the opposite direction when he writes: "There was no such love, no such romance. Mickiewicz fell in love with a betrothed woman, whom he met five months prior to her marriage. It was the love of a poet for a countess."\* What we can say is that poems are not the result of spontaneous combustion in a vacuum. Every work of art, however objectively distant from the author, still arises from the experiences of a human being; these experiences become fictionalised to a greater or lesser degree, and engender fictional works to a greater or lesser extent descriptive of those actual experiences of their flesh-and-blood author. In his discussion of the Great Improvisation, Roman Koropeckyj suggests that the outburst "articulat[es...] a 'personality transformation'" of the poet himself, and cites the recorded evidence of Mickiewicz's friend Edward Odyniec, who witnessed a mystical experience undergone by the poet while praying in a Dresden church in March of 1832, following which the Improvisation was written at one go, the following night."\*\* To return to our present discussion,

---

\*      Jarosław Marek Rymkiewicz, *Żmut* (Warszawa: Czytelnik, 1991), p. 175. Cited by Szelwach, p. 73.

\*\*     Roman Koropeckyj, *The Politics of Revitalization: Adam Mickiewicz between* Forefathers' Eve, Part 3 *and* Pan Tadeusz (Boulder: East European Monographs, 2001), pp. 13, 35, 43. Mickiewicz stated that the experience was such

whether or not Gustaw is Adam, and Maryla Maria, we can be sure that Mickiewicz the poet comes out strongly, here and in other places, in defence of the rights of the heart, of romantic love.

This is made abundantly clear in Mickiewicz's overtly Bürgeresque tale, "Ucieczka" ["The Escape," 1830]. It is a retelling of the *Lenore* tale, but with a surprising twist. After visiting a witch (*nota bene*: going beyond social and religious convention again), the young woman succeeds in conjuring forth her dead lover. As she "escapes" with him on his horse, he encourages her, again and again, to toss away the religious articles she is carrying with her — for they are slowing down the horse. This she does, without a blink. Even when they arrive at the graveyard, Mickiewicz's maiden does not repent like her earlier sisters in the genre; she follows her heart, and, rejecting the world, leaps into the grave with her lover, locked in a "fiery kiss." Her actions inspire awe; the constant refrain is *Panno, Panno, czy nie strach?* ["Maiden, Maiden, are you not afraid?"], but here the words are not accompanied by a wagging finger; rather, they are the spontaneous outburst of a third party, looking on at the decision in the awestruck manner of a person beholding an act of selfless heroism. The correctness of the girl's choice is confirmed the next morning, when the parish priest, walking about the churchyard, notes the fresh grave — and goes off to celebrate a Mass "for two."

Mickiewicz's bold — and constant — agitation on behalf of Romantic love does not make him a suffering anomaly. Rather, it shows him as an early spokesman for the sort of erotic attraction at the base of all marriages that have a shot at success, and which we for so long now, have taken for granted.

### PART III

Mickiewicz himself "escaped" from Russia, in 1829. A year later, the November Uprising broke out. He did not take part in the insurrection, although he did travel, from Rome to the Prussian Partition, spending some time in the border city of Poznań (Posen) and the surrounding areas, before joining the exodus of Polish intelligentsia to Paris, where he was to spend most of the rest of his life Part III of *Forefathers' Eve* was written In 1832. This is the section of the cycle nearest to Polish hearts, as it directly

---

as if a *bania z poezją się rozbiła nad nim* ["a glass sphere of poetry had suddenly burst over him"].

references the struggle of their nation for independence. As the author writes in the introduction:

> For half a century now, Poland has been the scene of such ceaseless, unflagging, inexorable cruelty at the hands of the tyrants who oppress Her, and such illimitable devotion and endurance on the part of Her suffering peoples, as the world has not seen since the days of the persecuted Christians. It seems as if these kings had a Herod-like presentiment of the manifestation of a new light appearing upon the earth, and of their own imminent downfall, while the people believe ever more strongly in their renewal and resurrection.

Here we find, if not the beginnings, at least the greatest expression of what came to be known as Polish Messianism. The main postulates of this mystical philosophy — referenced by Mickiewicz's younger colleague Juliusz Słowacki and elaborated by the quirky mystic Andrzej Towiański — posits Poland as the "Christ of Europe." Unjustly slain by the empires of Austria, Prussia and Russia (with the Pilate-like acquiescence of France), Poland was understood to be fated to "resurrect" to liberty, which great boon she would then bestow upon the other "enslaved" nations of the continent. As the introduction continues, Mickiewicz strikes the quasi-biblical tone he was soon to develop in the *Księgi narodu i pielgrzymstwa polskiego* [*Books of the Polish Nation and Polish Pilgrimage*, 1832]:

> Round about the year 1822, the politics of Caesar Alexander, the enemy of all liberty, began to manifest themselves more clearly, ground themselves more firmly, and take a more determined direction. In those days a universal persecution was visited upon all the tribes of Poland, an oppression that became ever more violent and bloody. [...] The mystical, gentle, yet unshaken character of Tomasz Zan, the leader of the youths; the religious resignation, brotherly concord and love among the young prisoners; the divine wrath, which evidently fell upon the persecutors, all left deep impressions upon those who were either witnesses to or participants in these events; described, they seem to transport the Reader into ancient times: the ages of faith and miracle.

Yet even despite the new emphasis on the political aspirations of his country, Mickiewicz does not lose sight of the larger picture, the universally human theme of the individual and his place in the cosmos. As Gustaw (soon to rechristen himself Konrad) sleeps in jail through uneasy dreams, the presence of his Guardian Angel reintroduces the "heavenly" vistas that complement the earthly, in both genres of epic, and Polish Monumental Drama:

> Alas, thou no good, heartless child!
> Such force has the incessant care
> Of thy sweet earthly mother mild,
> Her works on earth, in heaven her prayer,
> That thou hast lived a youth secure
> From tempting itch and deed impure.

In speaking of these scenes, Wacław Borowski notes wryly that here, mysticism runs the risk of devolving into a cloying "infantilism." Yet he recognises immediately that the references to "child" and "mother," and indeed the entire superstructure of familial references, constitute a defining characteristic of Part III: "It is a grand poem about children and parents, about the fatherland-family, about human sonship and a Father Divine."\* In short, the grand family of the Communion of the Saints, of which Gustaw/Konrad is himself a subject-agent. As in the case of Dante, both traditional, canonical creatures (the Guardian Angel) and familiar, but now blessed individuals (his sainted mother, like Dante's Beatrice, Faust's Gretchen) make up the living links of the chain that connect the earthly "militant" with God. Polish Monumental Drama, an integrally Catholic manner of looking at the world, is based on the conviction of the interpenetration of eternity and time, the realm of the spirit and the realm of flesh. As Gustaw/Konrad dreams on, fitfully, a philosophical struggle is carried on above his head, no less real in the world of the fiction than the battles of the gods above the Homeric plains:

> NIGHT SPIRITS.
> Black down, soft down, lay here — his head to press.
> Let's sing — but soft! — cause him yet no distress.

---

\*    Borowy, II, p. 79.

[...]

ANGEL.
We've asked the Lord to press
Thee in thy foeman's hands:
Solitude feeds the soul.
Here, in thy loneliness,
As if on desert sands,
Think on thy destined role.

[...]

[Night Spirits]
Let's sing over the sleeper, sons of night!
We'll serve him until he our slave becomes.
Bore through his heart, seep through his inner sight:
He'll be ours yet — ah! may his sleep be long!

ANGEL.
On earth, in heaven, prayers are raised for thee —
Soon from these tyrants thou shalt be set free.

Very interesting, this scene from the prologue, which sets the plight of the main character as a test. Mickiewicz's protagonist has been "pressed / into his foeman's hands" at the request of the heavenly host, something which makes of him a kind of Job figure — and places his rebellion in the same context as the trial of Goethe's Faust — it will endow the climax of his prideful soliloquy with a salvific element of volition, and it also emphasises the sufferings of the entire Polish nation as a kind of theogony. There is a sense to the Partitions, to the repression, and, since sanctified by God, it all must end in victory.

Before the victory, however, comes the struggle. The reality of the world of spirit, so strongly foregrounded in *Forefathers' Eve,* is most apparent, most pregnant with meaning, in this Prologue to Part III. The holistic, Christian ontology, which understands the human individual as a composite being of body, soul, and mind, inhabiting (potentially *and* really) the quotidian world and the realm of the spirit, is seen here more strongly than even in the conjuring scenes of Part II. There, we see the earthly community still viscerally tied to the community of those who have passed on — to glory or torment — here, the Communion of the Saints is depicted in a manner that suggests that no individual is overlooked; all of us, singly as well as communally, are of particular concern to God. The Christian image of the Guardian Angel — a spiritual being surpassing us in power as well as holiness — created specifically to guide the individual to God, is an idea so familiar and common to have been washed pale of the grandeur of its implications. To think: each human being has been accorded his own, individual, spiritual guardian, whose one sole reason for existence is to care for that particular man or woman — how can one not think of oneself as special, after realising this? And yet — of course — it's not all skittles and beer. The special grandeur of the individual human, created in the image of God, which is to say, created with a completely unfettered free will that is respected even by the Omnipotent Himself, implies just as great a responsibility for one's actions.* As the Spirit intones:

> Ah, mortal! If thou only knew thy power!
> When but a thought, like a spark in the mist
> Shines in thy mind unseen, great stormclouds lour
> To pour forth gentle rain or savage tempest.
> If but thou knew, that as each thought alights
> There gather round in silence, and stand by
> Like storm-hounds, angels both sooty and bright:
> — Wilt dash to hell, or flash out in the sky? —
> Yet thou, like a steep cloud, fliest on aloof,
> Knowing not where thou art borne, nor what thou do.
> Ah, mortals! Each of you might, imprisoned, alone,
> By thought and faith overturn the stoutest throne!

The lesson is not lost on Mickiewicz's protagonist, although, as will be seen, his understanding of what this means is far from perfect. It is at this point that Gustaw becomes Konrad, and the thrust of *Forefathers' Eve* shifts from the personal and erotic to the political, the patriotic. Rising, Gustaw comes to terms with the fact of his imprisonment. He understands it to

---

\*   Vide Borowy, II, 86. Further, Borowy notes a statement made by Mickiewicz himself to Mikołaj Kamieński in 1843, which illustrates how seriously he took this issue: "If a man only knew, how great an influence he wields on nature, he might be led to abuse his knowledge." And thus it is good that this is hidden from him! Borowy, II, 89: *Żeby człowiek wiedział, jaki on wywiera wpływ na naturę, to by mógł nadużywać swojej wiedzy.*

signify the end of the life that went before. He shall no longer see Maryla, shall no longer wander about his native fields. But instead of despairing at this thought, he accepts it, and turns to a new life, new goals:

> They've torn my only weapon from my hands.
> No, not quite. But they've broken it, beaten it blunt.
> Alive, but for my Fatherland, a corpse.
> My thought will fester in such shadows dun,
> Like diamonds deep in rockbeds dull and coarse.

When these "diamonds" will be unearthed for their proper use, is something that he cannot know at the moment; he does, however, take the first step on his new road by walking over to the wall, and, literally, assuming a new name, a new persona. He writes:

D. O. M.
GUSTAVUS
OBIIT M. D. CCC. XXIII
CALENDIS NOVEMBRIS

*/and on the facing wall/:*

HIC NATUS EST
CONRADUS
M. D. CCC. XXIII
CALENDIS NOVEMBRIS

Yet he is not entirely "new." In this dramatic cycle of shifting names, shifting modes of existence, the ontological identity of Mickiewicz's protagonist remains constant.* This is made explicit near the culmination

---

\*     Gustaw takes on the "role" of Konrad, as it were. The new, nationalistic orientation of his love is uppermost, but, as Borowy points out, the exact date — 1823 — is important. "This is still the period of the Śniadeckis," he notes, referring to the brother-professors of Wilno University, *bêtes noires* for Mickiewicz because of their adherence to the outdated strictures of Classicism. (The "wiseman" seeking out spirits, or rather seeking to disprove them, in "Romantyczność" is usually taken to be Jędrzej Śniadecki). And so it is a cultural statement as well;

of the Great Improvisation, which we are about to consider, when the
frustrated Konrad threatens God Himself:

> Now I call Thee forth to battle!
> Contemn me not — though exalted, I'm not alone:
> On earth I'm brothered to an awesome nation.
> I've armies and dominions, powers and thrones,
>                And if I choose to blaspheme,
> I'll grip with Thee more bloodily than did Satan!
> I fight at hearts'-point, where he could but scheme.
> I've suffered, loved; torture and love my leaven;
> For when Thou'd torn from me my happiness
> Against my own breast I bloodied my fist,
>                And shook it not at Heaven.
>                    [...]
> Th'art silent! Behold my cleft heart, open wide!
> Now, give me power! Just its baser part,
> A crumb of what on earth was won by pride,
> And with it, how much happiness I'll fashion!

    To what might those lines about "bloodying my fist against my own breast" refer, if not the suicide of Gustaw in Part II? And thus, whatever the change of names, the identity of the protagonist remains the same, and will so remain in Part IV, when he once more assumes the name of Gustaw; in this way coming full circle, from universal man to Pole, and back again to a man with whom all of us can identify.\*

    There is nothing more challenging for the reader, used to logic and linearity, than the matter of that bloodied breast in *Forefathers' Eve*. Is it

---

Gustaw, in taking upon himself the new identity of Konrad, is enlisting himself on the side of the Romantics in the battle with the Classicists. See Borowy, II, 83.

\*     It would be interesting, and instructive, to compile a catalogue of "conditional suicides" in literature. Usually — as in Tasso's *Aminta* (1573) — the desperate person, dead or near dead, is revived by the remorseful caresses of the party who originally spurned him. This usually happens at the climax of the story, providing it with a "happy ending" that precedes unjustly maligned Hollywood by whole centuries. Against such a catalogue, the revolutionary, and deeply philosophical, uniqueness of Mickiewicz's revenant Gustaw/Konrad would be thrown in to high relief.

a physical wound, or a symbolic one? Was it fatal, or not? In this cycle where the dead and the living enjoy the same rights on stage, it is best to simply throw up one's hands and suspend our disbelief: in the traditional, Catholic world of *Forefathers' Eve* (which is more traditional and Catholic than we denizens of rationalist ages are willing to admit), reigned over by an Omnipotent God who — to paraphrase Scripture — is not a god of the dead, but the God of the living, anything can happen.

From a literary point of view, here, the act of suicide — from love's despair in Part II — is sublimated into a sacrifice on behalf of the nation. In the three lines preceding the ellipses in the citation above, Konrad merely says that he did not blame God for his misfortune, although he does — obliquely — indeed blame him for "tearing that happiness from him." In the four which follow, the ripped heart becomes something of a ghastly parody of the Sacred Heart of Jesus, or the pierced Immaculate Heart of Mary. The wound has been made, Konrad implies, so as to allow passage of the power he desires of God. As we shall see, the "power" he demands is not divine at all.

To deal with the Great Improvisation from a cold, interpretative perspective is to risk eviscerating it. Perhaps this is true of all poetry; perhaps nowhere is the dictum of T.E. Hulme more apropos than in reference to close readings of truly remarkable poetry. When we engage with the poem on its own terms, as poetry, allowing it to speak directly to us, we come in contact with a real, living object. Criticism is taxidermy.*

And yet it is inevitable. The same thing might be said for the entirety of *Forefathers' Eve*, and since we so deal with the other sections of the work, there is no reason to exempt the Great Improvisation. Our hesitation to do so springs from the consciousness of what this soliloquy has meant, and continues to mean, for generations of Poles. We refer the reader to the often contradictory statements given by Poles from across the political spectrum, and through the years since 1832, highlighted in "The National

---

\*        "In prose as in algebra concrete things are embodied in signs or counters, which are moved about according to rules, without being visualized at all in the process. [...] Poetry [...] is not a counter language, but a visual concrete one. It is a compromise for a language of intuition which would hand over sensations bodily. It always endeavours to arrest you, and to make you continuously see a physical thing, to prevent you gliding through an abstract process. ... Prose is in fact the museum where the dead images of verse are preserved." Writing in the *New Age*, 19 August 1909, cited by Noel Stock in *The Life of Ezra Pound* (New York: Avon, 1970), p. 99.

Context" above. Like the Bible — and Konrad, in his raving, implies that his writing is no less inspired than the canon of Scripture — it can be made to mean practically anything. The one thing it cannot be made to mean is that the superhuman claims of Konrad have any real basis in fact, or the approbation of their author.

On the one hand, the soliloquy is the chief expression of Polish frustration at the nation's continuing dismemberment and subjugation to the Prussian, Austrian, and (especially) Russian Empires. It is the chief expression of Polish "Prometheanism," in which the poet Konrad dares to take God Himself to task for the oppression of his people; here we have the artist assuming the mantle of statesman. Curiously, if the mantle is prophetic, the vatic statement flows in an unusual direction. A message is not being transmitted from the deity to the people; rather, the national "prophet" is informing God of something, acting as the spokesman of humans. But the soliloquy cannot be said to be the chief expression of Polish Messianism. That will be reserved for the soliloquy of Fr. Piotr, in which Konrad's implicit claims of the innocence of Poland's suffering will be developed into an explicit claim of the nation playing a role in God's plans: through her "crucifixion," Poland will resurrect the enslaved nations of Europe to freedom. (*That* is prophecy; that message is moving in the usual direction). What is true is that, while Mickiewicz does allow Konrad a long leash in this soliloquy, and thus permits him to enunciate the frustration that many of his countrymen were feeling, he does not fully buy into the claims made by his shaman, nor does he invite us to do so. Konrad's words are beautiful, inspiring, and daring. They are also chilling, as when he demands "soul's rule" from God, and would so act, if he were granted it, in a way that is at opposite poles with the gentle influence of God. God respects our free will; Konrad would make us into automatons, if "happy" ones. In short, Konrad is raving; indeed, possessed. After that very real exorcism scene, we are left to wonder: how much of what Konrad said was dictated him by the devil? Some of it? All of it?

One thing is true: in so framing his Great Improvisation, Mickiewicz razes the superstructure of Byronism. There are no supermen, no Manfreds. Toward the end of Part III, as we shall see, Konrad learns that, while grand schemes for bettering the life of his countrymen (through "soul's rule," for example) are impossible, small acts of charity can lead to an actual betterment of their situation. And this plays into the very homey, real atmosphere of *Forefathers' Eve*. Konrad's small act of charity at the end of this section, in which he donates his ring to Fr. Piotr for the living poor and the suffering souls of Purgatory, is a real participation in the Communion of the Saints no less palpable than the offerings spread before the revenant souls in the nighttime chapel.

The Great Improvisation begins with a paradox: the poet, who is to challenge God Himself on behalf of his nation, sees himself as set apart from them, and speaks of them with disdain from his lofty perch:

> "The people." Ha! Do I sing for the crowd?
> Show me the man who's grasped
> My song's thoughts whole —
> Unblinded by the sun-flash of its soul!
> Wretched is he who jabbers for the rout:
> Tongue belies voice, voice belies thought,
> Thought springs from soul, then is broken, caught
> In words, swallowed by words brooding, aquiver,
> Like the earth above a secret river.
> From topsoil trembling, can men sound the stream's depths?
> Or whence it's rushing — can they even guess?

Konrad proceeds to speak of his "songs" in words that recall the bibliolatry of Islam: they are not simple literary compositions such as one might scribble down on a cocktail napkin; they are something of an eternal word, creative, and past all contemplation:

> O my song, you're a star past the world's farthest bounds.
> Earthly eyes, even fluttering on wings of ground glass,
> Think to soar to you, but merely hop off the ground.
> And even if they reach your Milky Way at last
> > They've learned to glimpse your sun's bright treasure,
> > But flag at calculation, scope and measure.

Again the paradox. If he is a great poet, how can we tell, if we mere mortals are unable to evaluate his output? He immediately answers our question with these haughty lines:

> My songs, you have no need of human eyes—
> > Flow through the recesses of my soul,

> Shine at the zenith of her starry pole,
> Like underground rivers — like stars of the night skies.
> Thou God, thou Nature! I would have you hear —
> Such a song as mine is worthy of Your ear.

Nowhere, perhaps, do we have such a brash assertion of the creative power touted by the Romantics who, following Fichte, would claim that the worlds created by their imaginations are no different in real existence from the world we walk upon daily. Konrad continues his praise of his "song-creation:"

> A master, I stretch forth my hands,
>     Stretch forth unto the heavens, and place my hands
> Upon the stars, as if upon the crystal wheels
>     Of a harmonium, and roll
>     Now softly, swiftly now, stars, with my soul.
>     A million tones, and of these myriads
>     Each I coax forth, and am aware of all,
>     Binding, sundering, chords, triads,
> Spilling out rainbow mists and thunder peals!
>
> I take my hands away and lift them up
> Over the world's edge — and the wheels stop.
>     The spheres are silent. I sing alone.

At this moment, he turns to the people; not just his own, but the entire "race of man." Whatever he might think of the impossibility of mankind understanding his poetry, he claims the right to be our spokesman before God:

> Long, drawn-out, like the wind's deep tone;
>     I hear my songs engulf the race of man:
>     They moan in mourning, scream in rage,
>     Accompanied by age on age
> And each note a seraphic firebrand!
>     It's in my ear, it's in my eye,
>     Just like the whistling wind that sweeps
>     The billowed waves across the deep,
>     The burly clouds across the sky.

And again we have that curious prophecy *à rebours*. It is not Konrad's task to transmit God's will to his people, or even, like Milton, to justify His ways. Rather, Konrad transmits the mourning and rage of suffering mankind to God. But now he starts to unravel. It's one thing for the great soul to scorn the grey masses. More than one "superman" has made similar claims, shown similar contempt. Konrad, however, begins to scorn *God Himself* by asserting a kind of collegiality between himself as creator of songs, and God as creator of the universe — (which, paradoxically of course, includes Konrad):

> Worthy of God, such versification!
> This song, this great song, this Song-Creation.
> Such song is strength — causality —
> Such song is immortality!
> I feel the Eternal — the Eternal I've wrought —
> What greater thing might'st Thou have done, O God?

As we note above, not even Manfred will make such a startling claim. Commanded to bow down before the evil genius Arimanes, he replies "Bid *him* bow down to that which is above him, / The overruling Infinite — the Maker / Who made him not for worship — Let him kneel / And we will kneel together." It is not inconceivable that this is exactly what Mickiewicz was aiming at: the destruction of the Byronic hero, by pushing his overreaching past its limits and discovering him, to our eyes, to be a mere mortal, no different from anyone else. Konrad — consciously or not — speaks of the confrontation he is speeding towards as a test:

> Am I almighty, or just overproud?
> — Tonight I'll know. This moment is my fate.
> Tonight I flex the sinews of my soul —
>     This is my Samson hour, my weight
> Is pressed against the columns of my prison.
> I'll cast my flesh aside, and when I've risen
>     On spirit wings, I'll soar
> Out of the sluggish round where star and planet roll
> To where Created borders on Creator.

Here we recall the Job/Faustian context of the angelic claims in the Prologue. If Konrad has been handed over to his enemy in order to be sifted, perhaps these — unfettered — exploratory ravings are not sinful per se, as they have been implicitly sanctioned by God. Whatever the case may be, very quickly, he admits (despite his earlier claims) that he is not quite the equal of the Ancient of Days. He is "just a man," and despite his "great powers," still he lacks the means to influence his people in a direct way that would impel them to liberty and happiness. Whatever the desired outcome, the emphasis here is on compulsion, rather than influence.

Throughout the entire soliloquy, Konrad has been arguing from "feeling," rather than reason. The latter he considers, like a true Romantic, too calculating; a brake to progress and happiness, rather than a spur. Feeling, on the other hand, is more direct; it impels one to actions that may be rash, but are nevertheless true for the direct way they suffuse the person and impel him to do something. However, the power that Konrad seeks goes beyond the ability to stir an object's free agency. He seeks an "influence" that will be immediate, and irresistible:

> I want to wield the Heart that burns in me.
> I want to rule as Thou dost — always, secretly:
>> What I will — let them but understand,
>> Do it directly, and count them blest
>> With each task, and should they protest,
>> Then let them suffer for it, and be damned!
> Let people be to me as word and thought:

---

\*   Beyond the theological question of whether Konrad is sinning or not, Mickiewicz, subtly yet strongly, draws forth Konrad's insanity by having him shift between acknowledgement of his humanity, and wild claims of — why avoid the word? — deity. Not long after this admission of humanity, he queries God: "Didst Thou bestow it on me — this eye, sharp and strong, / Or did I seize it myself?" Those who are able to resist the strong charm of Konrad's passionate words will hear, in these lines, a claim as laughably irrational as that of Milton's Lucifer, who, when called by Abdiel to renew his acknowledgement of the God Who created him, petulantly responds that neither he, nor anyone else, remembers his creation. Perhaps it was different than what Abdiel suggests? Perhaps he created himself? Cf. *Paradise Lost,* V:856-863. There Satan suggests that he and the angels might have been "self-begot, self-rais'd / By our own quick'ning power" which of course makes no sense whatsoever.

> Bricks of song-structures to be willed and wrought!
> Such is, they say, Thy governance!

Whether or not Mickiewicz read Milton, Konrad surely didn't. Nor is he well-grounded in Christian moral theology. For the claim that God's "governance" is such that it takes possession of the human's will and compels him to action — and this is exactly what he is claiming, and claiming for himself, in the above-cited lines — is as far from the traditional understanding of the Judeo-Christian God as it can be. As Alina Witkowska succinctly puts it, "Konrad's dreams for making people happy bear the traits of a tyrant's love, who desires to subject others to the dictatorship of the heart."[*] Even the heterodox Milton points out that God, while foreknowing that Adam and Eve would betray His command, still did not force them to do so. For had He done that, He would have destroyed their free will — which is what makes human beings both human, and created in the image of God — and turned them into robots, automatons, things.

And here begins Konrad's raving in earnest. In the lines which follow, while continuing to stake the claim for his exceptionalism (even though there are others on earth, he admits, like him, there is no greater) and even though he admits here that God may be more powerful than he, still, he wishes to meet the Lord on equal terms, and makes the surprisingly irrational claim that, if he really tried, he could destroy the entire cosmos:

> Give me souls'-rule! How I contemn this shed
> The mob calls "world" and has grown used to praise it;
> How can it be that I have not as yet
> Attempted with my mighty hand to raze it?
> And yet I feel that, should I tense my will,
> Screw it down tight,
> Then, burst it forth, I might snuff out one hundred stars
> And another hundred alight,
> For I'm immortal! And in creation's round

---

[*] Witkowska, p. 119. See also Borowy, II, 109, for the ironic contradictions in Konrad's speech: the Great Soul who wishes to "make his nation happy" would do so by depriving his countrymen of the very faculty upon which happiness is predicated: free will. "I would [re]-create my nation like a living song," he states at one point, "and if they rebel against me, let them be damned," he says at another!

> There are such others — but I've never found
> A greater. O Thou, greatest by far
> Here in the heavens! It is Thee I've sought
> Here at the cosmic axis,
> I who stand greatest in the earthly vale.
> I haven't met Thee yet; that Thou dost exist
> I sense, I know — let us meet! Let me feel
> Thy exaltation!
> 'Tis rule I want; such power is my lot —
> Give it to me, or but point out the road
> That leads to this my fated destination!
> There have been prophets — soul-rulers, I know —
> They've done great things, well, so can I!
> I want to rule as Thou dost, from on high,
> And as Thou dost, I want to rule the soul.

God, however, is silent — predictably so to all of us, save poor raving Konrad. He returns to his hobby-horse of feeling, and yet, paradoxically, comes to the conclusion that, if God will not respond to his feeling with feeling, He must be devoid of feeling; He must be the greatest "wiseman" of all. And if something internal impedes Konrad, at the end of the soliloquy, from blaspheming, overcoming him with a paroxysm before he can get the last word out which would compare God to the Tsar, here he succeeds in blasphemy, by sneering, "Thou art love? A liar [i.e. Christ Himself] Thee so named!"

We have seen the word "test" used twice in reference to Konrad. Tests, in reference to human agents, imply self-control, free will, in the human subject. One of the greatest tests known to our culture is that to which Job is subjected in the Old Testament. Borowy, indeed, compares Konrad to Job, highlighting the fascinating fact that, whereas Latin translations, beginning with St. Jerome, translate VII:20 of that book thus: "And though I have sinned, what have I done to Thee, O guardian of man? [*custos hominum*]," the Hebrew text replaces the last vocative with "tyrant of humanity." But

---

\* The Hebrew word is *natsar*, at the root of which is "protection." It also has a secondary meaning of "concealment," which is tempting in the context of Konrad's complaints. However, it seems that Borowy, after Fallek, is not on the solidest of grounds here, and that St. Jerome is probably correct, after all. We

if it is a test, Konrad is subjected to it, not saved from it, as Konrad Górski mistakenly suggests: "At the last minute, God halted Konrad's wild career" and, while "thrusting him into the abyss from which Fr. Piotr was to raise him," still preempted the blasphemous expression.* What Górski overlooks is that, if this were true, Mickiewicz would be making God into the very sort of tyrant that Konrad assumes Him to be, depriving, at the same time, Konrad of his human nature and replacing it with that of an automaton — just as he wished to do to his "nation." No, even if prevenient grace allows Konrad to tense his flagging strength and restrain himself from the damning word, still it is Konrad who wills to restrain himself, and is able to.

Free will, which tears Konrad from the clutches of the devils who had animated him like a marionette all the long way through the Great Improvisation, must be imputed to him. *He* overcomes the temptation to curse God as the universal "Tsar;" his freely willed refusal to spit out this last, fatal word is what saves his life, his soul. Otherwise, there is nothing heroic about him at all. He is still quite sick, but it is this last inch of free earth, in which he fixes fast his heel against the onslaught of Hell, that allows Fr. Piotr to enter his cell and finally and fully to exorcise him from his tormentors.

What a difficult lesson to learn, and how arduous a struggle to learn it. But it had to happen; at this point, one sees the wisdom of Alina Witkowska's interpretation of Gustaw's conscious self-recreation at the beginning of the Great Improvisation, and the Improvisation itself, as brutally honest self-exploration:

> Both improvisations, and especially the so-called Great Improvisation, possess a confessional character, in the sense of honesty and deep confession, an opening of the soul [...] The analytical process, though violent and auto-reflexive, of Konrad's improvisation grants him, in its extraordinary outburst of poetic power — perhaps — a vision of himself, his aspirations and goals.

---

must add to this the question of whether or not Mickiewicz knew Hebrew in the first place, so any similarities between the Great Improvisation and the Hebrew text of the scriptures looks to be coincidental rather than intended. For Borowy's argument, see II, 127.

\* Konrad Górski, *Racjonalizm i mistyka w Improwizacji Konrada*, p. 90, cited by Borowy, II, 132.

Near the conclusion of the Prologue, when the prisoner writes on the wall of his cell "Gustavus obiit [...] hic natus est Conradus," he conjures up in himself a new man, who is to be the essential opposite to Maryla's lover. But just who and what are hidden behind this new name, we will only come to know thanks to the Great Improvisation. In a certain sense, Konrad will only come to know it that way, too, for the Great Improvisation is an act of auto-creation. For this reason, one can consider it an examination of oneself; it fulfils the same function as the "visions" of the other characters in the work, such as Fr. Piotr, Ewa, and the Senator.[*]

Konrad will not revert — yet — to his previous identity as Gustaw. At the end of it all, he is cured, and it is this that allows him to move from the unrealisable dreams of Prometheanism to the practical work of charity. As he is being led off to exile, Konrad once more catches sight of Fr. Piotr, present, in the same room, by chance:

KONRAD.
That's odd — I've never seen that priest before,
And yet, I seem to know him. I'm as sure
As if he were my brother. Once, I dreamed...
Yes — now I do remember where I've seen
That very face, those very eyes of his...
His was the hand plucked me from the abyss.

/to the Priest/

Father, though we don't know each other well
— At least you don't know me — please, deign accept
The thanks of one who in his conscience knows
The grace poured out on him while his reason slept.
Friends are always well met, even such as those
Seen in dreams only, when so many foes
Surround us. Take this ring, Father, and sell it —
Give half to the poor, half for the suffering souls

---

[*]     Witkowska, p. 120. Jan Walc calls the Improvisation "the deepest act of self-criticism, condemnation, and rejection of self-pride." Walc, p. 144.

> In Purgatory. Well I know their dole,
> If Purgatory be imprisonment —
> And who knows if I'll ever hear Mass again.

Konrad has learned his lesson, and Mickiewicz offers it to us. Perhaps Konrad's claims, during the soliloquy, that his verse is sublimely unintelligible to the vulgar masses, was not mere raving, but a preparation for this scene. We cannot contact, let alone identify ourselves, with Konrad in his Byronic, poetic trance, which is sterile anyway, in that the claims he makes are shown to be empty. We do recognise Konrad in his Christian humility, here. Bettering society by "soul's rule" is out of our grasp (fortunately!); there remains the less dramatic, but infinitely more efficacious, method of small, concrete acts of charity. All of us can do that, and if enough of us did, the world, which will never be perfect, would at least be better.

Scholars of Polish literature like to generalise in dividing the nineteenth century into two periods. The earlier, Romantic Age, dominated by Mickiewicz, is revolutionary in nature. After 1863 — the last "romantic" insurrection against Russia — the Positivist Age foregoes revolutionary gestures for "organic work" — the kind of less flashy, patient approach to reality, working on behalf of others, which would prepare the entire nation for re-integration when the Partitions would finally disappear. As is often the case, such cultural shifts don't suddenly come into being when the clock strikes twelve. They are precipitated by human beings, and although they may be more pronounced in one cultural period than in another, they are, as human traits, always accessible. And thus here, Mickiewicz reveals his universalism in striking fashion. He's allowed himself the paroxysm of revolutionary claims; from them he returns to the sober truths of human nature.

Gustaw/Konrad is indeed a representative man, no less than is the character of Dante as written into his *Comedy*, or that of Goethe's *Faust*.[*]

---

[*] One would also like to write "Byron's Manfred," but that character is consistently too outside the normal parameters of humankind for us to consider him our representative. In that work, the Chamois Hunter better fits the bill. In Czech literature, Karel Hynek Mácha's Vílem (from the narrative poem *Máj*, influenced by both Byron and Mickiewicz) is a representative man. This is not so much true of his acts — a bandit and an unwitting parricide — as of his situation on the night before his execution. Mácha develops such an exquisite portrait of a

Although during his rant he declares himself to be his nation incarnate, he never sets himself up as the acme of Polish suffering. In other words, while he may, in his possession, be tempted to equate himself with God the Father, he never suggests that he is a Christ figure. He is just one among many, and as Part III continues, each of them is accorded his place on stage, in person, or in the memories of others. There is the young martyr Cyprian Michał Janczewski:

> A year ago he was a carefree child.
> Now, gazing through the bars, like from some wild
> And lonely cliff — a Caesar! — and his eye,
> Proud, calm, contemptuous of the drabs, and dry —
> As if he wanted to cheer up his mates,
> And with a bitter smile, but sweet, he bade
> Farewell to the onlookers, as if to say
> "It doesn't really hurt."

There is Adolf Cichowski; in what is perhaps one of the first literary descriptions of PTSD on record, Mickiewicz describes and deplores not only his unjust imprisonment, but indeed the ruination of the rest of his life, once freed, by the experiences he underwent:

> So many tortures had he to endure,
> So many talks with his own self, unsure
> Whether the walls had ears, his one defence
> Against incrimination — stubborn silence,
> With only shadows for his company,
> That, no month in the town, however gay
> Could undo lessons rote-learned day by day
> For fifteen years. He saw the sun's bright eye
> As the unsleeping gaze of some great spy;
> His servants — keepers, each guest an enemy.
> When someone would drop by for conversation,
> He'd think it was for an interrogation.

---

human being facing unanswerable, final questions of death and what comes after so that not only we, but even his jailer, are moved to the core with empathy, seeing in him, ourselves.

> He'd turn around and so avert his gaze
> That what his lips said not, nor should his eyes
> Betray; withdrawing deep inside himself,
> He'd concentrate his strength, so as not to tell
> A word unweighed. You'd ask him any question —
> He'd think himself again back in his prison,
> Rush off as if he were still in his cell,
> To cower in the corner, crying "I won't tell!
> I don't know!"Ah, how many tears his wife
> Poured out, convincing him that all was well!

There is the character known as Wasilewski, for whom Mickiewicz reserves a Golgothan scene:

> Now, Wasilewski didn't faint, or sag,
> Or droop, he just fell outright on the flags.
> There on the soldier's breast, his arms around
> His neck, he looked like one just taken down
> From the cross. His eyes were a horrible sight —
> Round and wide-open, and completely white.
> The crowd as well opened wide their eyes and mouths
> And from a thousand breasts there then rushed out
> A common sigh — a deep, underground moan
> As if it seeped out from beneath gravestones.

The crowd, witnessing with pity this "deposition from the cross" (even the Russian guard who lifts him from the ground has to wipe tears from his eyes) seems like a congregation participating in the Stations of the Cross on a Lenten Friday. Yet they are no mere spectators; as the final lines of the citation indicate, they too are victims, trampled down beneath the hard earth of Russian oppression. Thus Witkowska perceptively notes the constant repetition of eye-witness statements in this scene "I saw... I saw... I saw..." which constitutes for her a republican, and patriotic strain in Mickiewicz's poetry:

> Not only bards, folk-visionaries [*wajdeloty*], "chosen" ones can be sentinels of [national] remembrance; anyone can, any ordinary pedestrian who can say "I saw it myself" [... This is] a universal

attainability of participation in history, which most clearly links the Dresden *Dziady* with the conception of a contemporary Polish martyrology.*

Mickiewicz's catalogue of Polish sufferings under the heel of the Tsar extends even to a certain Ksawery Łebski, who committed suicide rather than face the torments of such a Russian prison as broke Cichowski for good:

> ADOLF.
> Remember Ksawery, who blew his pate
> Apart rather than fall into their web.
>
> FREJEND.
> Łebski! Who lingered with us 'round the wine,
> But come the gall — he's gone, with hasty step!
>
> FR. LWOWICZ
> Prayers for him too would not be out of line.

Uncharacteristically for the time, the imprisoned priest, Fr. Lwowicz, encourages prayers for his soul too, as one more sinned against, than sinning.

All of these examples of Polish "martyrs" are a conscious contextualisation of Konrad. He is not a great, Napoleonic or Byronic soul, but one of many innocent victims of oppression. The implications are quite clear: all of Poland is in this together. And as their suffering is shared, so will be their victory. It also accords well with what we have seen of the "backwards" quality of Konrad's prophetic stature, which does not have him delivering messages to the people from the Lord, but rather representing them, as their mouthpiece, before Him.

Nor is Konrad's frantic soliloquy exceptional, saving its violent qualities. Three other characters are accorded similar spiritual experiences, and consequent vatic utterance, in Part III. The innocent young girl named Eva, and the vicious tsarist viceroy, Senator Novosiltsov, are visited in sleep by dreams which are, respectively, comforting and terrifying. Most

---

\*      Witkowska, p. 116.

importantly, or at least most dramatically, Fr. Piotr, the priest who exorcised Konrad of his demons, is granted a glorious vision by God. Unlike the other two, this occurs not as a dream, but a trance, while waking. It is prompted by, or at least granted during, prayer. Traditionally (and beautifully), Mickiewicz shows Fr. Piotr gaining access to God, not through the prideful claims of the poetic shaman, but the humility of the pious servant:

> Lord, what am I worth in Thy sight?
> Dust, not a mite.
> Yet should I but confess my worthlessness,
> Then grantest Thou converse with Thy holiness.

Immediately following this comes the vision: first, of Poland's suffering, and then, of her resurrection and final victory. Here, in recording Fr. Piotr's vision, Mickiewicz is really toying with prophecy. Up until now he has either been narrating a fictionalised history of personal, and national, trials, or he has been creating (in the Great Improvisation) a convincing psychological portrait of megalomania. Fr. Piotr's vision is a vision of the future. Like El Greco's famous "Opening of the Fifth Seal," Mickiewicz is engaged in the fascinating task of describing something which has not yet taken place. In this case, it is the reestablishment of Polish liberty, something that he states will be brought about by one of the innocent "children" oppressed by the Tsar:

> But look! — one child's escaped — and he shall bring
> Salvation to his nation suffering!
> Of foreign mother — heroic blood of yore —
> And his name shall be forty-four.

Only a mystic would dare indulge in the unverifiable — and unscholarly — question of whether Mickiewicz actually *was* a prophet, and, if so, set out to identify that child of liberty. Since Polish independence was not regained until 1918, it would logically have to be after that date. Did the "prophet" foresee Marshal Piłsudski? Lech Wałęsa? Karol Wojtyła?\* The sticking point has to do with the "foreign mother" stipulation. This, and the

---

\*   Such mystics are never lacking. In 1978, countless Poles were ready to canonise Juliusz Słowacki a prophet for his 1848 poem "Pośród niesnasków"

numerological designation "44," not to mention the fact that Mickiewicz succeeded in escaping Russia for the west, have led many to wonder whether or not the poet was referring to himself. It is said that Mickiewicz's mother was of Jewish ancestry — which would cover the "heroic foreign blood;" as for "44," Czesław Miłosz tells us that these numbers are an equivalent of the Hebrew letters DM. Given that vowels are not written in Hebrew texts, "Does it stand for Adam, for Mickiewicz himself?" he asks. "We do not know, and the author confessed that he had known only at the time of writing." This is not unlike the story of Coleridge's experience writing "Kubla Khan." In both of these cases, the poets imply that they were under the mastering influence of extra-rational perception. For Coleridge, the vision was prompted by an opium dream; in Mickiewicz's case, whence did that fleeting illumination come? Impossible to know; what is certain is that at the time of writing, the arrival of this salvific child on the scene was yet to take place. As Fr. Piotr begins his description of the Passion of Poland (which will underpin the ideology of Polish Messianism), he begs the Lord to speed on the happy event:

> O Lord! Wilt Thou this child's advent not hasten,
> To cheer my people chastened?
> No — the people shall suffer — I see the rout
> That drags along to judgement my Nation bound —
> All Europe tears and drags him, mocks,
> "To the Tribune!"— innocent, to the stocks.
> There at the bench, mugs heartless, handless, sit:
> His judges!
> "Gaul!" cries the people, "the trial! Get on with it!"
> Gaul finds no sin in him, and yet begrudges
> The verdict — washes his hands
> While the kings cry out, "Death is our demand!
> Torture and death! May his blood be upon
> Us and our sons!
> Crucify the Son of Mary; give us Barabbas!

---

["Amidst strife"] which foretells the election of a Slavic pope, who will bring equity and peace to all peoples.

\*      Czesław Miłosz, *The History of Polish Literature* (Berkeley: University of California Press, 1983), p. 223.

Poland is traditionally Francophile. So much so that, in the hegemonic past, the Russians were wont to classify this stubborn recusant to Pan-Slavism and sometime rival as a "Latin traitor" to Slavdom; in our own times, the Polish intellectual Krzysztof Zanussi has called his country "a Romance nation that happens to speak a Slavic tongue."* Poles filled the ranks of Napoleon's Grande Armée, in the hope that their participation in *Gallic* hegemony would lead to a resurrected Poland, and it is no coincidence that the Emperor chose the honour guard permitted him in his final exile from among his Polish officers. With that in mind, we can see that Fr. Piotr's vision has a tang of the immediate present. Poland is crucified by Prussia, Russia, and Austria; with the exaggeration permitted to venting, "all Europe" drags her along and mocks her, while France herself — from whom the Poles had hoped so much — plays the role of a cynical Pilate.

From here on out, we're in the nebulous future, and nothing certain can be ascertained concerning the validity of the continuing images:

> While Mother Freedom stands below and weeps,
> "I thirst" — Austria vinegar, and Prussia
> Gall offers — Look! and now a Russian
> Leaps forth and stabs him — blameless blood
> Flows out my Nation's side in a salvific flood.
> What have you done, most stupid, brutal knave!
> Yet he alone repents, and shall be saved.

Well, perhaps we can say that, at least from the perspective of the present moment, that last line is proof positive to many Poles that Mickiewicz certainly was *not* a prophet! What can have prompted his sentimental casting of Russia in the role of Longinus, except for his sincere affection for his Russian friends, expressed, among other places, in "To My Muscovite Friends," with which the *Passages* come to an end? For the trials of Poland at the hands of Russia were to continue all throughout the twentieth century, and remain far less than cordial in the twenty-first.

No less problematic are the concluding lines of the priest's vision, in which resurrected Poland is personified:

---

\*     In conversations with the author.

> His pupils three a starry trinity,
> His punctured palm aloft for all to see.
> Who is this man? — Thy deputy on earth,
> I know him — since his very birth.
> But how he's grown! His soul — how grand!
> He's blind — an angel leads him by the hand.
> A fearsome sight: three faces — look!
> He has three brows.
> Above him, like a baldachin, a book,
> A book mysterious shades his head,
> And on three capitals he rests his foot.

It would be hard to find a more confusing bit of hermetic writing than this. Moving past the contradiction of the person having a superlative number of eyes and being blind all the same, the description of the three-faced "deputy" or "vicar" is far from awe-inspiring; the reader is immediately reminded of Dante's grotesque description of Lucifer, whose three faces are meant to be as repulsive and farcical as the unfathomable mystery of the Trinity is beautiful.*

Eva's vision, that of a little girl who lives not far from the southeastern city of Lwów, is a more peaceful complement to Konrad's raving. She has just learned of the persecution of the students from a Pole visiting her father. She prays for them, and especially for a "poet" who suffers along with them. As she falls asleep, she is rewarded with a visionary dream appropriate to her age and innocence:

> I see — the Blessed Mother! — brilliant
> With glory, as she takes up in her hand,
> Looking at me the while, the humble garland,
> And gives it to the Babe, who, laughing, throws
> At me narcissus, lily, rose —
> How they have swelled in beauty at His touch!

---

\*      To add to the confusion, we are told that the has "three pupils" and "three faces." Does this mean he is some sort of triple cyclops, with one eye in each brow? Or has he three eyes in each face, for a total of nine? Or is it merely that each eye has three pupils, instead of one? In any event, the descriptions are far from attractive.

> How many there are now! How much
> More lovely as they spin,
> Each searching for his twin,
> My darlings,
> Twining new garlands!
> How lovely it is here, like paradise!
> How happy I am here, my God, my Christ!
> May this garland ever wind me round!
> May I die, by rose and lily bound,
> Gazing in the white narcissus' eyes.

This is certainly not as dramatic as Konrad's ravings, but it is more comforting and believable. The heaven that she contacts in her vision is not the abode of overwhelming power, but the seat of love. The God she beholds is the Baby Jesus, who is presented to her — quite in line with the *Salve, Regina* — by His Mother, our human sister and mediatrix, the Virgin Mary. The girl's name is Eve, which is not coincidental; and her vision supersedes that of Fr. Piotr as well. The latter's vision implies an earthly reckoning, while Eve's returns us to the lost Eden of the "peace that passeth understanding" toward which mankind has been yearning since the Fall. Need we also mention that our poet's name is Adam? Heavy-handed allusions aside, it is important to note that this vision, the least commented upon by critics of *Forefathers' Eve*, might be the most important of the three. Konrad's literally diabolical ravings are a non-starter, and lead nowhere. Even Fr. Piotr's messianism is shown as wanting in comparison to the vision of the little girl.* We have here a repeat of the Christian messianic story, according to which Jesus was rejected by the Jews, not because of His messianic claims, but because of the manner in which He presented Himself. The Jews were awaiting a Messiah — but one of an earthly kind, who was to restore the Davidic kingship, chase the Romans from Palestine, and settle old political scores, here and now. Is that not the sort of Messiah of whom Fr. Piotr dreams? Christ's kingdom, however, was not of this world, nor is His triumph, nor that of the individual Christian, nor that of the Christian

---

\* Whether Mickiewicz intended it or no, one is tempted to relate the priest's name, Peter, with that of the prince of the apostles, St. Peter, and likewise, his clumsy hopes for earthly reckoning with the missteps St. Peter frequently takes in the Gospels.

community, to be expected "here and now." Eve's vision reminds us of the spiritual, transcendent significance of the Incarnation and salvation history as a whole; in this way, her vision links, in power and importance, with the last words we hear from Konrad at the end of his exorcism, and those at the end of his story. The exorcised shaman learns his lesson, as soon as he comes back to his senses following the expulsion of the devil:

> You lift me up? — who... Take care, lest you tumble
> Into this same abyss! He gives his hand,
> And we fly upwards — through the scented breeze,
> Bird-like, I soar, and shine with the sun's rays —
> Who gave his hand? An angel, or a man?
> Who dared descend among the hellish rubble
> Where I had landed, senseless and forgot?
> Contemning men, the angels I knew not!

It is a lesson of practical love, one human being's grateful recognition of another. It is a lesson of help, of one soul for another, played out not against a political background, but on a level both more prosaic and sublime: that of the struggle between heaven and hell, good and evil. It is a lesson that Konrad internalises, and which permits him, in lines that we have quoted before, to perform an act of love, in donating his ring for the relief of others, living and dead. It is a small act, but infinitely larger than the impossible deeds he aspired to not so long ago.

Eva's vision, devoid of nationalism and politics, and Konrad's final act of charity, so mundane and human, elevate this poetic cycle to a general human level that surpasses its significance for Polish literature, and sets it in the company of the universally applicable texts of Dante, Goethe and Shakespeare.

Konrad's farewell to Fr. Piotr constitutes the last time we hear him speak in Part III. It is not the last time we see him, though. Once more, near the conclusion of the segment, Mickiewicz returns us to a gloomy graveyard in early November. That year's rites are about to come to a conclusion; we are privy to a conversation between a young woman and an elderly *guślarz*. It's time to go, the latter suggests. There is nothing more to see now:

> WOMAN.
> I'll stay here, guślarz, even so,
> Here in this darkling cemetery —

There's only one soul I would see:
The one that, long ago, appeared
Among the spirits, in the year
That I was married — suddenly —
Pale and bloody, silently
Measuring me with a wild eye.

GUŚLARZ.
It's possible he hadn't died —
That's why he wouldn't answer me,
Despite my strongest conjuring.
For it is possible, you know,
To conjure, on Forefathers' Eve,
The spirits of the living, too.
The dust remains at cards, in fight,
Or at the table; all the same,
The living spirit thence takes flight
When it is conjured by its name,
Appearing like a shadow thin.
As long as its time hasn't come
Though, it can't speak — it stands there, dumb.

With this brief exchange, Mickiewicz identifies Konrad of Part III with Gustaw of Part II, and reinforces the tantalising, confusing (yet perhaps, after all, irrelevant) game of death-in-life, suicide literal or metaphorical. Witkowska, while not explicitly denying the reality of Konrad's (Gustaw's) self-slaughter, sees in it a metaphor of an "unwillingness to agree to a compromise with life."* The identification of Konrad with Gustaw (i.e., the fact that there is *one* hero of *Forefathers' Eve*, not two) is made even stronger a few lines hence. The *guślarz* tries one more time to conjure the soul of the one person the woman most wants to see. When he doesn't appear, the girl despairs, "He's a dead spirit!" But no, the *guślarz* replies:

---

\*      Alina Witkowska, *Literatura romantyzmu* (Warszawa: Państwowy Instytut Wydawniczy, 1987), p. 97.

> Ah, woman! There might be another
> Cause — your lover must have changed
> Either the faith of his fathers,
> Or perhaps his given name.

As we have seen, that is exactly what has happened. Konrad has regained the faith of his fathers, thanks to Fr. Piotr, but he has changed his given name. Part III ends now, coming full circle with reference to the wounds of Gustaw/Konrad. Here, metaphor gains the upper hand over literalism:

> GUŚLARZ.
> Such gore was dripping from his chest,
> So many wounds are in that breast:
> His suffering is beyond words —
> He's wounded with a thousand swords,
> And each has pierced him to the soul.
> Perhaps his death will make him whole.
>
> WOMAN.
> Who thrust him through with all those swords?
>
> GUŚLARZ.
> Our nation's foreign overlords.

Once again, Mickiewicz turns toward Christian metaphors in his political understanding of Konrad's "passion" as representative of the entire Polish nation. That image of the "thousand swords" piercing his heart recall, at least to the Catholic mind, the familiar image of the suffering, pierced heart of the Blessed Virgin. This is more important than may seem at first glance, this allusion to the Catholic iconography of the Immaculate Heart of Mary rather than the Sacred Heart of Jesus, wound about with thorn. For in associating Konrad with Mary (so powerful and important a saint, yet human like us all the same), Mickiewicz makes impossible the identification of his hero as some sort of Christ-figure. Having exploded Byronism in the Great Improvisation, here he undermines Polish Messianism.

The physical description continues, with the addition of another wound:

WOMAN.
There was one wound between his eyes,
One only, and of no great size.
I thought it but a smudge at first.

GUŚLARZ.
And that's the wound that pains him worst.
I saw it, and its depths did sound:
It is a self-inflicted wound,
And even death won't ease its pain.

WOMAN.
Ah! Make him whole, great God, again!

If the image of the three-eyed "44" beheld by Fr. Piotr in his vision described above reminds us of the *tilak* worn by some Hindus to mark their "third eye," the fact that Konrad's new wound is found in the centre of his forehead further distances him from the Messianic figure seen by the priest. Instead, as the *guślarz* explains, it is an indelible mark of his presumption. What can this be but a visible sign — not unlike that of Cain — indicating the sinfulness of Konrad's self-elevation to deity during the Great Improvisation scene? And once more, in destroying the exceptionalness of both Konrad in particular — and the mystical conception of the Polish nation, in general — Mickiewicz once more broadens his work to a universality that makes it accessible to all.*

At the end of Part III, Mickiewicz continues the story with the seven lyrical *Passages* (*Ustęp*), which describe in classical couplets the journey of the Polish exiles to the interior of the Russian Empire, and their life there. These *Passages*, as beautiful, tight and effective as they are in the original

---

\*   Mickiewicz is often understood — or decried — as someone who would elevate the Polish nation to the level of a "chosen people." Certainly, he toys with this motif as a literary device, in *Forefathers' Eve*, and, especially, the later *Books of the Polish Nation and Polish Pilgrimage*. Yet it is wrong to exaggerate these characteristics beyond their significance as literary tools, to be taken up, and put down, when appropriate. Mickiewicz is above all about the liberty of the human person (again, Eve's inclusive vision is most important). This can be seen from the very generous way he treats Russians in *Forefathers' Eve* (see especially the ballroom scenes), the *Passages*, and his great epic *Pan Tadeusz*.

Polish, are still a wrenching, unexpected generic shift from the dramatic verse of the immediately preceding segments. They (logically) lack the immediacy of dramatic verse; from the first-hand viewpoint we enjoyed just moments ago, setting us so close to the *guślarz* and the Girl as almost to touch them, watching the string of penal wagons speeding along into exile, we are suddenly shut out from the present moment, and the poet speaks to us at one remove, at arm's length, through descriptive, narrative poems. That is just the point. By wrenching the reader out of the present moment as he does, Mickiewicz makes him undergo a sensation similar to the families of the deported, as their sons and husbands are torn away from them. By emphasising our distance from the people and scenes described in the *Passages,* he is recreating for us the sense of distance between those left behind, and those now in exile.

The *Passages* are seven, or six, if one wishes to consider the concluding poem "To my Muscovite Friends" as a verse letter, generically separate from the preceding classical narratives. It certainly is metrically different, for in it, the poet resumes a more emotive, romantic style that is palpably distinct from the foregoing couplets.

The *Passages* consist of, in order: "The Road to Russia," "Suburbs of the Capital," "Petersburg," "The Statue of Peter the Great," "A Review of the Troops," "On the Day before the Petersburg Flood of 1824," and the aforementioned verse letter, "To My Muscovite Friends." As mentioned above, the *Passages* are characterised by an acerbic, classical wit that bites with the immediacy of the couplets of Pope, or Byron. For example, in his "Review of the Troops," the poet thus describes the ranks of Russian soldiers. First come the tall grenadiers, and then,

> Behind them stand the smaller fry in rows
> Like cucumbers behind tomato stalks;
> At further sorting my untrained mind balks.
> A sharp, zoologist's eye is what it takes
> To sort the genus of so many snakes.

These are the words of a man not too kindly disposed towards the subject he describes. Adam Mickiewicz is the national poet of Poland, and, whether or not he saw himself as such, it is his identity as a Pole that takes the upper hand in the descriptions found in *Passages*. We ought not to expect even-handedness, or detached observation in what will follow.* He himself allows his awareness of his bias to slip out in places like that we have just cited. All of the men he sees before him are "snakes" — vile, deceitful, noxious. He groups them together in a single lot, simply because they are wearing the uniform of the Empire he despises. It would take an impartial, scientific, eye, he says, to sort them into subgroups, intimating at the same time that he is unable to see them as anything but The Enemy. The impartial, "zoological" observer might be able to find among the vipers garter snakes as well: harmless fellows conscripted into the Tsarist ranks (like the old Polish Corporal of Part III, by the way), against their will, who are victims too. Indeed, the *Passages* are the most nationalistic portion of *Forefathers' Eve*. In them, Mickiewicz veers away from universalism, and strikes an anti-Russian, chauvinistic tone like nowhere else in his magnum opus.

Russia, as Mickiewicz describes it in the *Passages*, is a nullity of empty spaces:

> Nor town, nor hillock here to cheer the heart;
> No monument of nature or of art.
> The land is flat, empty, unpopulated,
> As if but yesterday it were created.
> ("The Road to Russia")

There is no Romantic rapture at wild unspoiled places; even the mention of freshness, the youth of the country round-about "as if but yesterday it were created," has nothing of the enthusiasm for Eden that animated Bierstadt, Moran, and the painters of the unspoiled American West. These descriptions are, rather, one of the more charitable comments of a man who sees himself as a cultivated Western European, looking upon the realms of savagery. It is not a wilderness, but a wasteland. This theme continues even as we near the capital itself. In "Suburbs of the Capital," the narrator states:

> The clock shows midday's already grown old;
> The sun is now descending in the west;

---

\* As Borowy points out, the value of the narrator's bitter criticism of even the architecture of St. Petersburg is "doubtful." II, 166. "The same can be said of the unoriginal architecture of any modern city."

> The vault of heaven looms empty and vast;
> No cloud, all's clear and quiet, colourless,
> A grand transparency, that pale sky —
> Just like a frozen voyager's dead eye.

The sun itself seems eager to leave these Arctic wastes behind. No Ovid banished from Rome has so bitterly reflected upon his new surroundings, where the heavens themselves offer the hungry eye no cheer.

The narrator is slightly more charitable to the natives of this Ultima Thule, the Russians themselves:

> I've met the people: shoulders broad, a girth
> Of chest expansive, napes sinewy, thick —
> Just like the beasts and trees of Northern birth;
> They're fresh and hale and strong; they're never sick,
> And yet their faces are like their native lands:
> An empty, open, and a wild expanse.
>      ("The Road to Russia")

Now, Mickiewicz was no xenophobe. The authentic humanity with which he infuses the chastened Konrad at the conclusion of Part III seems to have been a part of his own character. As we will see, he can be, and often is, generous in his descriptions of the Russian people, considered as men. As Borowy points out:

> Above all, the poem expresses compassion for those who suffer, and engages us in that compassion as well. [...] Thus the Russian question, as taken up by Mickiewicz, is treated by the poet as a portion of the question of humanity in general.*

But in the lines just quoted, there is a wariness that is hard to miss. As he will describe the land itself as a *tabula rasa*, so indeed these strong and hale denizens of the North. What a strength lies dormant in them! The narrator seems to shiver here: what if the idea that will finally animate them to action be the evil impulse of a wicked leader? In the same poem, he continues his description of them, musing:

---

\*        Borowy, II, pp. 168, 170.

> Seen from afar, they're splendid, full of grace,
> But once inside — one finds but desert wastes.
> Their bodies, weft of sturdy fabric, firm,
> Are winter quarters for their soul: a worm,
> That must mature in that cocoon's soft night
> Before it sprout wings for the springtime flight.
> And when the sun of liberty will arise,
> What sort of wings will attempt the azure skies?
> A splendid butterfly, a pied delight?
> Or just a dirty moth, that shuns the light?

As for now, they are an inert, slumbering mass, little better than chattel. There is no better example of this unformed, as yet unconscious elemental force of the Russian masses than the rather heartbreaking vignette of the batman, found frozen on the parade ground on the day after the "Review of the Troops:"

> Half soldier, half peasant, long beard and shaven head,
> Half buried in the snow, but wholly dead —
> Batman to some forgetful officer,
> He sat there guarding his master's warm fur;
> Wearing but cap, and soldier's overcoat
> He guarded it, and never thought to throw't
> Over his own back; left there, his command
> To "Wait!" and so he waited, with one hand
> Clutching the coat, the other he'd keep warm,
> But didn't slide it in his uniform
> Until he froze quite through and through, and thus
> His own dog found him, and raised this sad ruckus.
> The frost sealed fast the lid of his right eye,
> His left froze open, as if he'd still yet try
> To keep his master's property safe and sound
> (He faced, as ordered, still the parade ground)
> Awaiting his lord and master! As is right;
> "Sit there!" was ordered, and so he sat, all night.
> Masters give orders, servants must obey;
> And so he'll sit on till the Judgment Day,
> Still faithful to his master's voice, though dead —

> "Make sure that no one steals that coat!" he said,
> And so he did — though by his lord forgot —
> Who left, without wasting a second thought!

This pitiful episode prompts Mickiewicz's narrator to rise above his nationalistic bile, and react to the scene on a purely human level. It is the one time in the work where he identifies with a Russian *qua* Russian, addressing him as a "brother Slav:"

> Poor, frozen hero! such a death, by God,
> Shames your humanity, and but befits a dog.
> And your reward? Your master's laugh: "That's rich!
> Faithful to death even. An exemplary bitch!"
> Poor, frozen man! Why is it my heart bleeds
> And my eye tears at this your faithful deed?
> My heart is rent for you, poor brother Slav;
> Poor nation! — thus I mused beside his grave —
> Who know but such heroism: of a slave!

"Slave" here is not used merely to aid the rhyme: it is Mickiewicz's diagnosis of the corrupt system of the Russian empire. The Russian word for "peasant" may have its roots in the word for "Christian," but these Christian souls are not treated in a Christian manner. They are bestialised, used and exploited, left behind to freeze "without wasting a second thought." The faithful, dog-like batman is no exception. He was not the only one to fall victim to the review of the troops; some twenty other men are scraped off the parade ground to be disposed of, like so much offal:

> Now all are gone: actors and audience.
> On the vacant grounds are found but the remnants
> Of twenty corpses — this one dressed in white
> (Cavalryman), while that one's colours might
> Be any — boot and hoof trampled him so
> He's buried deep already in the snow.
> These men, set up as course-guards for the rows
> Of infantry and horse — stood still, and froze;
> This one misstepped — "Right face!" — faced left instead:
> Struck by his neighbour's rifle, dropped down dead;

> All of them, tossed on wagons, that are driven
> By police lackeys — the dead, the barely living —
> All to be tossed into a common pit,
> Tamped down again — and that's the end of it.

It is a systemic injustice. The Tsarist *polis* is an oligarchy of the worst sort. The tiny chosen few on top are not only raised above the *hoi polloi*, but they feed off them like parasites. The bestialisation of the Russian peasantry is nowhere more clearly seen than in this passage of the "Review of the Troops," where the narrator decries the preference given by the aristocracy for horses over people:

> For as to worth, as Zhomini writes, of course
> It's not about the rider, but the horse.
> This fact is well known in the eastern marches
> Of our old Republic — guardsmen's chargers
> Can be had for the price of a mere three souls,
> While an officer's mount will cost one fourfold;
> For such a horse one must toss in a scribe,
> A lutenist, and an acrobat beside;
> In tougher times, you need to add a cook.
> Official nags and mares, such as you'd look
> Suspicious in the mouth, and even such
> As pull sick-wagons still can be worth much
> As antes in a hand; and mares, of course
> Can be had cheap: for as little as two whores.

Again Mickiewicz is fair-minded. In his notes to this passage, he points out that the same sort of attitude can be found among the Polish nobility of the former Eastern marches of the old Republic. As with his scathing characterisation of the Nobleman from the Dantesque Part II (who is Polish, not Russian), the poet castigates cruelty and injustice wherever it is found. It is not his fault if Russia seems to be the epicentre of all injustice. As the crowd presses forward to get a better view of the Review about to take place on the "Tsar's baiting ground,"

> a dragoon
> Hastens to butt back with his lance's knob

> The more impertinent gawker; leather thongs
> Whip down across the backs of the bolder throngs;
> And he who, like a frog in spongy fen
> Stuck out his snout, retracts it once again.

We are used to Police barricades set up all along of Fifth Avenue for the St. Patrick's Day parade; we don't bat an eye as it draws close to evening on December 31, and policemen seal off the roads leading into Times Square, directing us further down the sidewalk (and far out of our way) to reach an open side street to take us west, or east. Their presence — almost always courteous, never physically violent — is there to keep public order on especially hectic days, and for our own safety. The picture that Mickiewicz gives us here, of an implicitly common scene (given the frequency of troop reviews) has nothing of courtesy or concern about it. The crowds are scourged (literally) for their "impertinence," their "boldness," as if some law had been broken by their taking a step or two beyond the unseen line. They are being shown their place, roughly, and that place is among the rest of the chattel. It is tempting to think that Mickiewicz had Dante in mind here too: the concluding image of the "frogs" quickly ducking to safety beneath the waters of the bog reminds one of a metaphor Dante employs for a sinner avoiding the angry talons of a devil. If so, the allusion is scathing: Petersburg, in short, is Hell itself.

It is an age-old tradition, this Russian cruelty. Earlier on in the very first *Passage,* "The Road to Russia," the narrator muses on the antiquity of these empty steppes, and of the peoples to whom it gave birth:

> That from this very land, so desolate
> More than one nation its genesis took.
> But as the flood receded from these plains,
> Leaving no trace of those colossal rains,
> So did those swarms abandon their demesne,
> Leaving no trace of ever having been.
> But far away, a lonely Alpine gorge
> Bears witness to the passing of those hordes,
> And further yet, on Roman monuments
> One reads the record of their violence.

What was Russia's contribution to civilisation, the narrator muses? The Dark Ages. Now that Europe has rebounded since the High Middle Ages, the barbarian flood has receded to its original, stagnant pool: Russia itself. Heaven help the West, he implies, should those waters swell again!

The Tsar himself is a relic of these dark ages of humanity. While Europe has, for the most part, left behind the absolutist nightmare of arbitrary rule, the Russian Tsar continues to tyrannise the lands under his sceptre as if he were still one of the despots that consolidated Muscovy beneath their heavy knout. Reflecting on the straight military routes that criss-cross the Russian Empire to foster — not trade, as in Roman times, but oppression — the poet reports:

> Straight through the desert wastes the highways shoot.
> They grew there from no well-trod merchant paths,
> Nor scuffed out by the plodding caravan's foot.
> The finger of the Tsar decreed these swaths,
> And if a Polish town lay in their way,
> Or Polish castle challenged its ruled grade,
> Their walls were broken down without delay
> And with their rubble were the highways paved.
> ("The Road to Russia")

And he is a tyrant, this Russian monarch, in the best, Aquinian sense of the word. He is not a king (who expends himself on behalf of his people), but that worst sort of ruler, the tyrant, who exploits his subjects for his own pleasure and profit:

> In Rome, to build a theatre for Caesar,
> Treasures were poured out in a golden flood.
> These castles — of the lackeys of the Tsar —
> Arose from a torrent of our tears and blood.
> To fund these obelisks and orangeries,
> They had to feign — how many conspiracies?
> How many innocents had to be damned
> To death, or exile, to confiscate our lands?
> ("Suburbs of the Capital")

The Russian Tsar, whose title, as is well known, derives in corrupted form from the Latin "Caesar," is depicted in the *Passages* as the triumphant

Peter the Great of Falconet's famous equestrian statue. In the words of the "Russian bard," who stands arm in arm with the Polish pilgrim in front of the monument, the sculpture is a paean to tyrannical egotism. It depicts a desire to glorify one's self, to satisfy one's desires without giving a thought to the rights of others, which, in the case of an absolute despot, means subjection at home, and imperialism abroad:

> The Tsar, already poured in bronze, a giant
> Astride the back of his giant bronze steed,
> Awaited but direction for his ride.
> For Peter couldn't rest on his own turf,
> His Fatherland not sufficiently wide —
> So land was sent for, beyond the Northern surf.
> ("The Statue of Peter the Great")

It is interesting to note that it is not the Pole, the victim of Russian Imperialism, who describes the statue so bitterly, but the Russian. He calls the Tsar to account for crimes against foreign princes and peoples, and (perhaps especially) against his own people, those entrusted to his care: "How many backs were trampled in the brawl / To spring atop the perch from which he strains?" he asks, rhetorically.

This equestrian statue of the eighteenth century calls to mind another: the famous, calmer bronze of Marcus Aurelius, which has graced the Capitol in Rome since the third century. And a comparison of the statues leads, inexorably, to a comparison of the men. The advantage, in both cases, goes to the Roman:

> Not thus, in ancient Rome, did there uprise
> Aurelius' bronze — that man of all beloved —
> Who first won fame by banishing the spies
> And all informers from the state removed!
> Then, when he'd crushed the parasites at home
> And routed on the Rhine and the Pactol
> Those hordes, whose fierce invasions threatened Rome
> Did he return to the peaceful Capitol.

The wars of the philosopher-emperor, in the telling of the narrator, were not for self-aggrandisement. Rather, he sallied forth to the Rhine and the Pactolus disinterestedly, on behalf of his people, in their defence. Likewise, his reign was propped by no secret police apparatus, just the opposite: he banished all spies and informers. To what degree these praises are deserved of the Antonine may be a matter of debate. There can be no question, however, of the negative reflection cast on the Tsar: spies, informers, and wars of conquest are part and parcel of the world that gave birth to *Forefathers' Eve*.

The steed that bears the weight of Marcus Aurelius is no frenzied, trampling mount. It is a stately, considerate beast, careful not to harm the minions as they crowd round their "father" on his triumphal way:

> The stallion fierce, so pliant to his command,
> It's obvious that his lord was crowded round
> By an adoring populace, who cheered:
> "Behold Caesar! Our Father's drawing near!"
> And so he does, restraining the steed's bound
> To gently ford the living stream of praise,
> Including all in his parental glance.
> The horse, though fiery, proud-maned, fain to prance,
> Yet seems aware (as he his vim restrains)
> That on his back he bears the Best-Beloved,
> So nothing spooks him: children crowd and shove
> To draw close to their father: still calmly, straight
> And proud he steps. Such a stately, even gait,
> So loved this man of the commonality,
> His road ends surely, at immortality!

The aesthetics of equestrian statues are such that the gestures, especially those of the rider, are symbolically fixed. Almost invariably, only one hand is on the reins. The other is extended — in open-palmed blessing, as in the case of Marcus Aurelius, or gripping sceptre, staff of office, or (as our narrator would have it in Peter's case) a "knout." The one-handed ease with which the rider controls the mount is intended to convey the legitimacy of his rule: the powerful beast represents the state, and the fact that the ruler can control him with but one hand invests him with an authority and an aura of meetness that elicits a vote of confidence in the beholder. In this passage, the image of the horse is key. In the case of Peter, he is rampant, violent, implicitly ready to trample down whomever might foolishly place himself in his path. In the case of Marcus Aurelius' steed, he is almost preternaturally cautious, carefully restraining himself so as not to tread on any of the "best-beloved's" adulating subjects. When we recall that the horse symbolises the state, the political eloquence of the image is obvious.

Thus the most famous of the *Passages*, which purports to record an actual conversation between Mickiewicz and his friend, Aleksandr Pushkin — the "greatest bard of the North." It sparked Pushkin's own poem on the statue, "The Bronze Horseman," as well as "Mickiewicz," Pushkin's bitter rejoinder to the Pole's "To my Muscovite Friends." In this latter poem he castigates his "once quiet" Polish friend for now "singing with hatred verses soaked through with poison." One might wonder whether or not Pushkin would have felt moved to write this poem were it not for the fact that in "The Statue" Mickiewicz places the reproach of despotism in the Russian's mouth. After all, Mickiewicz is sniping from afar; Pushkin has to live in Tsarist Russia — and he was on a short leash as it was — a situation certainly not helped in the slightest by being associated with a reactionary poem, in which he himself voices criticism of the *batyushka*. If so, we have here a curious confirmation of one of the theses of Mickiewicz's critique of Russian despotism. The absolute, arbitrary Tsar is a villain, no doubt; but much worse than his own influence, is the manner in which it is magnified, and spread throughout society by those who emulate him, or heed him in fear. Mickiewicz first speaks of this in "Suburbs of the Capital," where the summer palaces are now empty, because

> [...] The summer being spent,
> The courtly flies, buzzing after the scent
> Of the Tsar's carcass, fly to him in town
> Where he shall winter. Nothing spins around
> The parquet but the winds. For where the Tsar
> Is, there the vultures gather.

To mix metaphors, the Tsar is a poisoned spring, which taints all of the waters that flow from its font:

> Each one resplendent — but with borrowed light
> Reflecting splendour falling from his eyes
> (The Tsar's); a swarm they are of fireflies
> That gad about on balmy St. John's Night,

> But when the Spring of the Tsar's favour's past,
> These insects, one by one, lose all their flash;
> They don't migrate to some more clement clime,
> But in what Russian muck they bide their time
> Buried, who knows? The general, breasting fire
> Basks in the warmth of the Tsar's smiling eyes,
> But should those eyes cloud over with royal ire,
> The general pales, and — sometimes — up and dies.
> ("A Review of the Troops")

The unhealthy atmosphere of social contagion fostered by grovelling absolutism is spoken of more to the point in "Petersburg," where the narrator gives an account of the promenading city-folk:

> First come the servile officers of the court:
> This one in warm fur — though frozen to the bones —
> His coat wide open (How else might he sport
> His shivering bemedalled breast before
> The envious eyes of all?) His own eyes seek
> Only an equal, to whom he'd deign speak.

In his introduction, Mickiewicz speaks of the Mandarin-like castes of the Tsarist civil service, and the various levels of prestige associated with each rank. Such a caste system, which dehumanises the person, reducing him to a mere station, is possible only in a caesaropapist system such as that of Russia, where the ruler is invested with quasi-divine status. The rot which is such a gradation of human worth seeps through the entire body politic. It characterises not only the upper echelons of the civil service pyramid, but also the very lowest levels of society, where each man seeks solace in finding someone still lower than himself to scorn:

> Then much more humbly slouched shuffle chinovniks,
> With furtive glances seeking their own cliques
> For bows obsequious, or the odd-lot sample
> Of lower life-forms yet, whom they might trample.
> Nearly bent double creep they by, each one;
> Their spines so elastic — like a scorpion.

Since such is the human architecture of the corrupt Russian Empire, what wonder if Mickiewicz's narrator finds the very surroundings in which he is engulfed unbearable? What sort of civilisation can be expected from a tyrant who raises a monument to himself on the bones of his despised slaves?

> How did this Russian capital begin?
> What was it drew these hordes of Eastern Slavs
> To found this last of their icy enclaves
> Here, torn from ocean's wave and northern Finn?
> [...]
> No peasant coveted this excrement
> Dredged from the sea — it was the Tsar's command
> That bade a city (not theirs, his) to stand
> To his all-mighty whim a monument.
>
> On shifting sands and marshes thick with mud
> He bade them sink one hundred thousand piles,
> Tread firm the muck with peasant bone and blood;
> And thus, the ground made firm, an army toils
> (Yoked, Moscow-style, to barrow, cart and ship)
> Bearing great loads of wood and building stone
> From distant lands, and the sea's bosom ripped;
> Whole ages enslaved to build the Tsar's new home.
> ("Petersburg")

Which is not to say that the Western-looking Tsar did not seek to modernise his nation on a European model. Yet even in this his *Drang nach Westen* was in total disregard of human rights, and if there were any European models that he aped perfectly, they were the worst imaginable: for example, France's Reign of Terror under Robespierre:

> "I'll Europeanise Russia! Look here —
> Shorten your kaftans, boyars! Cut your beards!"
> His word is law; those who refused to wear
> French frocks learned why the French feared Robespierre;
> His word is law; those who saw *that* grew pale

> With terror, and beards fell like thick brown hail.
> ("A Review of the Troops")

Is there something of the priggishness of the European *parvenu* in Mickiewicz's description of the Russian urbs? Poland belongs to the periphery of Western Europe, and the disdain shown by the Polish bard for the Russian East can be an expression of the insecurity he himself feels for his Lithuanian-Polish culture, so frequently overlooked by Paris and London. Whatever the psychological case may be, in his descriptions of Russian civilisation, Mickiewicz's narrator mocks the game of catch-up he sees in the architecture of the Russian capital, in which one finds a mimetic hodge-podge of everything, covering a hollow indigenous core:

> On both sides of the grand, proud boulevard
> Stand rows of palaces. — A kind of chapel
> With dome and cross is here, and there stand guard
> — Like hay ricks — statues wrapped in straw and snow;
> And there, Corinthian columns in a row:
> The Summer Palace, flat roofed, Italian,
> Next to some Chinese kiosks, and there: Japan,
> While further: ought of classic Catherine's doing —
> Some freshly-aped Neoclassical ruin.
> All orders present, buildings of all shapes,
> Like beasts brought here from all the world's wild ranges;
> Giraffes and bison, crocodiles and apes,
> Exhibited in individual cages.
> ("Suburbs of the Capital")

Mickiewicz's narrator has never had a kind word to say about the works of Russian hands. Everywhere he looks, he finds sham, discord, or a poverty that barely rises above the level of beasts. The first time he had the occasion to mention the appearance of Russian civilisation was on his way into exile, in "Road to Russia," the very first of the *Passages*:

> [...] here and there, one sees a rough-cut fall
> Of timber leant-to in haphazard dome,
> A strange mass, which recalls a roof and walls,
> With folk inside. They call this thing a "home."

> And then, further on, thousands of these ricks
> Are grouped together on the arctic plains
> Like shakos fallen, from their smokestack strains
> A wisp of steam against the cutting air;
> A gleam of light anaemic here and there
> Wanes in a window; hovels bunched in pairs,
> With thin-planked fences circling them around,
> And such a huddled mess they call a "town."

We must not forget that we are seeing things through the eyes of a victim of Tsarist oppression. The speaker of these lines is being carted off, against his will, into an endless landscape he has no desire to contemplate, let alone visit. Such images of rural poverty might be found in his own native Poland — as well as other places throughout the "civilised" world — but he mentions them not. In recollection, the lands he is being torn from constitute the pinnacle of human culture, while here, in his anger and resentment, his eyes eagerly seek out each blemish in the landscape in order to magnify them into constituent characteristics of the land he despises.

Yet it is for Petersburg, the very tumour from which the Russian malignancy spreads, that the narrator reserves his deepest scorn. And here, even in his critique of the eclectic, not to say haphazard, architecture of the city, everything once more devolves upon the baneful head of the Tsar. It started with Peter:

> Now it is Paris that the Tsar recalls,
> And so they raise some mock Parisian walls.
> Once, on his journeys, he saw Amsterdam,
> And so he floods the town again, and dam
> And dyke are piled to regulate the flow.
> In Rome, he hears, are palaces. And so
> He has them built here too. Does Venice rest
> In her lagoon, like some alluring siren
> Lolling in waters lapping at her breast?
> No sooner does his sceptre dredge the mire in
> Canals and rios crisscrossed, far and near,
> Replete with bridge, and boat, and gondolier.
>     ("Petersburg")

As with the buildings, so the inhabitants. In the same poem we read:

> "Here resides Achmet, the Khirgizan Khan,
> Senator for the Department of Poland."
> There, one can "Learn from le Monsewer Jock
> French lingo, as echte Parisians talk."
> The "Tsar's Own Scullion" next "Vodkas and Wine,"
> "Bass-Baritone" and "School Inspector." A sign
> Reads: "Here lives Piacere Gioco, Italian,
> Once Purveyor of Sausages and Scallions,
> Now Welcoming all Girls of Good Repute
> To Clean, Cheap Lodgings."

All is debased. To the natural cosmopolitanism of a London or a Paris, Mickiewicz opposes a kennel of mongrels, of whom none seems to have a professional reputation based on tradition or learned expertise; the "purveyor of Sausages and Scallions" turns hotelier, grabbing at whatever scam looks likely to turn a quick buck. And how on earth, did "Achmet," the Khan of Khirgizia, become a senator from the Department of Poland? Either his appointment was obtained through graft, or he was raised to his eminence by the Tsar according to the same logic that sent Caucasian troops into the Lithuanian regions, and Lithuanian conscripts into the Caucasus: so that no ethnic sympathies should impede them in the prosecution of their (harsh) duties. Either way, Mickiewicz underscores a mongrelised culture, and neither of the options redound to the praise of the Tsarist state.

To paraphrase a saying from the American West, Mickiewicz would have us believe that there is no law on the banks of the Neva, and no God to the north of the Niemen. Russia, as it is described in the *Passages*, is a place that draws the dregs of European society, eager to make a fortune in lawless regions (or occupations) unregulated by any concern for human rights. Consider the description of the foreign officers in the Tsar's army:

> Their officers? — Here in this coach, a Kraut
> Hums something by Schiller (a sentimental air)
> And thumps a straggling soldier's back; while there:
> A Frenchman buzzes through his Gallic snout
> A liberal ditty; the errant *philosophe*,
> He's scheming ways to batten his career,

> Now whispering into quartermaster's ear
> To gypsy down the rations, skimming off
> The half not spent on soldier's food — to line
> Their pockets, half by half — So half this kine
> Will starve? *There's more where they came from!*
> ("The Road to Russia")

> Europe looked on in rapt fascination:
> "Peter the Great's invented civilisation!"
> So well had Peter built, indeed it's true,
> That his successors had little else to do:
> Send brother despots a regiment or two,
> Incite a pogrom here, some arson there,
> Covet their neighbour's goods — and fleece them bare —
> Impoverish more the poor; staff regiments
> With well-paid Krauts and mercenary French;
> Astonished Europe all but overwhelm
> With such a strong and wise, enlightened realm.
> ("The Road to Russia")

Here Mickiewicz picks up the familiar strain that resounds throughout Polish literature (and diplomacy) whenever the more Western nations begin to sing the praises of Russia. *We Poles have known these people at close quarters for ages. Trust us: don't be sucked in by appearances, lest you learn, too late, their true nature*:

> Ah, French and Germans! Just you wait your turn!
> Soon Tsarist *ukases* your ears will burn;
> When on your napes you feel the scourge's blow
> And behold your cities in the lurid glow
> Of firestorms glinting off sharp Russian swords!
> Then, I reckon, you'll be at a loss for words —
> When your great fan the Tsar requests to hear ya
> Warble your Alexandrines in Siberia!
> ("A Review of the Troops")

During the Communist period, the Polish People's Republic (1945-1989), such sentiments expressed by the national bard, and others, were inconvenient facts in a geopolitical system of dependence. Poland had no truly autonomous existence separate from the USSR, which was officially and non-negotiably presented as the most progressive state in the world, and the one true friend of the Polish people. Some complicated intellectual acrobatics were necessary, at times, to square this with the facts of Polish-Russian history. In cases like this, educators and editors went out of their way to stress that Mickiewicz was criticising, not the Russian masses (for whom he had the highest regard), but rather the Tsarist apparatus, which the Poland-friendly, white-hatted Russian people themselves abjured and overthrew for the good of their country, and Poland, and the world as a whole. As a matter of fact, there is a lot of merit in this sentiment, as far as Mickiewicz was concerned. He did not hate Russians as Russians, and here and there in his writings he goes out of his way to present "good" Russians as fair-minded people, who are suffering under the tyranny of their government no less than the Lithuanians and Poles. For example, the Russian officer Rykov in *Pan Tadeusz* is presented as an honourable sort, while the poet's disdain is generously poured upon the head of Major Plut — a Russianised Pole whose adopted, Russified name has the word for "spittle" at its root. In the *Passages,* the "bard of the North" who muses over the monument to Peter the Great along with the Polish "pilgrim" represents the "good Russian:"

> Evening it was, a lightly falling rain,
> Two youths, one greatcoat sheltering the twain;
> The one — that pilgrim fresh come from the West,
> The unknown victim of Tsarist violence;
> The other — the Russian bard of greatest worth,
> Whose songs are famous all throughout the North.
> They stood there arm in arm. Of recent date
> Their acquaintance — so soon grown best of mates.
> Their lofty souls, all earthly obstacles
> Far above — the summits of one Alpine range,
> Though sundered by an angry flood that falls
> Between them (yet they barely hear her rage),
> Each to each bent in natural sympathy.

We again recall the fact that it is the Russian, not the Pole, who delivers the implacable condemnation of the Tsar in this poem. It is he who, true to the Decembrist sympathies of Pushkin, Rylov, and others of the generation of Mickiewicz's "Muscovite friends," wonders about the future of a Russia warmed by the liberalism of the Western nations:

> Peter here, gives the stallion the reins.
> How many backs were trampled in the brawl
> To spring atop the perch from which he strains
> For — where now? Your eye waits for them to fall,
> The maddened steed, who champs his bit to froth,
> The rider, who controls the stallion not;
> For one whole century the fall's been stayed.
> They stand there, like a frozen stone cascade
> Upon a bitter shore where cold winds blow.
> But — should the sun of freedom chance to glow?
> And this land's warmed beneath a western breeze?
> What then, with this cascade of tyrannies?

This is Mickiewicz's attitude as well, as can be seen from the sentiments enunciated by his narrators in the *Passages*. His is no implacable hatred of all things Russian. Like Clausewitz, he foresees a future in which the enemies of today become the friends of tomorrow. Russia, and the Russians, are depicted as a young nation, without significant traditions and history. Yet the very emptiness of the desolate Russian landscape is turned into a hopeful metaphor by the poet as early as the "Road to Russia:"

> An open region, white and desolate,
> A sheaf on which no pen has ever writ.
> Is God's hand to illume the virgin scroll?
> His characters — the honest human soul?
> Inscribing here truth, faith, and holy peace;
> That loving-kindness shall be mankind's law,
> The trophies of the world: self-sacrifice?
> Or will it be that God's primordial foe
> Shall come with sword, not pen, the page to stain,
> Declaring man forever to be chained,
> The trophies of the world: from quarter-draw?

Such sentiments are echoed by one of the most intriguing characters found in the *Passages,* the charitable Lithuanian who, while condemning Tsarist tyranny, stints not in his love for the poor Russians of the capital as human beings, and foresees a day when that longed-for liberty, though still afar off, will come to pass:

> On the further side, across the street from him,
> There was another man. He no pilgrim,
> But seemed to be a native of the town,
> Or one who's lived here long. He went around
> Dispersing alms to all the poor. He called
> Each one by name, and chatted with them all,
> Asking them how their children were, their wives,
> Turning none away.
> [...]
> He seemed and angel from the realms of glory
> Among the suffering souls of Purgatory,
> Beholding nations whole in their torments,
> And knowing their relief still ages hence;
> Till freedom come — so many generations,
> So many long years until their salvation.
> ("Petersburg")

And yet that day will be long in coming. Before it does, will the just God not send a merited chastisement against this wicked nation? In the very odd poem "The Day before the Petersburg Flood of 1824," the prophet-painter Józef Oleszkiewicz (1777-1830) foretells just such a day of wrath:

> "Who lives to see what morning shall reveal
> Shall see — not the last, but the second ordeal:
> The Lord will shake the Assyrian throne,
> And quake the foundations of Babylon.
> And yet, O Lord! Spare these eyes the third trial!"
> [...]
> Hark! — There! — The winds rise, there they raise their heads
> Like marine monsters from their Arctic beds;
> Of icy mists they've fashioned their swift wings
> And from their fetters they unchain the seas;

> Hark, hark! — And hear the abyss roar oceanic,
> The steeds of icebergs press on, driving panic
> Before them: rearing, tearing icy reins.
> Their mad destructive rush nothing restrains:
> Burst, all but one of their gigantic chains
> And soon those links will snap beneath the strain...

Is this the singular fellow foretold by Father Piotr to Konrad, before the latter's exile to Petersburg? Is this the new mystagogue, whom Mickiewicz's hero is to seek out? It seems likely; that is the sense one gets from the actions of the "pilgrim" who, after hearing the chilling prophecy of this *guślarz* sets off, alone, in pursuit of an explanation.

Interestingly enough, he does not catch him up. Although he hears, from afar, the Jeremiad launched against the Tsar by Oleszkiewicz, as soon as the latter becomes aware of the fact that he is being overheard, he douses his lantern, and disappears into the nocturnal fogs of the capital.

Why did Mickiewicz not allow Konrad — for it surely must be he — to contact the wizened old artist-prophet, to converse with him, and obtain from him a new trajectory for action? The answer is perhaps to be found in those lines from "Petersburg" in which the narrator averts his gaze from the pompous streams of promenading Russians to fix them on the group of "Polish pilgrims" gazing up at the buildings of the hated capital:

> A few there were among the passers-by
> Differing from them by clothing and by mien;
> Who never on the gay crowds cast an eye,
> Yet gazed around in wonder at the scene:
> The walls and the façades and the foundations,
> The iron fences and granite crenellations,
> As if they weighed the tensile strength of each,
> Searching between the bricks for a chance breach,
> Then, letting their arms fall down in despair,
> As if they thought: "A man don't have a prayer
> To knock these down!"

One in particular catches his eye, and the sentiments expressed in the concluding lines of the passage above seem distilled, in his character, to a chilling potency:

> Eleven there were in all,
> Then one remained, his smile bitter as gall;
> He raised his fist, and beat the limestone wall
> As if in striking one, he cursed them all.
> And then he crossed his arms upon his chest,
> His eyes upon the Tsar's palace fixed fast,
> With piercing glance — stilettos two, his eyes —
> A Samson he, among these Philistines.
> Like Samson snatched by treason and enchained
> Who, gripping the pillars, just begins to strain.

Just a few years before Part III of *Forefathers' Eve* was published, circa 1828, Mickiewicz composed *Konrad Wallenrod*, a long narrative poem set in the middle ages, during the Germanic crusades against the pagan Lithuanians. It is a rather transparent *roman à clef*, in which the Lithuanians stand for the Poles, and the invading Teutonic Knights, the oppressive Russians. The hero of the work, a young Lithuanian named Walter Alfa, receives the following instruction from his mystagogue, an old *guślarz*:

> "Free knights," he said, "can choose which arms they please
> And on the open field fight man to man.
> You're a slave. Your only weapon's guile.
> Stay on and learn the German arts of war.
> First get their trust, then we'll see what comes next."

"What comes next" is the young Walter's deceptive assumption of the identity of a deceased knight, the eponymous Konrad Wallenrod. Eventually, he rises to a position of leadership over the people he inwardly despises, and treacherously leads them all into destruction. Even though this will precipitate his own death, he is quite happy to sacrifice his life on the altar of his nation. In *Wallenrod*, Mickiewicz calls this the "strategy of the fox." Is it possible for us, in our post 9/11 world, to call this anything but terrorism, effectively carried out by that most terrible of enemies, the sleeper cell? Terrifying, because — like the Boston Marathon killers — indistinguishable from us until they uncover themselves in their horrible act?

Such are the "Samsons" of Mickiewicz's innocent nineteenth century — "heroes" with whom it is practically impossible for us to sympathise these days, given the present danger in which we are forced to live our lives.

But perhaps Mickiewicz himself has little sympathy for them. It is interesting that the Konrad of the *Passages* is described in terms that recall his raving in the Great Improvisation. There, still in the possession of those legions of evil spirits, he claimed that it was his "Samson hour;" here, he is like a "Samson who just begins to strain." Perhaps this is why Mickiewicz does not allow him to come into contact with Oleszkiewicz. Although he has been freed of his demons once, Konrad is still a mere man, and the bacillus of hatred — spin it as you will — remains in his soul, ready to be set into motion again should the right (or really wrong) circumstances so conspire. The day of revolution has passed; Konrad can no longer precipitate the change he so longs for: he must wait for its arrival, as patiently as he can, like everyone else. That is the Christian attitude, and that is the attitude toward which all of *Forefathers' Eve* tends.

Revolution in Russia, if it is to come, will not be imposed from without, by Poles or Supermen or anyone else but the Russians themselves. That is the envoi of "To my Muscovite Friends," in which Mickiewicz speaks in his own voice to the liberal strata of Petersburg society in which he moved and made friends during his sojourn in the capital:

> Now this cup of venom I pour out in bitter flood.
> Burning is my speech, and corrosive its every sound.
> I distilled this poison from my homeland's tears and blood.
> May it burn — not you — but the chains with which
>     you are bound.
>
> And should it so befall, that you complain of my songs,
> I'll take it as a dog's barking when, too long resigned
> To pinch collar, and the hand that's yanked it for so long,
> Bares his teeth at long last — *Come on. Yank it one more time!*

### PART IV

In the usual ordering of the sequences, Part IV comes immediately after Part II, and before Part III. Read in this way, it suggests that the romantic, self-centred hero Gustaw evolves from the Wertherian love-sacrifice into the other-centred, national hero Konrad. With Part IV complete, Mickiewicz washes his hands of Maryla and mewling, and moves on to more important things, such as the future of his crucified nation.

By following the standard numerical order of the parts such as we propose, Mickiewicz's multi-faceted hero takes on a new appearance, no less logical. His love for the Young Wife is the main theme of Part II. In Part III, he famously turns his back on that love, "sacrificing" it for love for the nation, "all of its generations," past present and future, which is symbolised by his self-Christening as Konrad. However, as we have seen, the shamanic route proves to be a false road. Denied the power to "wield souls," he comes to learn that small acts of real charity are much more effective than the bombastic claims of "souls'-rule," to which no one can aspire. And thus, by concluding *Dziady* with Part IV, we return Gustaw-Konrad to his Lithuanian village. He comes full circle, like the Campbellian hero, and returns to the love of his youth.* This time, however, he is sure of not being frustrated. From the perspective of eternity, he understands that she has been fated to him, and that they will be reunited after her death. With his reemphasis of the (riskily trite, but nonetheless true) dictum that love conquers all, and with the concluding plea of the revenant Gustaw that his old tutor, the priest, have more human compassion on his flock (the present *and* the departed) than devotion to the letter of his Church's law, Mickiewicz elevates his monumental drama beyond parochial, Polish history into the ether, where Dante and Goethe respire. *Forefathers' Eve*, which stoops into Polish particularism in Part III, rebounds in Part IV to be a "great European" work of literature.

Part IV begins with otherworldly, Romantic action. Gustaw's appearance at the priest's cottage elicits a preternatural terror among the children gathered at evening prayer: "A dead man! Dead! A ghost! A vampire! / In God's name!... Get away from here!" they cry. Yet as soon as the uncanny signal is sounded, the priest takes control of the situation with his calming address to the new arrival: "Tell us your name. Come. Have no fear." It would seem as if we had here an adult coming upon a scene of childish panic, turning on the lights and demonstrating that

---

\*      See Alina Witkowska's above-cited argument about the transformation of Gustaw into Konrad in III.2 as a trying on of a new persona. As Konrad failed at the superhuman saviour routine, he returns here to an individual love, which, ironically, proves itself to be the greatest of them all.

there is no monster lurking under the bed. He is, after all, Gustaw's old teacher, which is to say, a person dedicated to learning and reason.

But even more importantly, he is a man of God. He is no representative of the Enlightenment, as is the "wise man" of the lyric "Romantyczność," who derides the supernatural vision of the young girl because he cannot see the ghost with his sensitive lenses of glass. Mickiewicz's priest possesses an intellect which admits a wider breadth of reality than the materialistic *philosophes* of the preceding era. Although in this scene the children are more perceptive than he — they recognise a ghost when they see one — they are still wrong in shrinking from it in terror, as a threat. By the same token, the priest himself is "wrong" in supposing Gustaw a mere vagrant with mental problems, and yet he assents nonetheless to the spiritual premises proposed by the revenant soul, which proves him amenable to the otherworldly lesson of charity he will be confronted with at the conclusion of the play.

*Forefathers' Eve* is a very Christian play, never more so than in Part IV. The lessons are simple, and might indeed be boiled down to the two great commandments of Christ: Love God, and Love your neighbour as yourself. These two simple commandments presuppose an acknowledgement of, and responsibility towards, the human community in which we all share. They are the foundation of all great Catholic letters, from Dante to Eliot; one which posits the individual, eternal, fate of each man and woman on the acts, for good or ill, performed by them in time. Mickiewicz is formulating nothing new when he places the following lines in the mouth of Gustaw:

> O children, it's not right for you to laugh!
> Listen, I once knew a girl, when I was half
> Your age, as sad and luckless as you see
> Me now, broken by the selfsame misery!
> She wore just such rags, and in her hair
> Such leaves and twigs as now I wear.
> When she would come into a town
> The whole village would gather round
> To laugh at her misfortune.
> Jeering, pointing, they'd chase her out
> Into the fields. Once, I too joined the rout,
> Just once! I mocked her too. Maybe
> That's why I've come to share her portion?

> Who knows? God in His majesty
> Takes the side of misery;
> I was so happy, so carefree, then —
> Who knew that it would fall to me,
> Such a just punishment?

But neither are they old. Rather, they are timeless, the Christian equivalent of the laws of karma, a restatement of the striking lines from Part III which begin with "Ah, mortal! If thou only knew thy power!" presented in a manner applicable to each of us, in our far from heroic, quotidian lives.

But Part IV is not a sermon. Like all works of literature, it is the child of its age, and the theme of romantic love, unhappy love, and the (somewhat sentimental) torments it bears along in its wake, which form a Leitmotiv for the entire sequence, is never far from view. As Gustaw pulls out his stiletto for the first time, the priest grabs his wrist and cries out:

> What are you doing!... Have you lost your mind?
> Put that blade down! Grab his hands — Stop!
> Are you a Christian? Such a godless thought!
> Do you know the Gospels?
>
> HERMIT
> /putting the knife away/
> And you — Do you know pain?

In what is both a critique of Romantic sentimentality and the German idealism which no less coloured the milieu in which he was formed, Mickiewicz, through Gustaw, assails the "bandit books" which had seduced him in his adolescence, and to which the Priest had innocently introduced him:

> Those books wrenched out my wings at the very roots,
> Twisting them to upward flight,
> Foiling descent, strain however so I might!
> I dreamt a lover glimpsed only in a dream,
> And her I longed for, holding in despite
> All earthly creatures, all of the common rout;

> I searched, ah! Where did I not seek her out,
> That love divine, found not beneath this sun
> But only on the sea-foam of my imagination!
> [...]
> So I flew off to the golden climes
> Sung into being by poets and sages,
> Goaded by hunger that nothing assuages
> Until, after wandering through lands far and near,
> I found her — and I found her here!
> Oh, just as I was about to cast myself down
> And in the filthy stream of luxury to drown,
> I found her! Whom I never thought I'd find.
> I found her! Just to lose her for all time!

The patron saints of the eighteenth century erotic imagination are singled out for censure: Abelard, Heloise, Rousseau and *his* Heloise. The ballads of the great Weimarians, Goethe and Schiller, are also referenced or directly cited as Gustaw strongly implies that poetry is to be found at the root of his woe. Poetry taught him suffering, formed in him a dangerous understanding — or perhaps misunderstanding — of the nature of love no less than in the case of poor Tatyana, the heroine of Pushkin's marvellous *Evgeny Onegin*. Once more we come across that characteristic of Slavic Romanticism which warns against the tragic conflation of fiction with real life. How curious that the "Slavic soul" should ever be stereotyped, as so often in the West, with heedless Romantic bravura...

Every action has an equal and opposite reaction, in the moral sphere no less than in that of physics. The *Kythera deina* of Sappho finds her illustration in Gustaw's present state, so eloquently described by the extended metaphor of the ringlet of hair he carries about with him.

> So slight a bond — the slim windings
> Of a girl's braid!... Yet no sooner had I lain
> It on my breast, that it grew about me, to constrain
> Like a hairshirt, my chest,
> Sinking into my flesh, rooting in my breast.
> I can barely breathe, so tight this lovelock spins!
> I suffer greatly! Yes, for great are my sins!

There is a moral here, yet it is elusive. What are these great sins he bemoans? This is no romantic exaggeration; we must continually remind ourselves that, just like the revenant spirits we came across in Part II, Gustaw is a soul suffering purgation. He has died — by his own hand — and has been sentenced by God to an indefinite period of suffering, until the guilt incurred has been burnt away, and he can enter Heaven. We do not learn what these sins of his may be. Of one thing we can be sure: the love itself was no sinful thing:

> Pray — what might be my sin?
> Pure love? And are its wages eternal death?
> That same God created love, whose creative breath
> Gave life to her delightful graces
> And bound two souls in the embrace
> Of such chains — for all time!
> Before He plucked them from the slope of light
> For them to wither in this fleshly blight
> He bound them fast together — for all time!
> Now, as we're parted by evil hands
> The chain's stretched taut — but such bands
> No one can break!

Whatever the cause of his harsh penance, whether the sins he speaks of predated his affair, were contemporary to it, or resulted from it, he can no more be censored for his love than he can be for having two arms and two legs. It is part of his nature; here again Mickiewicz returns to the Leitmotiv of a love established in Heaven. If it went awry, it did so neither because of the lovers' fault, nor that of God, but because of the "evil hands" who parted them, opposing themselves in this to the very will of God.

This eternal bond between Gustaw and Maryla is stronger even than the unbreakable, sacramental bond of matrimony. The Priest himself had been married; whether that be before he entered Holy Orders, or concurrently with his vocation (is he a priest of the Roman Catholic Church? or the eastern, Uniate Church, whose priests, like those of Orthodoxy, are permitted to marry?).* At any rate, Gustaw's interlocutor

---

\*      Although there is ancient precedent in the Roman Catholic Church for widowers to take Holy Orders, the opinion of critics and historians favours the Uniate option. So Pigoń, p. 18, so Czesław Miłosz, in his *History of Polish Literature*

has known the love of a woman and thus, as both widow and ghostly father, he is in a unique position to understand the significance of human erotic relationships in the Christian conception of reality. Yet when he expresses pain at the recollection of his departed wife, Gustaw mocks him:

> Wherever I go, someone's mourning his wife!
> It's not my fault! I've never seen your wife!
> /*coming to*/
> Take comfort, blubbering husband, in your woe—
> Your helpmeet was dead already, during life!

Fairly harsh that, and yet perfectly in line with his ideas of a love sanctified in the mind of God when the two souls in question were first formed. In this manner — and here the Romantic overcomes the Catholic in Mickiewicz — matrimony is transformed from the evangelical uniting of man and woman into one person, into a criminal separation, at least potentially, of woman from all other ties:

> Dead, as soon as they pronounced her "wife!"
> Marriage tamps living maidens down below
> The earth, cutting them off from kin and friends
> And... everybody else. The girl's life ends
> As soon as she the stranger's threshold crosses.

Husband becomes, ironically, "stranger." Gustaw rails against the marital convention that "cuts the girl off from kin and friends," but his real complaint is her being cut off from "everybody else" — signifying, in this odd bit of periphrasis, her destined lover, as if "husband" and "predestined lover" could never be one and the same.

It seems odd that this poster-boy for romantic love and soul-mating should so strenuously object to the exclusive claims of the marriage bond. It seems like a case of sour grapes. But we must guard against inflating the particular into the general. It is an individual case, his individual case, that he is explaining here, and in the context of this play, he is not so much arguing against marriage *per se* as arranged marriage, marriage based on

---

(Berkeley: University of California Press, 1983), p. 216, to give but two examples from our contemporary criticism.

anything other than all-encompassing, unique love. Gustaw is separated from Maryla here on earth, but — as we shall learn — they will be reunited in Heaven. As she is the (perhaps) unwilling cause of his present torment, Maryla will be the effective cause of his salvation. We have come across similar cases before. Dante was not married to Beatrice, nor was Petrarch to Laura. In this subtle, yet unmistakeable, allusion to the sanctifying graces of the Neoplatonic understanding of love as teaching the human soul of the love of God, Mickiewicz's *Forefathers' Eve* can confidently take its place alongside *La divina commedia* and *Il canzoniere*.

Yet what distinguishes ideal love in Mickiewicz from that found in Dante and Petrarch, is its erotic admixture. Dante never really dreamed of possessing Beatrice, nor did Petrarch approach Laura, except from afar. By the rules of the troubadour tradition, from which both Italian poets emerge, by definition the *donna ideale* is untouchable. Not only is it irrelevant whether she has an earthly husband or not — one might almost say that she must — her adoring poet, who looks upon her not entirely dissimilarly from the way the worshipper contemplates the Virgin Mary, *cannot* possess her physically. If he does, she ceases to be an ideal, he ceases to be a poet, and their passion leads no further than the satisfaction of coupling, which we share with the animals. Despite the fact that Dante is upbraided in the *Commedia* for looking at Beatrice "the wrong way," his sin is not so much of an adulterous nature, as it is idolatry. He finds his be-all and end-all, his goal, in the finite, if glorified, person of Beatrice, and not the infinite God to Whom she points the way. When Dante the character finally achieves the Beatific Vision, it is noteworthy that Dante the poet takes time to point out that in his ecstasy, he has completely lost cognisance of the presence of Beatrice. Likewise, although in one of the poems of his cycle Petrarch boldly calls for Laura to stand by his bedside when he is dying (rather than St. Joseph, the patron of departing souls), he would evoke her presence at his death, i.e. when he has become physically incapable of corporal amours, and is on the point of entering the spiritual world himself.

Mickiewicz, on the other hand, not only does not deny corporal eroticism, he glories in it. In the case of Gustaw, Maryla had been created for him, and he for her, before their very birth; separated in this life, they will be reunited in Heaven (even the Priest acknowledges this), but unlike his Florentine and Provençal predecessors, he rages against Maryla's earthly husband, who has taken her from his arms; he rages against the "evil hands" who participated in the separation, and, in his jealousy, he rages even against her:

That's one sort of death, my children.
But there's another kind, far worse,
When one does not die all at once
But piecemeal, slowly — How it hurts!
Two souls together bear the brunt
Of its dart, but only one is killed;
Only in one all hope is stilled;
The other dances free, unscathed.
And she lives on, free, fresh, and gay.
Oh, tears she'll shed, a few — she must!
But then her feelings slowly rust.
At last, her heart crumbles away.
That kind of death would two at once slay,
But only one of them is killed,
Only in one all hope is stilled;
The other dances free, unscathed.
And she lives on, free, fresh, and gay.
That sort of death killed... I won't say who!
But it's much worse than death is, true?
A corpse, who turns his gaze on you...

Corporeality is such an important part of our makeup, corporal love so crucial to that unique communion between two persons which is matrimony, it is hard not to see in Mickiewicz's version of Neoplatonic love a more perfected, more human, more Christian understanding of love, than that developed by Dante and Petrarch. In their emphasis on the disembodied love of the poetic worshipper for his *donna ideale,* in their downplaying of the physical delights of material, earthly love, they sail close to the Gnostic position, which sees matter as evil, and only the spirit as good. This might have been all right for the age of faith; in his play, Mickiewicz provides us with a much more relatable, modern lover. While not rejecting the traditional Christian cosmology or the hope of eternal reunion, he does not neglect this earth. He wants Maryla here and now, as well as there and then — with all the more urgency as, if we accept Christ's words in the gospel, in the Resurrection they will "be like angels" and there will be no more "marrying and giving in marriage."

The enforced celibacy, sterility (it is for this reason that he disguises Gustaw as a "hermit" in this portion of *Forefathers' Eve*) is what makes the metaphor of the animated corpse so fitting. By her rejection of him, Maryla has cut off Gustaw from physical contact with the one woman for whom he was destined; she has deprived him of life-giving potentiality, and made him no more valid in this regard than a dead body. The metaphor goes beyond sex. In a very human way, emphasised, but not invented, by Romanticism, we see that the physical satisfaction of two people becoming one in the significant erotic union which is marriage is the very foundation of human endeavour. With the support and wholeness and strength that marriage provides, a person may turn his or her hand to other tasks and succeed where he might not have, had it not been for the support of his spouse. By depriving him of herself, of the one woman to whom he was destined, Maryla has stifled all creative urges in Gustaw, not merely erotic ones. What good are her words at farewell, urging him on to great exploits? You might as well encourage a corpse to get up and run a four-minute mile:

> Had she not all ideals in me killed —
> With one light breath overturning battlements
> Raised for the dwelling places of giants.
> Nothing remains now but the tottering walls
> That crumble beneath the footfalls
> Of butterflies.
> And now she tries
> To raise castles on eggshells?
> To my atlas-career she brought a halt
> Transforming me into an ant! The vault
> Of heaven, now, she would have me bear?
> In vain! Man has but one spark of strength that flames
> In youth. Should Minerva blow
> Life into his soul, a new Plato
> Arises; if the torch is lit by Mars,
> A hero bursts forth, who in scarlet wars,
> With virtues great, and sometimes, greater crimes,
> Towards the shining Pantheon he climbs;
> Sceptres are dashed down by a shepherd's rod
> And thrones overturned by one imperious nod.

Deprived of the love that, if requited, would have enabled him to do great things, the spurned lover is locked in a state of obsession with the desired, yet absent, object of his love. He is stopped in his tracks, unable to move forward. The spiritual reality of their God-intended union will be (as we shall see) a source of some comfort to him; it is also a source of maddening frustration.

The existence of a spiritual realm, where the destined lovers make contact, are aware of the other's presence, however slightly, which was first signalled in Part I, is taken up here again, in Part IV. She "appears to him suddenly;" she is near, yet never to be grasped, like the grapes above Tantalus' head, like the waters just beneath his chin. He cannot forget her, even if he would, which is the same thing as to say that he cannot get on with his life, for she constantly stands in his way. He moves about like one living, but he is as invalid as a corpse. So immobilised is he by this obsession, that she affects him like no *donna ideale* we have ever come across before. She nearly makes him forsake idealism. This becomes apparent when the Priest finally realises who his guest is, which elicits an unexpected rebuke from the former pupil:

> PRIEST
> Gustaw! It's really you? So long! And whence?
> Where have you been, my dear friend, these long years?
> You vanished like a stone that disappears
> When chucked into a pond. And then — silence —
> No word from you, no letter, no scrap of news
> From the one star pupil of mine, in whose
> Talents I dared to hope such great success —
> And — nothing! Then, today! So lost — so dressed...
>
> GUSTAW
> /angrily/
> Old man! And shall I pay you back in kind?
> Speak out my charge, haul you to an assize?
> It's you that killed me! Teaching me to read —
> Both lofty books, and Nature's lovely screed.
> It's you that made earth hell,
> /mournful smile/
>       and paradise!
> /strongly, with contempt/
> While it's just dirt!

There follows an exposition of Maryla's sin, now that the identity of the Hermit has been revealed. Gustaw relates to the priest the seemingly unexpected nuptials of his predestined lover, with the man into whose arms those "evil hands" thrust her. The wedding has taken place, a wedding supper of sorts is being held, and Gustaw creeps up to the window and peers inside. What he sees there — Maryla, the smiling bride beside her husband — makes him fall insensate to the ground. As if Mickiewicz had emerged from the same rationalist background as the author of the *Manuscrit trouvé à Saragosse,* in which the most fantastic, seemingly supernatural events find their rational explanation in the end, so here are we provided with a reasonable explanation of the "revenant" motif:

> A corpse stretched out next to the wedding feast
> I lay, the grass bedewed with tears of gall —
> A paradox of agony and tenderness,
> Just as the sun arose bloody in the east,
> So did I rise — around me all was calm —
> I realised, the wedding night was past!
> Lightning-fast, age-long, that moment of gloom!
> I expect another such on the Day of Doom!
> /pause, slowly/
> Then the angel of death led me out of the garden!

Yet unlike Potocki, Mickiewicz is a Romantic. The walking dead may be an apt metaphor of the spurned lover deracinated from, made useless in, the world of the living, but that is not the whole story. Mickiewicz's Dantean interpenetration of the world of the spirit and the world of matter is sincere, and is the foundation upon which Polish Monumental Drama rests; no less sincere is the Romantic idolatry of the beloved in which Gustaw partakes. He continues with his upbraiding of his faithless love with such lines, which belong entirely to the Romantic period:

> Had I an equal say in our fates
> And God should offer me such a girl
> Whose beauty never had been seen before,
> The type that set the ancient Greeks to war,
> More gorgeous than the angelic ranks that swirl
> About His throne, in dreams, in poets' lies,

> More gorgeous even than you! I'd still despise
> Her for your sake!
> If as a dowry, all the gold
> Of fabled river Tagus were told
> Into a sack, and with it also given
> The kingdom of Heaven,
> I'd spurn it for your sake!

Romantic as well is Gustaw's fantasy of confronting the bridal pair at a banquet, which both foreshadows Poe and recalls the shaman-claims of Konrad, from Part III:

> What? Kill her? How I prate on!
> For that I'd have to be blacker than Satan!
> Iron, away!
>
> /puts away the stiletto/
>
> Let her own memory gore
> Her heart like a stiletto, to the core!
> I'll go, but I'll go without a knife;
> I'll go myself to cast on her my eye —
> [...]
> I merely stand and stare —
> Ha, ha! A venomous, viper's glare
> To blind her, strike her petrified!
> Like smoke, my stare wafts deep inside
> Her brain, seeping through her eyelids white
> There to brood forever,
> Staining each waking thought, and at night
> Waking her in fever.

As Konrad during his trance-induced conversation with Rollison, so Gustaw here touts the power of his "basilisk eye." Likewise similar to Konrad's situation is the inconsistent, contradictory nature of his rambling thoughts. Earlier on, as we have seen, he blamed her for rejecting him, and thus taking away whatever creative power he might have possessed to do great things. Now, he blames himself for not winning her, by never having done great things to impress her, or rather make him worthy of her:

> What for, these ravings? Have I any right
> To dream of her — a wretch like me — however slight?
> Where is my virtue? My great deeds? My fame?
> I've none, I've nothing, as no longer have I
> This one love of my life. Did I ever try
> To win her hand, my passion to requit?
> I was not bold above friendship. That was it —
> I only wanted her near
> Even as kin with kin — a sister dear
> To a brother — God's my witness — Had I her thus,
> Then was I satisfied: the two of us
> Together chastely, only for to say
> "I see her, saw her, will see her today
> And each tomorrow;"
> Morning and noon and evening to bid
> Her first Good Morning, next to her to sit —
> No space between for sorrow!

Alas, it is the one, or the other; it cannot be both. Either she is to blame for not remaining faithful to him, and thus hobbling him on the route to achieve the full potential he could only achieve at with her at his back, or he is to blame for doing nothing to win her. Perhaps what he really blames himself for is found in the concluding lines of this section. He failed in timidity; the "great thing" he should have done was to engulf her in a world-shocking erotic passion. Instead, with a worshipping shyness that sets him behind even the cherry-coated sylph-like swains of Fragonard's worst canvasses, he was content merely to limp along, satisfied with "brotherly" love.

Yet that one thought (boldness in love) does not logically follow from the lack of great deeds, virtue, and fame. Gustaw is buffeted by, aswirl in, tormenting regret. His moods, too, shift from tenderness to hostility, from adoring love to vituperation. If Mickiewicz achieves anything here, it is in his portrait of the destructive force of love, when unrequited. We have said that the animated corpse is used in *Forefathers' Eve* as a metaphor for continued existence when life has lost its sense; in Gustaw's incoherent torrent of accusation and self-blame, explanations and contradictory assertions, we have a vivid elaboration of the metaphor.

He only regains lucidity after the dramatic reenactment of his suicide. One wonders whether the sudden reappearance of the prized pupil — in such a state! — was not enough shock for one evening for the poor old vicar; instead, Gustaw takes up his stiletto again, and runs himself through as the priest looks on. It is certainly the most theatrical event in this part of *Forefathers' Eve*, and the Priest reacts with all the horror and panic that a normal person would experience at such a juncture. Jan Walc is correct that Gustaw is "playing a role before the Priest" here, and that he is a "methodological madman," such as Hamlet.[*] Gustaw allows the fear to run its course, and then, calmly, lucidly, leads the (somewhat, if not entirely Rationalist) clergyman back to balance with an appeal to his reason. After all, he's still standing, is he not?

> GUSTAW
> Charms,
> Magic perhaps? You know, there are such arms,
> Costly ones, that slit the very soul
> Although they seem to leave the body whole.
> By such a weapon I was run through twice.
> /*pause, he smiles*/
> Such weapons here are wielded by a woman's eyes,
> /*gloomily*/
> And after death, by a sinner's vain regrets!

The most remarkable thing here is the sudden, palpable, transformation of Gustaw's intellect, from raving babble to calm, smiling, instruction. Gustaw cannot kill himself, because he is dead already. We learn that we are dealing with a revenant, after all. Yet according to the world-view of Polish Monumental Drama, of which *Forefathers' Eve* is the earliest, and greatest, example, and the Christian faith, from which it grows, the end of this temporal life is not the end of life, period. As a matter of fact, Gustaw's temporal death has been nothing if not the gateway to a greater life. This, again, is evidenced by the dramatically immediate shift in his elocution,

---

[*]    Walc, pp. 41-42. He is following Zofia Stefanowska in making this assertion. Cf her *Próba zdrowego rozumu* (Warszawa: Państwowy Instytut Wydawniczy, 1976), p. 36.

from confused and frenzied to calm and instructive. It is as if he were reaffirming Dante's great dictum of existence, grasped from beyond the mortal plain, as a logical book, bound by love, while here below we can only comprehend (to our confusion and frustration) scattered leaves.

Gustaw has been freed from the physical, and mental, torment of unrequited love by the blade that pierced his heart. By the same token, although he has been freed of that pain, he has not been absolved of the responsibility of his sin, and that a great one, of self-slaughter. By God's mercy, Gustaw has not been damned to Hell. But he is not in Heaven yet; like the Ghost of Hamlet's father, he is in Purgatory. He will not rest in the blessed regions until Maryla expires, and he, devoted to her in life, will slip in through the pearly gates, as it were, by clinging to her hem:

> Now let your suit be
> For them, not me, as you offer up your Mass.
> Nothing more than your remembrance do I ask.
> On earth, my sin met retribution fair —
> Now, is it penance, or reward, my share?
> For he who, still on earth, has tasted Heaven,
> Whose soul to her predestined half was given,
> Who every earthly limit soared above,
> Heart and soul losing himself in her he loved,
> Thinking her thoughts alone, breathing her breath,
> Retains not his identity after death,
> But to his one and only love sealed fast
> Becomes the shadow that she casts.
> If, during life, his mistress was a saint,
> He shares her heavenly glory.
> If she were spattered by sin's gore, he
> Sinks into hell marked by the self-same taint.
> I'm fortunate in that God indentured me
> To her, an angel. For both her and me
> The future's bright. Meanwhile, a shade, I range
> Beside her, the diapason of pain
> And ecstasy; when she recalls me, sighs,
> And drops a tear discreetly from her eyes,
> I near her lips; I gently part her hair;
> I mix my substance with the fragrant air

She breathes; I become one with her! And then,
Heaven!
But oh...! Only those who love, who part and yearn
Will understand the envy with which I burn
When...
Still must there pass by many a long season
Thus, before she's called to the embrace
Of Him Who made her. Then, keeping her pace,
I too shall steal into the Blessed Regions.

/the clock strikes/

Heed well the wisdom you've been given,
The daughter of the Lord's own breath:
Who during life has tasted Heaven
Won't get there quickly, after death.

Those for whom the Priest, and his children, ought to pray are other souls in Purgatory. Gustaw accepts the penance due for his sins, and is working it out now, until Maryla's death will release them both to eternal life. Once more, as if we needed reminding, we are firmly back in the Dantean-Petrarchan realm of Neoplatonic love, in which the most effective saint for the lover is his *donna ideale*.

As in Dante's case, when he finally is able to see past his obsession with Beatrice and orient his eyes in the proper direction, toward the fount of all love, the Holy Trinity, so here Gustaw's travails have opened his heart beyond Maryla, to embrace others. He has not only arrived at the Priest's door as part of his yearly penitential reenactment of his "passion," but to fulfil a mission on behalf of others:

Hear now what's led me across the great divide.
When I arrived here, when I stepped inside,
You and your children were offering prayers
For those who wander the Purgatorial vales...

PRIEST
/grabbing a crucifix/
Yes, yes! We'll finish them —

GUSTAW

All right, but first, confess:
You believe in Hell, Purgatory, and the rest?

PRIEST
I believe in everything the Good Lord preaches
In His Gospel, and our Mother the Church teaches.

GUSTAW
And in the old rites? Do you still believe
What your grandfather did? Forefathers' Eve?

PRIEST
That ritual was once a pagan feast.
The Church enables, nay commands, her priest
To enlighten her folk, and stamp out superstition.

GUSTAW
/*pointing to the ground*/
And I, Father, am entrusted with a mission
By others to convince you to relent.
Return us our Dziady! The Judge Omnipotent
Rates one true tear of pity shed here below
More than seas of mourning poured out just for show —
Paid keeners and horses beribboned in black.
When a sincere hand sets on a gravestone one,
Just one, votive lamp, it gleams like the sun
In the eternal realm — I tell you truly —
More than thousands set there out of irksome duty.
When simple folk bring offerings of honey,
Milk and some poppyseed on that hallowed night,
Far better will that ease a poor soul's plight
Than modish funeral breakfasts, that stink of money.

As Gustaw's heart broadens, so does *Forefathers' Eve* broaden outward, from the particular and the national, to the widest human universality possible: a recognition of the interconnectedness of the human world in both the material, and spiritual spheres, which prompts a request for pity for all the suffering souls of Purgatory, familiar and unfamiliar, kindred and stranger; for the men and women of all ages and all climes suffering in the hope of glory.

Even the appeal to the Priest to lift the ecclesial ban on the ancient Forefathers' Eve rites is more than just Romantic Catholicism, more than just nineteenth century fascination with folklore and the gothic. It is an illustration of the law of love enunciated by Christ in the gospels, who brushed aside all pharisaical commandments, all the hundreds of positive and negative commands that held the people rule-bound, replacing them with the simple orientation arrows: Love God with all your heart; Love your neighbour as yourself. Gustaw is encouraging the Priest to break out of his rule-bound theology, and to allow for the existence of other conduits of solace to the suffering souls. Here again Mickiewicz approaches the breadth of Dante, who specifically bends his own rules of logic in the *Divine Comedy* to underscore the feebleness of man's reason, and man's great presumption in daring to confine God's sense of justice in his own.

Dante reserves some of the worst torments of Hell for the suicides, and yet at the gates of Purgatory, he places Cato. Dante is constrained to shut the gates of Heaven before his beloved, virtuous Virgil, simply because the Roman poet was born before the advent of Christ, and was unable to follow Him, and yet, in Heaven, he places the righteous Trojan king Ripheus. "My thoughts are not your thoughts," Dante paraphrases Isaiah, and after him, so Mickiewicz. In his unwillingness to look beyond the rules of his Church[*] — which Gustaw, like Dante before him, does not reject — the Priest is in danger of having the faith of his soul stifled by the rationalistic tendency of his mind:

PRIEST
For sure. And yet those midnight gatherings
In chapels and caves are ripe with pagan things,
White magic, heretical rituals
And superstition. Then the folk, chock-full

---

[*] Stanisław Demichowicz, who grew up in an area of Eastern Poland inhabited by Orthodox, Uniate, and Roman Catholic believers, and who witnessed Forefathers' Eve celebrations in the early twentieth century, revealed to Stanisław Pigoń that it was the Catholic clergy who were rather adverse to the folk rituals accepted by the Eastern churches. See Pigoń, p. 17.

> Of fables, unenlightened, will believe
> In ghosts and wizards. Ha! Forefathers' Eve!
>
> GUSTAW
> You don't believe in spirits?
> /*ironically*/
>                 A soulless world?
> It lives, but as a skeleton, that's whirled
> On its dottering career by hidden springs?
> Or like a clock wound up, whose pendulum swings
> It on its way in dull perpetual motion?
> /*smiles*/

In other words, the intellectual Priest has become so convinced by the proofs of science, that he runs the risk of misapplying empirical questioning to the realm of the spirit, where it most definitely cannot return the proper results. While remaining to all intents and purposes a good village priest, he comes close to falling away from miraculous Christianity and into ethical Deism. Witkowska is spot on when she notes: "the Priest, as Gustaw sees him, incarnates the philosophical sins of all rationalist-wisemen."[*]

To show him the error of his ways, Gustaw resorts to the "empirical proof" of miracle. He gathers the whole family around a counter and evokes the voice of a spirit who is suffering for the sins committed during his earthly life:

> Children, come close to the counter here.
>
> /*to the counter*/
>
> Little soul, what do you need?
>
> VOICE FROM THE COUNTER
>                 I beg three prayers.
>
> PRIEST
> /*terrified*/
> Glory to God on high!... He speaks! A wraith!

---

[*]     Witkowska, p. 98.

And the Word became flesh! Run! The sacristan!
Wake him up!... And the people!...

GUSTAW
                      Shame on you, man!
What's happened to your reason? And your faith?
Who fears the Lord need not fear anything.

PRIEST
What is it that you need... Ah! a goblin! You —

GUSTAW
I? I need nothing. But so many do!

There is no greater image of the intimate interpenetration of the worlds of the spirit, and that of matter, than this scene in *Forefathers' Eve*. Stanisław Pigoń sees in this immediacy of the spirit world a particularly Eastern Christian understanding of the soul's lot after the death of the body:

> To this way of thinking, Purgatory doesn't actually exist, at least not as a place where souls win expiation through purifying flame. According to this belief, the souls of the dead remain in a state of expectation upon their judgment, which they will hear only on the Day of Judgment at the end of time. Until then, such is their state in the cosmos.*

Whatever the case may be — and the distinctions between East and West seem to be more of a semantic than a theological, nature — this can be understood in a Catholic manner as well. Purgatory is not, as Dante has it, a mountain in the southern seas, the tip of which, crowned by the earthly paradise, touches heaven. It is another mode of existence, here and now. The suffering souls, who are in need of the merciful prayers of the Church

---

\*     Pigoń, p. 15. Are the souls of the dead, in the Orthodox way of thinking, unsure of whether they are saved or damned? If they have consciousness, that would seem odd. Rather than "waiting upon their judgement," it might be better to say "unsure of when they will enter into their reward," for (in the case of the saved, but not yet purified, souls) both East and West teach that the prayers of the living can hasten on the dead to their place in heaven. They cannot do it themselves; they can only suffer patiently.

Militant, are not locked in some prison far, far away; they are everywhere about us, here and now. The reaction of the priest is not so much one of frightened surprise, but one of joyous wonder. "Wake up the sacristan!" he calls in shock, "wake up the people!" How ironic that is, for it is the simple people of his flock that have always known this truth. It is he, their shepherd, who is in need of enlightenment, in the broad, Catholic sense, not that of the eighteenth century *philosophes*.

Most striking is the Priest's sudden blurting out "What is it that you need?" — a verse from the very rituals he was so intent on stamping out. His unconscious mind, or his better nature, rushes out in love to the suffering soul and contacts him — not as a priest, but as a fellow mortal, who will one day himself stand in need of the prayers of others once he has passed over into Purgatory. His spontaneous cry at this moment is natural. It is natural to acknowledge the existence of life beyond this material plane, as our very nature rebels at the idea that all life ends with death. It is natural to worship God according to the rites of the Catholic Church, of which the Priest is an important representative; it is also natural to assume that God is not confined to any one Church, any one ritual, and this assumption must lead us to tolerance and sympathy for the well-intentioned desires and expressions of others.

It is, in short, natural to love. *Forefathers' Eve* is all about love: the individual, universally experienced, erotic love of one man for one woman; the more particular love for one's fatherland, and the universal love, again, for all mankind, the living and the departed. Read according to the numeration of segments established by Mickiewicz, the story of Gustaw-Konrad takes us on a cyclical journey from unclear awareness of a destined human love at arm's reach (Part I) through the religious duty we, the living, owe the suffering souls of Purgatory (Part II); thence through the charity we owe our nation and immediate friends (Part III) and at last to the Neoplatonic idea of love, which uses erotic attachment as both a didactic tool, and a gateway to, the love of God and others (Part IV). By imitating and creatively engaging with the Great Europeans of his acquaintance — Dante, Petrarch, Goethe, Shakespeare, Byron — Mickiewicz has created a work wholly deserving of his being ranked among them.

*San Francisco*
May 25, 2016

# FOREFATHERS' EVE

# FOREFATHERS' EVE, PART I

## THE SPECTACLE

*On the right side of the stage — a Girl in a room, alone — Quite a few books around and about, a piano. The window on the left gives way to fields; on the right there hangs a large mirror. On the table, a candle burns out. An open book — the novel* Valérie.

GIRL /getting up from the table/.
    Cheap candle! What a fine time to go out!
    Now I can't finish reading. And I much doubt
    I'll fall asleep, so unsatisfied I am...
    Ah, Valérie! Gustave, angelic man!
    How often have you filled my waking dreams!
    In sleep, I'd join you both. But, God! It seems
    I'll toss and turn all night. Your tragedy,
    Wellspring of tragic wisdom...

/pauses, with distaste/
                                What's with me?
    What can such lovers hope for here

/points to the ground/
                                      but pain?
    The ending's clearly visible — like a train!
    But you are lucky, Valérie, adored
    By such a lover as all girls pine for
    In vain, seeking his traits in each new face,
    And in each voice, straining to catch a trace
    Of his, to join with hers in harmony —
    Vainly, in my experience. All I see
    Are faces cold as stone — Medusas all!
    And hear: words colder than the sleet in fall!

Each night returning to my lonely abode
I bear with me that day-long's tiresome load
Of boring people and their boring schemes.
I come back here, to my books and — to my dreams,
As to his lonesome cave a castaway
Returns after plodding fruitlessly all day
His desert island, seeking someone there
Who isn't — finding only waste — and despair.

The man condemned should learn to love his chains.
By jerking them, he but augments his pains.

Greetings, old cell! Since for life we're condemned,
Let's learn to call it self-willed imprisonment.
We've nothing to busy us with? From man's earliest age,
Such seclusion's been sought out by the fervent sage
Intent on finding wealth, medicinal balm,
Or poison... Young wizards, let us test the scope
Of our talents — to find poison for our hope.
And as our faith forbids our suicide,
Let's inter our soul alive, still on this side
Of the grave; from which one may yet resurrect —
Such graves lead to the Fields of the Elect.
Life among the shades of an imagined earth?
The real, tedious one, has not half its worth.
Shades only? In this world where we draw breath
Walk there no souls hid from our eyes by death?
I shall not so insult grand Nature's wealth,
Blaspheme her Maker — or misprize myself.

In all of Nature, that majestic whole
Of flesh and spirit — each has a kindred soul:
Each flash of light, each voice that threads the air
Impelled by laws harmonic, finds its pair;
Each note that's wafted through the desert parts
Of space falls, finally, on a kindred heart —
Ah! Can it be, the tender heart of man
Must yearn forever, for all ages banned

To solitude? Though no one understand
This heart of mine, I have it of the Lord —
He gave it me, and it would be absurd
To think that nowhere, never, should there be
Some kindred heart, long journeying to me!

Oh, if we but with yearning wings might push
Apart the clouds, and feel the passing rush
Of pennons — share one word, exchange one glance —
Oh, that would be enough of a romance:
To know, for sure, that both of us exist!
Then would the soul, whose flagging joys desist
Almost to feel, so tightly are they wound
About by torturous pain, unchained, rebound,
Their shackles shed, toward the skies,
And this deaf cave become a paradise!
How sweet it would be, Ah! to get to know
That kindred spirit, and whatever should glow
In one's thoughts, spread before him — all that's lain
In one's most secret heart; now to make plain
Before his eyes, a splendid, glittering trove
Of jewels spread out before the one I love!
Then — were it but a moment — we might connect
Past memories with future hopes, collect
All in this present Now, and resurrect!
Then would we be like vapours that the dew
Respires at dawning when the day is new —
Unseen and light, yet as they meet, they rise
To spark, to flame, and soar the starry skies!

*Stage left, enter a Chorus of Villagers bearing food and drink. At the head of the chorus, an Old Man [the Guślarz]*

GUŚLARZ.
    All is darkness, all is quiet;
    With wary ear and careful eye
    Haste we to the secret rite.
    Soft our singing, slow our tread,

Ours no festive revelry.
The chants we raise are for the dead.
We're not ringing in New Year's;
We approach the graves, in tears.

CHORUS.
All is darkness, all is quiet —
Haste we to the sacred rite.

GUŚLARZ.
Haste we silently and slow,
Past the church and past the manor.
The priest our spells would disallow;
The lord would waken at our clamour.
Only the departed hasten
Where the guślarz shall command;
The lord appoints live men their station,
The graveyard's under the priest's ban.

CHORUS.
While it's dark, and all is quiet,
Haste we to the sacred rite.

CHORUS OF YOUNG MEN.
/To a Young Widow — see "Romanticism"/

Leave off your mourning, dry your eyes
Sweet girl, and wring no more your hands.
You'll hear many a young man's sighs,
And wear, ere long, a new wedding band.

From the dark forest race two doves —
And close behind, an eaglet flies.
You're safe now, sweet, but — look above:
Hark! your silver-feathered husband cries!

Weep not, fair dove, in useless mourning.
A second husband to bill and coo,

Spurs at his heels; blue sash adorning
His breast, he hastens close to you.

A rose beside a violet growing
In summer fields; now, scything slow
A peasant slashes at his mowing;
He slits the husband, lays him low.

You weep and sigh in vain regret:
Slender Narcissus — see? — bows low
To you, his flashing pupil set
Amongst the fields like a moon aglow.

Leave off your mourning, dry your eyes
Sweet girl, nor plod along as if in trance;
The one you seek no more can sigh
To you, nor take you by the hands.

His right hand now grasps a dark cross;
His eyes turned to blest Heaven's expanse —
Buy him a Mass to mourn your loss
And give us living lads a chance.

/to the Old Man/

Cease yearning, old man, beg the young;
Yearning blights heart, and thought, and tongue.
Set forth some cheery models rather;
Show us some shining treasures, father.

The old oak sheds his leaves in fall
Deaf to the grass and blooms that call
For shade. "Young sprigs, I know you not —
Nor if you merit a sheltered plot.
Not such the blooms that graced the glade
Of yore, reposing in my shade."

Stop your complaining! So it goes —
"The good old days!" Were they? Who knows?
These wither, those grow green and fat.
Less beautiful? Well, whose fault is that?
We are the only blooms you see —
Enrich us with glad histories.

Stop sighing, old man; vain your mourning.
Men die, and new men are a-borning!
Not all your kin lie in the grave;
Consider all the joys you have!
Take some from us, our happy throng,
And seek your dead among the young.

GUŚLARZ.
Whoever wandering on life's road
Strove to hold true to the straight path
While thorns and nettles would be thrown
Before their feet as it may hap
Too often — who through decades whole
Of pain and trouble, labour, tears,
Forgot the longed-for distant goal,
To find it after many years;

Whoever scorned earth for the sun,
Eyes fixed forever on the mess
Of stars, the tracks the planets run
And tumbled into the abyss;
Who sought to excavate with tears
What's lost forever in the past;
Who would unravel future years,
What jealous destiny holds fast;
Who recognised missteps too late
But strove to better his worse thoughts,
Half-closing eyes, to penetrate
In dreams, what waking, he vainly sought;

Whoever sick with dream-disease
Became his own implacable foe,
Flailing round about to seize
What he'd held always in his soul;

Who in his heart old memories churns,
Who would catch sight of destiny —
Forsake the world for graveyard urns,
Wisemen! for white necromancy.

Darkness and secrets everywhere;
We're guided by both faith and song.
Onward, with us, you who despair;
All who remember, all who long.

CHILD.
    Did you see that? Let's go home! I think we should —
    That flash — Hear that? — There's something in the woods...
    Tomorrow we'll come back, — in the morning hours;
    You'll — ponder, as always, and I'll lay flowers...

    I heard them say, tonight we might see spooks.
    I don't know them, or how Mummy looks,
    She's dead so long now — And your eyes are blind
    In sunlight! How'll you see at nighttime?

    And near deaf, too! Remember? On Sunday
    Two weeks past, kin and friends all came to say
    Happy Birthday to you — and you just sat
    There, glum and dumb, just as if the cat

    Got your tongue; not a word, not a single sound
    Until — "Who's all these people milling round?
    And on a workday? Is the sun down yet?"
    And your guests so merry! And the night as black as jet!

OLD MAN.
>From that day on, ah! how far away I've sailed!
Familiar lands and islands, slipping by the rail;
I've watched my heritage past the horizon drown —
Your faces, voices, hands, which now surround
Me — What are they worth? Those I knew in youth:
The stroking hands, the voice that shot me through,
Where are they? Weak, or snuffed, the flames that fed
Their vigour; is it they, or am I, dead?
I leave a world much changed from that I'd known —
Wretched, who piecemeal to grave-mould is grown!

Only your voice, my grandchild, yet remains —
A childish echo of dear, long-dead strains;
Through it there bubbles your late mother's laugh!
Still, you too will leave me, as the others have.

I'll make my way alone. For he who by day
Heeds not the living, in the night won't stray,
Guided by voices dead. I've trod each year
This ground; first, like you, with childish fear;

Then, a young buck, full of boldness and daring;
Then, in yearning sadness; now, beyond caring,
I tread the selfsame path. Tonight, what leads me?
Some dark foretaste of my own mortality?
I'll find the graveyard. Something deep inside
Tells me, once there, I'll no longer need a guide.
But now, kneel down, my son, before we part —
Receive my grateful blessing with glad heart.

O Lord, who in thy servant's hands wast pleased
To thrust this cup — I've drowned it to the lees,
The bitter gall of life — I beg Thee here,
As I creep near Thy judgment, bend Thy ear
To my pious request: Bless my grandson,
Of Thy great mercy: Lord, let him die young!

Be well! But wait — Press once more Dziadek's hand!
And let me hear your voice. Sing once again
That song we both love, the Unhappy Knight
Who, by love's enchantment, was petrified.

CHILD /sings/.

*The Enchanted Youth*

Shattering the rusty lock,
Twardowski braves the gloomy portal.
In soaring tower and dungeon dark,
There's much to daunt the boldest mortal!

In one cave — such a thing of fear! Or
Pity — There in penance strange,
A young man stands, facing a mirror,
A young knight wound about in chains.

He stands there in the musty keep,
A strapping lad of flesh and bone
And yet, upwards, enchantments creep,
Turning him slowly into stone.

Up to his chest he's petrified;
His face retains its softness yet;
Courage and strength dart from his eyes;
His pupils shine with tenderness.

"Who might you be?" he asks, "Who fords
These glooms, their threshold boldly crossed,
Where broken lie so many swords,
And lives uncounted have been lost?"

"My name? The whole world knows my story,
And cringes at my blade, my word.
Great is my power, and my glory,
For I am happy Twardów's lord."

"From Twardów? Where's that? In my days
I never heard one of that name
Reap any sort of martial praise,
Nor tilting at our knightly games.

"How many years, I cannot guess,
Have I been kept, imprisoned here;
But you come from the world a-fresh,
And of that world I'd gladly hear.

"Does daring Olgierd still lead out
Our Lithuanian men, and wield
The sword that wreaks the German rout
And sweeps the Mongol from the field?"

"Olgierd? Two centuries have come and gone
Since the world trembled to its knees
Before him. Jagiełło, his grandson,
Now sweeps to greater victories."

"Two ages? Pray, but one more word:
As you wend on your errant way,
Has it chanced — happy Twardów's lord —
You near Świteź' banks to stray?

"If so, do folk there still sing lays
Of Poraj and his mighty sword?
Of beauteous Maryla's grace,
Which the same Poraj long adored?"

"Young sir, indeed I've travelled, I
Have roamed these Niemen lands all over.
Yet nary a word — nor of Poraj
Have heard, nor of his gentle lover.

"But why waste breath? Dear time is passing —
Once from these chains I set you free,

The world will be yours for the asking,
And sate your curiosity.

"I've learned some lore of wizardry —
And understand that looking glass
Is hexed. I'll smash it, you'll be free.
When it's destroyed, your spell will pass."

This said, he marches to the mirror
And raises up his sword to smite —
"Hold!" cries the youthful knight in fear,
"If you would help me, gracious knight,

"Take down the mirror from the wall,
And give it here into my hands.
Thus only will these fetters fall;
Thus only will my torments end."

And so. In tears, his face bled white,
From Twardów's hands into his own
He took it, kissed it — the young knight
Then turned completely into stone.

CHORUS OF YOUNG MEN.

The guślarz bade us youths
To wait here in mid-road.
There shine the village roofs;
There: grave-stones in the grove.

Midway 'twixt cradle and tomb,
Our youth suspended stands.
'Twixt gaiety and gloom
Stand we fast-centred, friends!

Return home? That's not right.
Nor plod with weeping throng.

Here shall we hold *our* rites,
Shortening the night with song.

We'll greet those who draw near,
And query who tread back.
We'll dissipate their fears,
And point them the right track.

The sun has set, the children run,
The old folk weep and moan.
But soon enough breaks the new dawn
And all are coming home.

Before those kids grow grey,
Or bell for oldsters toll,
More than one moment gay
Will yet delight their soul.

But whom among our lot
Cheers not sport's thrust and toss,
His heart, damp with sad thoughts
To this grand world is lost.

Who like a ghoul or owl
Seeks out the mouldy frost
Of graves to sob and howl,
He to this world is lost.

Who sings grave-songs when young
And visits tombs and urns,
He never sings gay songs,
Nor to this world returns.

Let infants and the old
Haunt church with bread and sigh!
We'll stand here in mid-road,
Beneath the pristine sky.

## SONG OF THE HUNTSMAN.

'Midst hills and meads
And woods and vales;
'Midst neighing steeds
And trumpet peals,

On a mount whose jump
The hawk outrushes,
With a gun whose thump
The thunder hushes,

As gay as a child
Or a bloodthirsty knight,
Sly, bold and wild,
Speeds to the fight

The huntsman! Sing
Your greetings, wold!
Lord of beasts, woodland king,
Long live the huntsman bold!

Does he aim at the sky?
Or the trees o'er the flood?
There, showers of feathers fly;
There gush rivers of blood.

Say who chased down the boar
That in deep forest glide?
Say who covered the floor
With the black bear's thick hide?

Say who caught in his springs
Airy squadrons by guile?
Say who netted their wings
With sly treacherous wile?

The huntsman! Oh, sing
Your greetings, wold!
Lord of beasts, woodland king,
*Vivat*, huntsman bold!

Press further, press further now,
Follow the trace!
Press further, press further now,
On, the gay chase!

*GUSTAW.*
I've hunted down a song! They won't be mad,
The rest, that I return with empty hands —
When I get back, I'll sing for my supper.
But where am I now? I can't tell. Up, or
Down — no path, just deaf woods. No horn, no shot...
Ha! For all your rhyming, see what you've got!
Chasing the muse, I strayed from the carried line,
And God, it's getting cold! A fire'd be fine.
Not just for heat, but light! To signal here
Another straggler — and then we'd see us clear;
Four eyes beat two!
                  And better far than four
Even one, my friend, that's fast fixed on the spoor
And not on the clouds of heaven! Those who chase
The quarry on firm ground don't stray to trace
Chimeras in the azure, cast drooping looks
At soaring mountain tops and purling brooks!
But single-eyed, chase on through brake and copse
After their prey — and never get lost!
They surely sit at table now, and regale
Each other with the tallest tales,
Boasting of past — or future — trophy hunts,
Passing round praise for hits; for misses, taunts!
Laughing out loud, or whispering low,
All gay and brash — except Father; when they grow
Tired of chewing round conquests of the field
They'll be off to see what sort of quarry yield

The manors round about; where, dancing, quaffing,
They'll chase the girls — and everybody laughing...
Sometimes the fiercest archer — Love — will smite
When least expected, striking in mid-flight...
And so their hours pass, their days, their years.
Thus was it always, thus shall be — the spheres
No more predictable along their way,
Such happy ones! —
                Why can't I be like they?
We all set out together; why did I
Break off alone, the wastes alone to ply?
Seeking adventure? No. Escaping *ennui*.
I crave not excitement, but — difficulty.
To change my thoughts, or, at least my place;
To find somewhere no one my dreams might trace,
Or see these empty tears that — who knows why? —
Will of a sudden crowd into my eye;
Or hear these sighs, which — where is it they go?
Not to the neighbour girls — To the winds that blow
Across the trees — to dreams!
                      Well, *that's* not strange...
And yet it always seems that someone hears
These sighs, and someone, somehow, sees these tears —
Someone, who like a shade about me ranges.

How many times I've heard the meadows rustle
Softly, as if a nymph's feet there did bustle;
I look: the flowers sway and nod their heads
As if someone had lightly mussed their beds;
Or when in some lone place I'm at a book
And, drop it! As I feel somebody look
And — Yes, something flashed in the looking glass;
I heard her filmy fabric sigh, as she passed!
Or lying in my bed, already sliding
Into black dreams, and somebody comes gliding,
Breathing my breath, heart keeping time with mine —
I even hear a muffled word at times,
Like a fly that buzzes past my drowsing ear.

I fall asleep in bright mist, when a clear
Flash falls, from on high and far away,
But what its shape might be, I cannot say...
But feel her eyes' beam — her smile, I see!
Where are you? Lonely daughter of mystery?

O, let your soul take on, at least
The vain and passing stuff of flesh;
Cover yourself with but a crease
Of rainbow, or a spring's bright flash!

O, let your myriad glories
Long, long into my parched eyes sink!
O, your lips' subtle melodies,
Long, long my thirsty ears would drink!

Shine unto me, dear Sun! I long
With your image to scald my eyes!
Sing, Siren! At your thrilling song
I'll slumber, dreaming of the skies!

Ah, where might I seek you? I flee the vulgar herd;
Be you with me only, and I'll reject the world!

BLACK HUNTSMAN /sings/.
  Too high, little bird, you fly too high.
  Your wings you'd boldly test?
  Look down: the earth you so defy
  Is spread with lures and nets!

YOUNG MAN.
  Wait! Someone's singing! Over here! Halloo!
  Sing out once more, my brother! Hey! Who are you?

HUNTSMAN.
  A huntsman, like you... With a bit more might,
  Though just as eager. But while you cover

The woods by day, I'm out hunting at night.
You skulk for beasts, while I ambush... lovers.

GUSTAW.
I don't know if round here you'll find much game...
Well, I'll be off now. Good luck all the same.

HUNTSMAN.
Hey, friend! Hold on! Why suddenly so queer?
Is this ill breeding? Or is it just plain fear?
It's you that called me! And now you run away?

GUSTAW.
You say I called you?

HUNTSMAN.
                Yes. "Over here! Hey!"
Wasn't it me you called? Then I don't know.
Enough that I heard you sigh, I heard you groan —
I'm a huntsman too. And once, I too was young.
I know your calling, and all that belongs
To your age — heartsore? Let's speak man to man.
So you're lost in the woods, are you, little lamb?
I've lost my way myself; I know the beasts,
Winged and pawed, on four, and on two feet —
What is it you're hunting? You're out after game?
And yet your pouch is empty. Aren't you ashamed,
So young and bold, and nought of which to preen?
Come clean — and I can help you in your plight.

GUSTAW.
Thanks, but I don't make friends so quickly, at night.
I don't need help from strangers. And what you mean
By saying that, I really just don't know...

HUNTSMAN.
Well, I'll explain it, if you are so slow.
You don't trust me. Well, I tell you true:

Know first, that someone watches over you —
A certain being, everywhere you stray,
Who'd like to take form that you might see,
And visit — If you're steadfast in what you say...

GUSTAW.
Dear God! What's that mean?! Get away from me!

*/here the manuscript ends/*

# FOREFATHERS' EVE, PART II

*The Living Dead*
    The heart is stopped, cold is the breast,
    Mouth closed, and eyes as dull as lead;
    He's here, and yet he's somewhere else:
    What kind of man is this? — The dead.

    Yet look — hope's spirit gives him life,
    The star of memory loans its rays,
    And to his youthful haunts he hies,
    Searching for a beloved face.

    The breast swells, yet cold is that breast,
    His lips and eyelids wide are spread,
    He's here again, yet somewhere else:
    Who is this man? The living dead.

    Those who live nearby his grave
    Know that each year his tomb is riven:
    He wakes each year on All Souls' Eve,
    And makes his way toward the living.

    But when four Sundays' bells will fade,
    Then he returns, his strength expired.
    Breast bathed in blood from wounds fresh made,
    He sleeps again in churchyard mire.

    Tales of this man who walks the gloom
    Are many — he was young, and still
    Live those who wept on his fresh tomb —
    They say he died of his own will.

Now torments must afflict his soul:
He moans in sorrow and sobs fire;
A sexton, not too long ago
Saw him, and heard his plaint entire.

As soon as he broke through the earth
His eyes sought out the morning star
And from his cold lips bursting forth
Such a complaint was hurled afar:

"Spirit accursed! Why do you send
Through the dumb earth the spark of life?
Splendour accursed! Snuffed, once again
Why do you shine to send me strife?

"O righteous sentence, yet fraught with fear!
To see her, just to part again;
To relive my pain year after year
And as I ended, each year end.

"To find her, I must err among
The mob, leaving my peace behind;
Living, I met with rough welcomes,
Now dead… I've really ceased to mind.

"Once, when she looked at me, I reined
Aside my thievish eyes; her words
Heard daily, yet I was constrained
To silence, like a coffin's boards.

"My friends would laugh at me, and call
My pain a modish heart's device;
Elders would nod and squeeze my arm
And offer me some… good advice.

"Scoffers and sober minds alike
I treated — how were they to blame?

Had I not frowned at lowing sighs
And sneered at 'woes too grim to name?'

"Another said 'It's just not right
Such love' — I scourged the prideful man —
And he, being suave and polite...
Pretended not to understand.

"But I'm proud too, that I could take
His measure, and know just where he stands;
I spoke in anger. When he spoke
I... pretended not to understand.

"But those who can't forgive my sin,
Who barely mask that they despise,
And screw a smile above their chin
And fashion mercy with their eyes,

"Only such I've never forgiven.
*My* lips have never borne the stain
Of grievance under smiles hidden,
Nor have I stooped to show disdain.

"Such will my lot be now, if risen
I show the foreign world this shade:
Some will chase me with exorcisms,
Others, amazed, will run away.

"With pride they charm, with mercy bore,
Some bend ironically their brows —
Going to One, why must I scores
Of others annoy and astound?

"Whatever will be, I go the well-trod roads:
Mercy for scoffers, for merciful — abuse;
But you, my darling! when you meet this ghost
Treat him as you always used!

"Look at me, speak, forgive my fault
That once again I dare to haste
To you, a past dream, for an hour
To trouble your new happiness.

"Your eyes, used to the world, the sun,
Perhaps won't fear this dead man's face.
Perhaps you'll listen, till I'm done
With my speech torn from out the grave,

"And twist about the past your thoughts
Like some parasitic vine
Which on an ancient structure's walls
Its widely-scattered arms will twine."

DZIADY. This is the name given to a solemnity which is still celebrated among the common people of many regions of Lithuania, Prussia and Courland, in remembrance of one's *dziady*, that is, one's deceased progenitors, in general. The beginnings of this ritual stretch back to pagan times, and it was once known as the *uczta kozła* or "goat's feast." The celebrant was called the *Koźlarz, Huslar* or *Guślarz*, a person both priest and bard. Today, since the enlightened clergy and landowners have striven to uproot a custom connected with superstitious and, at times, blameworthy practices, the common people observe Dziady secretly in chapels or abandoned houses near a cemetery. There, as is customary, a banquet of various foods, drinks, and fruit is laid out, and the souls of the departed are summoned forth. It is noteworthy that the custom of banqueting the dead seems to be common to all pagan peoples, whether we be speaking of Homeric Greece, the Scandinavian countries, the Orient, or the far-off islands of the New World. Our Dziady are exceptional in that the pagan ceremonies are now intermixed with notions borrowed from the Christian religion, especially as the feast of All Souls falls roughly at the same time as Dziady are celebrated.

    The common people believe that with meals, drink, and song they bring relief to the souls in Purgatory. The so-pious intent of this feast, as well as the lonely places where the ceremonies are held, the late hour, and the fantastic rituals at one time spoke strongly to my imagination;

I listened to the legends, stories and songs about deceased persons returning to the living with requests or warnings, and in all of the monstrous inventions one could yet discover certain moral tendencies and teachings set forth in a sensual, folkish manner. The poem which follows presents images in a similar way. As for the ritual songs, the sorcery and the incantations, these have been taken faithfully, and at times literally, from folk poetry.

*Guślarz — Old Man (from Chorus) — Chorus of Villagers*
*A Chapel. Evening.*

> *There are more things in heaven and earth than are dreamt of in your philosophy.*
> — Shakespeare

CHORUS.
    All is darkness, all is quiet.
    What will happen here tonight?

GUŚLARZ.
    Close the chapel doors now, tight,
    And place yourselves about the tombs.
    Snuff your lamps and candle light,
    Hang shrouds on windows, so the moon's
    Pale light won't enter through the cracks.
    But quickly, quickly! Come now — fast!

OLD MAN.
    All's been done as you have asked.

CHORUS.
    All is darkness, all is quiet.
    What will happen here tonight?

GUŚLARZ.
    Purgatory's suffering souls!
    Wherever in the world you be:
    If in flaming tar you roll,

Or in an icy river freeze,
Or if, for greater punishment,
Within a blazing log you're pent
That cries and whistles as the flames
Gnaw at its slow-consuming frame,
Come, hasten to our company!
— And now come closer, everyone —
Tonight we're celebrating Dziady!
Come now, into God's holy home:
Here is food, and drink and alms —
Here is prayer's most precious balm.

CHORUS.
    All is darkness, all is quiet —
    What will happen here tonight?

GUŚLARZ.
    Pour some incense in my hands.
    I light it now, and, hurry up —
    As the shooting flame expands,
    Help it on with gentle puffs.
    That's the way! You've got it — there.
    Let it burn up in the air.

CHORUS.
    All is darkness, all is quiet —
    What will happen here tonight?

GUŚLARZ.
    First, I call you lighter souls,
    Who within this vale of tears,
    Darkness, turmoil, painful dole
    And misery, streaked through your years:
    Flashed forth, burnt up, were wafted hence
    Like this handful of incense.
    Those who err in endless flight,
    Beating wings against Heaven's walls,

With this symbol, airy, bright,
You we conjure, you we call.

CHORUS.
Tell us what it is you need:
What will slake you, what will feed.

GUŚLARZ.
Look, ah, look up in the air —
Something shines against the coving:
Two children's souls aflutter there,
Like a pair of gold-feathered doves.
Within the copula they race
Like two leaves tossed round by the wind —
Like two doves flitting through the trees,
An angel dancing with his friend.

GUŚLARZ, OLD MAN.
Within the copula they race
Just like two leaves tossed by the wind —
Like two doves flitting through the trees,
An angel dancing with his friend.

LITTLE ANGEL.
/To one of the village women/
To Mummy we're flying, to Mummy—
What's wrong, Mama? Look — it's Józia—
Don't you know me? Your little bunny!
And here with me's my sister Rózia.
We fly through Heaven, Mama, now —
It's more fun than with you, and how!
Look at the sunny crowns we wear!
Our clothes are made from the light of dawn;
Look at the wings that we've got on —
Like two butterflies! Everywhere
We walk, the grass grows greener,
Where we step, flowers arise:
Heaven's fun! Everything's here —

And every day's a new surprise.
But even though everything's here,
We're bored sometimes… we're scared — a lot …
O, Mummy, your two little dears
Can't find their way to God!

*CHORUS.*
But even though everything's there,
They're bored sometimes, and scared — a lot;
O Mummy — your two little dears
Can't find their way to God!

*GUŚLARZ.*
O, little soul — what do you need
To help you find the holy gate?
Maybe you need a Glory Be?
Maybe you want a piece of cake?
Look — here are sweetmeats, cakes and milk,
Berries, fruits of every ilk.
Say, little soul — what will it take
To help you find the holy gate?

*LITTLE ANGEL.*
Nothing, no — no, we need nothing.
So sweet a life on earth we had,
Too sweet, and this is why we're sad.
Our life was just one long caress;
We've never tasted bitterness.
Cuddles and candies, romps and play,
Whatever I did was OK!
And all the work I had to do
Was sing, and skip; the same is true
For Rózia — she would dress her doll,
I'd pick her flowers, and that's all!
We've come here to your Dziady feast
Not for prayers or for treats;
We don't need any Masses said,
We don't need cakes, or milk, or bread,

But rather wormwood. Please, two grains,
And for your taking such small pains
Our penance will be completed.
For listen now to our bequest:
According to God's just command,
He who's not tasted bitterness
Will take no sweets from Jesus' hand.

CHORUS.
Listen, listen to their bequest:
According to God's just command,
He who's not tasted bitterness
Will take no sweets from Jesus' hand.

GUŚLARZ.
Little angel, little soul,
Take, and may it ease your pain.
A grain for you, another grain,
Now go with God; God bless you both.
And he who will harden his heart
Against prayers, in God's name, depart!
See the Lord's Cross?
You want no drink, want no sweetmeats?
Then go now, and leave us in peace —
A-huss! A-huss!

CHORUS.
And he who will harden his heart
Against prayers, in God's name, depart!
See the Lord's Cross?
You want no drink, want no sweetmeats?
Then go now, and leave us in peace —
A-huss! A-huss!

/The spirits disappear/

GUŚLARZ.
>  Now the dreadful hour's at hand —
>  It's midnight — strongly bolt the door,
>  Take the pitchy smouldering brand,
>
>  And set the cauldron on the floor.
>  Now, when you see me nod my stave
>  Then set the vodka-pot ablaze.
>  Now, quickly, quickly. Come now, fast!

OLD MAN.
>  I'm ready.

GUŚLARZ.
>               Now.

OLD MAN.
>                    A thudding flash,
>  A sizzling, and the moment's passed.

CHORUS.
>  All is darkness, all is quiet —
>  What will happen here tonight?

GUŚLARZ.
>  Now I call the densest souls:
>  Those who in this realm of pain
>  Bound soul and body in crimes's chains
>  Together in one sinful whole.
>  Although death smash your form of clay,
>  Although the angel of death call,
>  Your torment has no pause, no stay,
>  Your torture nothing may forestall.
>  Yet if the living might assuage
>  Somehow your punishment's fierce rage,
>  If we can cheat the gates of Hell
>  (To which you're drawing ever nigher)

>     We conjure you, casting a spell
>     With your own element — with fire!

**VOICE.**
*/From beyond the window/*
>     Away, she-eagles! Ravens! Owls!
>     Leave me here by the chapel's door!
>     Away, you cursed, glutton-fowls —
>     Two steps, at least two steps, no more!

**GUŚLARZ.**
>     Oh — all creation! What a beast!
>     There in the window! See the ghost?
>     Pale as a bone tossed in the streets —
>     Look at his staring eyes! Like coals
>     Covered with ashes. From his mouth
>     Fire like lightning shooting out!
>     Just as a burning sheaf of bracken
>     Tosses aloft its fiery glare,
>     So does a rain of sparks fall crackling
>     Comet-like from the damned soul's hair.

**GHOST.** */Behind the window/*
>     Children, ho! Don't you know me, children?
>     Come closer! Look here — now you see!
>     Now you remember! It's me, children!
>     Your old lord — you belonged to me!
>     Only three years have passed since when
>     You laid me in my stony tomb;
>     Now, when the night steeps field and fen
>     I walk there, seeking out the gloom,
>     Always in hiding from the sun —
>     Oh, divine justice is too rough!
>     Given over to the evil one,
>     Horrid, the torments that I suffer!
>     Thus am I forced to err and wend,
>     And of my errors there's no end.
>     Sore hunger is my element,

Where can I find something to eat?
　　My body's ever slit and rent:
　　Ravenous vultures' filthy meat —
　　Who, who will save me? Who defend?
　　And of my tortures there's no end!

*CHORUS.*
　　Ravenous vultures' filthy meat,
　　Who, who will save him? Who defend?
　　And of his tortures there's no end!

*GUŚLARZ.*
　　What then is needed, for your soul
　　To flee this horrid, tortured dole?
　　Do you need a Glory Be?
　　Do you need some blessed cake?
　　Look — here's sweetmeats, cakes and milk,
　　Berries and fruits of every ilk.
　　Speak! Tell us what it will take
　　To push your soul towards Heaven's gate?

*GHOST.*
　　Heaven? O, you blaspheme in vain.
　　I don't want Heaven! Not at all —
　　Only a loss would be my gain —
　　I only wish my soul would crawl
　　A little faster out of me.
　　A hundred times I'd rather be
　　Pinned to the very floor of Hell
　　Than wandering here about my woods —
　　I'd bear each type of torture well,
　　Yet I can't bear to see the goods
　　I once enjoyed, and every station
　　Of late-beloved abomination!
　　This is what you call starvation! —
　　And drag on — east-west, on: west-east
　　Nourishing these voracious beasts!
　　And yet, such is the Judge's will

That I must house my damned soul
Within this tattered corpse until
One of you pity my hard dole —
One of you, of my former serfs
Should feed my hunger, slake my thirst.
Oh, how this thirst parches my crop!
Oh, how my stomach twists for meat!
Oh, for some water — just a drop! —
Oh for at least two grains of wheat!

CHORUS.
Look how that thirst parches his crop!
Oh, how his stomach twists for meat!
If he had water — just a drop!
If he had just two grains of wheat!

CHORUS OF NOCTURNAL BIRDS.
In vain he begs, in vain he prays:
For we night-fliers, crows, eagles, owls,
His sable train, were once his slaves;
He starved us, now we feed his howls!
We'll eat the food and quaff the drink
That's offered him, with beak and claw
We'll tear it, be it on the brink
Of his parched, blistered, hungry maw,
Be it within his gripping mouth,
With my talons I'll rip it out!
I'll reach down to his very bowels!
You had no mercy on us, lord,
Nor shall we best you on that score!
Now, ravens, fall we to the feast:
Tear up each morsel, rip each piece,
And when there's no more bread or wine
Slice off his flesh: let his bones shine.

RAVEN.
You're hungry? Oh — a thousand pardons!
And yet — remember that one Fall

When I crept in your orchard-garden?
The pears were ripe, the apples red —
For three days I had gone unfed!
I gathered some of your windfall.
I saw no gardener, but he saw me!
And from the bushes raised a hue
And cry, and set your mastiffs free.
They chased me like a wolf through all
The garden — to the garden wall.
Thence was I hauled in front of you
(Them snapping, snarling all the while) —
They hauled me off to face a trial
And over what? Some apples, pears ...
Fruits of the field, like water, fire,
Which God intended Man to share!
And yet my lord cried out in ire
"Make an example out of him!"
With that they tied me to a plow
And whipped me so over frame and limb
With scourges twisted of willow-boughs
That, like the corn from stalks of wheat,
Like the peas from out dried shells,
Each bone was threshed from living meat
Before the eyes of all the dell!
You had no mercy on me, lord!

*CHORUS OF BIRDS.*
Nor shall we best you on that score!
Now, ravens, fall we to the feast:
Tear up each morsel, rip each piece —
And when there's no more bread or wine
Slice off his flesh! Let bare bones shine.

*OWL.*
You're hungry? Hunger makes you grieve?
Do you recall that Christmas Eve
So thick the snow, the wind so wild,
When I begged at your gate, with child,

"Lord, mercy!" through my bitter tears,
"Have pity on the tender years
Of this poor orphan at your door.
My man — his father — is no more;
My mother lies abed, weak, ill;
My daughter taken — by your will —
To serve you; here I weep, distressed
With this frail infant still at breast!
Lord, of your pity, help us poor!
Without your aid, we'll be no more!"
But you, my lord! You soulless beast,
Revelling at your drunken feast,
But called some lackey bully near
And whispered in his hateful ear:
"What is that screeching! Go see, lest
That howling bitch upset my guests!
Chase her away!" Right then and there
He dragged me roughly by the hair
And tossed me, and my child, below
The driveway, in the freezing snow.
Pummelled and frozen to the bone,
We could not make our way back home
Nor to an inn with dry, warm sheets...
We perished both, out in the streets.
You had no mercy on us, lord!

CHORUS OF BIRDS.
Nor shall we best you on that score!
Now, ravens, fall we to the feast:
Tear up each morsel, rip each piece —
And when there's no more bread or wine
Slice off his flesh! Let bare bones shine.

GHOST.
No help, although I need it badly!
You stretch your offerings in vain —
The birds snatch every crumb away.
'Tis not for me, solace from Dziady!

> Yes, I must bear my pain through age on age,
> How harsh God's just decree, though sage:
> For he who never stooped to be a man
> Hopes not for help from any human hand.

CHORUS.
> Yes, you must bear your pain through age on age,
> How harsh God's just decree, yet sage:
> For he who never deigned to be a man
> Hopes not for help from any human hand.

GUŚLARZ.
> If we may not allay your pain
> Be off into the night again.
> Who never heeds a just request
> Be off, by God's name, thricely blest.
> See the Lord Jesus' Holy Cross?
> You take no drink, take no sweetmeats?
> Go now then, and leave us in peace!
> A-huss! A-huss!

CHORUS.
> Who never heeds a just request
> Be off, by God's name, thricely blest.
> See the Lord Jesus' Holy Cross?
> You take no drink, take no sweetmeats?
> Go now then, and leave us in peace!
> A-huss! A-huss!

/The ghost disappears/

GUŚLARZ.
> Now take the wreath down from the pole.
> I set the blesséd herbs alight,
> It catches fire — a flash of light
> And upward clouds of incense roll!

*CHORUS.*
    All is darkness, all is quiet,
    What will happen here tonight?

*GUŚLARZ.*
    Now to you middling sprites I call,
    Who in this vale of storm and tears
    And darkness spent diffident years
    Among us; you were blameless all,
    Yet void of praise as well, like these
    Mallows and weeds and savouries
    Which bear no fruit, cheer with no flower,
    Possessing nor ill nor genial power
    Neither to make a maiden blush
    Nor mix in troughs for farmyard mush,
    Culled only then, when wreaths are wrought,
    Hung high on walls, and there forgot.
    Thus proud, clay maidens, and thus high
    You bore your chin and scornful eye.
    Whoever's stainless wing as yet
    'S not fluttered through high heaven's gate,
    By this light's flash, by this sweet smoke
    'Tis you we now invite, invoke.

*CHORUS.*
    Tell us what it is you need,
    What will slake you, what will feed.

*GUŚLARZ.*
    Mother of God! This image! Thine?
    Or is it an angel's feet that wind
    Down rainbow footpaths, cloud to cloud,
    To draw pure water from clear streams —
    So bright amid the gloom she seems!
    Folds of soft linen fall around
    Her feet, her hair plays in the wind,
    Smiles on her blushing cheeks abound,
    But sadness wells her tears to brim.

*GUŚLARZ AND OLD MAN.*
    Folds of soft linen fall around
    Her feet; her hair plays in the wind;
    Smiles on her blushing cheeks abound —
    But sadness wells her tears to brim.

*GUŚLARZ.*
    She wears a wreath upon her brow,
    She bears a green switch in her hand —
    Before her romps a playful lamb,
    A butterfly glides near, and now
    She chases it, above her head,
    But never catches it, instead
    It's always out of reach; she calls
    Her lamb to her, but her footfalls
    Scare off the playful toy — always
    Within her grasp — again it strays.

*MAIDEN.*
    I wear a wreath upon my brow,
    I bear a green switch in my hand —
    Before me romps my playful lamb,
    The butterfly glides near, and now
    I chase it — right above my head,
    But never catch it! No, instead
    It's always out of reach — I call
    My lamb to me, but my footfalls
    Scare off the playful toy — always
    Within my grasp — again he strays!
    Oh, once among the springtime dew
    Zosia would dance among her flocks,
    The sweetest girl who ever grew
    Among these woods and gay burdocks,
        La, la, la, la.
    Once Oleś gave a pair of doves
    To win a kiss from her red lips —
    She mocked both gifts and village loves
    And swung away on scornful hips.

La, la, la, la.
Józek would give her ribbons, bows,
Antoś held out a heart so true,
But empty as the breeze which blows
Her now, she would have none of you.
　　　La, la, la, la.
Yes, I was Zosia, born and raised
Among you, and my beauty's praise
Was ever on your lips, with spite,
For I held marriage in despite —
My beauty lost to everyone.
When nineteen squandered springs had run
Their course, I died, knowing nor care
Nor real bliss; nor wealth, nor dearth,
An earthling, yet I lived not on the earth!
My winged thoughts would never rest
Upon the earthy meadow's breast.
I chased each breeze, each butterfly,
Each lamb, but never lover's eye.
I liked the sound of pipes and song,
Tending my flocks, I'd often drawn
Near shepherds, who with tunes would vie
To beguile the hours, and catch my eye —
I sat while each, lovesick, so strove,
And smiled, but gave no one my love.
Now, dead, I burn with unfamiliar flame —
But it's not sadness, it's not pain.
I do whatever my fancy lists,
Spin ribbons from the rainbow's mists,
From morning meadows' purest tears
Craft butterflies and doves, and float
Wherever the breeze should hap to blow.
But whence does my great boredom grow?
Twigs snap, a leaf falls, and I seem to hear
Someone's approach — but he never appears.
It saddens me that I must twist and spin
At the behest of every breath of wind.
Up, and down, like feathers twirled

Am I of this, or of the other world?
Each time I seem about to alight
The wind sweeps me up again to flight
Up, down, and sidewise tossed and pressed,
Always a-wing, never at rest —
I never can climb the heights of heaven
Nor touch the earth: blown, blustered, driven.

CHORUS.
Up, down, and sidewise tossed and pressed,
Always a-wing, never at rest,
She cannot reach the heights of heaven
Nor touch the earth — blown, blustered, driven.

GUŚLARZ.
What needs your soul, so sorely driven,
To flee at last the wind, for heaven?
Do you need a Glory Be?
Do you need some blessed cake?
Look — here's sweetmeats, cakes and milk,
Berries and fruits of every ilk.
Speak! Tell us what it will take
To waft your soul through Heaven's gate?

MAIDEN.
Nothing — I have no such demands.
But — let those boys take my two hands
And hold me — pull me down to earth
For I have need of ... common mirth.
Consider well the fate I've found;
According to God's just command:
Whose feet have never touched the ground
Will never tread His promised land.

CHORUS.
Consider well the fate she's found;
According to God's just command:

Whose feet have never touched the ground
Will never tread His promised land.

GUŚLARZ. /*To a few villagers*/
In vain you rush — these are but shades.
In vain she reaches out to you.
The breeze lifts her aloft, anew,
But do not cry, my pretty maid!
Before my eye I see unroll
A portion of the future's scroll:
Two years more must you fly alone,
Blown by the winds on airy trails,
Then will you find your heavenly home.
Our prayers today will naught avail.
Go now, in God's name, thricely blest.
See the Lord Jesus' Holy Cross?
You take no drink, take no sweetmeats?
Go now, then — and leave us in peace.
A-huss, a-huss!

CHORUS.
He who heeds not a just request,
Away — by God's name, thricely blest.
See the Lord Jesus' Holy Cross?
You take no drink, take no sweetmeats?
Go now, then — and leave us in peace.
A-huss, a-huss!

/*The Maiden disappears*/

GUŚLARZ.
Now each and every soul I call
Without distinction, one and all,
With this my final incantation.
For you, these final ministrations,
This petty banquet that I spill
In each chapel corner — lentils
And a sift of poppy seed.

*CHORUS.*
>Take whatever you may need;
>What will slake you, what will feed.

*GUŚLARZ.*
>That's all, time's up. Open the door.
>Set your candles and lamps aglow;
>The gloomy sacrifice is o'er.
>Midnight is past, the rooster crows;
>It's time to sing of days of yore.
>But wait!

*CHORUS.*
>             What is it?

*GUŚLARZ.*
>                   There's one more!

*CHORUS.*
>All is darkness, all is quiet,
>What will happen yet tonight?

*GUŚLARZ.* /To one of the village girls/
>You there! Girl! You! In mourning dressed!
>Get up! You've sat down on a grave!
>Oh, children — look there! See? The pavement rises as if it were pressed
>From underneath — And now a white
>Spectre arises, bends it pace
>Toward the girl — full in her face
>He looks, standing right at her side.
>Complexion pale, expression drear,
>Like snow fallen at the New Year —
>A look both sorrowful and crazed
>He sinks deep in her fast-fixed gaze.
>But look! Just look there at his breast!
>A ruby stripe runs down his chest
>From where his heart was wont to beat

Even to his cold and clay-stained feet!
What it might be, I dare not guess.
His hand he lays upon his chest,
Upon the blackened cavity
And none but her he deigns to see.

CHORUS.
What it might be, we dare not guess.
His hand he lays upon his chest,
Upon the blackened cavity
And none but her he deigns to see.

GUŚLARZ.
What is it that you seek, young soul?
Perhaps you need a Glory Be?
Perhaps a bit of blessed bread?
Some milk, or berries, fruit, instead?
Tell us, young soul, what do you need
To reach at last your heavenly meed?

/The Spectre is silent/

CHORUS.
All is darkness, all is quiet;
What will happen yet tonight?

GUŚLARZ.
Respond, pale spirit! Answer me!
What? Will he then refuse to speak!

CHORUS.
What? Will he then refuse to speak!

GUŚLARZ.
If you disdain this Mass, this board,
Be gone, in the name of the Lord!
For who heeds not a just request,
Be off, in God's name thricely blest!

See the Lord Jesus' Holy Cross?
You take no drink, no sweetmeats?
Be gone then, and leave us in peace.
A-huss! A-huss!

CHORUS.
Yes, he who heeds no just request,
Be off, in God's name thricely blest!
See the Lord Jesus' Holy Cross?
You take no drink, no sweetmeats?
Be gone then, and leave us in peace.
A-huss! A-huss!

GUŚLARZ.
Now that's what I call a strange bird!
He won't be off, or say a word!

CHORUS.
He won't be off, or say a word!

GUŚLARZ.
Spirit blessed or sprite accursed,
Be off from this our sacred rite.
You see the floor gapes open wide —
Go in again, from whence you burst —
Beware! —
   He stands there, just the same!
— Before I curse you in God's name!
/pause/
Be gone through wood! Be gone through river!
Be gone and perish, cursed forever!
— I've never seen the likes before.
He stands there, dumbly, and ignores!

CHORUS.
He stands there, dumbly, and ignores!

*GUŚLARZ.*

    In vain I pray, in vain I thunder,
    He doesn't fear my exorcism.
    Hand me the holy water there.
    For this vexing, troubled vision
    Stands there rooted to the spot.
    Deaf and dumb and still past wonder
    Like a stone on a graveyard plot.

*CHORUS.*

    For the vexing, troubled vision
    Stands there rooted to the spot.
    Deaf and dumb and still past wonder
    Like a stone on a graveyard plot.
    All is darkness, all is quiet;
    What will happen yet tonight?

*GUŚLARZ.*

    This defies all human reason!
    Shepherdess! You know this person?
    Something horrid's here, or worse —
    For whom have you got mourning weeds on?
    Your husband and your folk are well?
    What? Silent too? Nothing to tell?
    Look here, and say something, my child!
    Hey! Are you dead? Why do you smile?
    What does this mean, this smile, this grin?
    What do you find so gay in him?

*CHORUS.*

    What does this mean, this smile, this grin?
    What does she find so gay in him?

*GUŚLARZ.*

    Hand me the candle and the stole —
    I light it, and again I'll bless...
    And all in vain! All fruitless—
    He won't be gone, the damned soul.

>     Take her outside. Come, grab her arms
>     And drag her from these hellish charms.
>     Why do you stare? Why do you grin?
>     What can you find so gay in him?

*CHORUS.*
>     Why do you stare? Why do you grin?
>     What can you find so gay in him?

*GUŚLARZ.*
>     Good Lord, the sprite is going too!
>     Wherever she, he's at her side.
>     What else will happen here tonight?

*CHORUS.*
>     Wherever she, he's at her side.
>     What else will happen here tonight?

# FOREFATHERS' EVE, PART III

This Poem
is dedicated to
Jan Sobolewski
Cyprian Daszkiewicz
Feliks Kółakowski

OF BLESSED MEMORY
FELLOW STUDENTS • PRISONERS • AND EXILES
PERSECUTED • FOR THEIR LOVE • OF THEIR FATHERLAND
WHO DIED • LONGING • FOR THEIR HOMELAND
IN ARCHANGELSK • IN MOSCOW • IN SAINT PETERSBURG
MARTYRS
OF THE NATIONAL CAUSE
THE AUTHOR

For half a century now, Poland has been the scene of such ceaseless, unflagging, inexorable cruelty at the hands of the tyrants who oppress Her, and such illimitable devotion and endurance on the part of Her suffering peoples, as the world has not seen since the days of the persecuted Christians. It seems as if these kings possessed a Herod-like presentiment of the manifestation of a new light appearing upon the earth, and of their own imminent downfall, while the people believe ever more strongly in their renewal and resurrection.

The history of martyred Poland embraces many generations and a countless number of sacrifices; bloody scenes unfold daily in all corners of our homeland, as well as on foreign soil. The Poem with which we present the Reader today constitutes a few small sketches from this huge canvas; a few events from the persecutions instigated by Caesar Alexander.

Round about the year 1822, the politics of Caesar Alexander, the enemy of all liberty, began to manifest themselves more clearly, ground themselves more firmly, and take a more determined direction. In those days a universal persecution was visited upon all the tribes of Poland, an oppression that became ever more violent and bloody. At that time the infamous Senator Novosiltsov stepped onto the stage. He was the first to understand the instinctive and beastly hatred of the Russian government towards Poles as something salvific, as eminently good politics, and thus he took it as the basis of all his actions, and set as his goal the destruction of Polish nationhood. In those days the whole area between the Prosna and the Dniepr, and from Galicja to the Baltic Sea, was locked away and governed like one huge prison. The entire administration of those lands was wound up like a huge machine for the torture of Poles, the wheels of which were set in motion by Tsarevich Constantine and Senator Novosiltsov.

The systematic Novosiltsov set himself to the torture of children and adolescents, so that the hopes of all future generations should be snuffed in their very cradle. He set up his central hangman's headquarters in Wilno, the academic capital of the Lithuanian-Belarussian provinces. At that time there existed certain literary organisations among the university students, which aimed at the maintenance of the Polish tongue and of Polish nationhood, rights such as were guaranteed to the Poles both by the Congress of Vienna and by Imperial privilege. Now, these organisations, aware of the ever more intense suspicion they aroused among the government officers, dissolved themselves before any edict should enjoin them to do so. But Novosiltsov, even though he arrived in Wilno a full year after the voluntary dissolution of these clubs, hurried before the Imperial presence and pretended to have found them still in existence. Presenting their literary endeavours as a clear rebellion against the government, he imprisoned several hundred youths and set up military tribunals, under his direction, with which to try the students. In the arcane "legal" proceedings of Russia, the defendant has no way of defending himself, for often he has no idea of the charges set against him. For the tribunal, as it sees fit, publishes only some of the accusations, keeping others secret. Novosiltsov, empowered by Tsarevich Constantine with unlimited authority, was prosecutor, judge, and hangman.

He closed several schools in Lithuania, and published a writ according to which the youths who had attended them should be considered "civilly dead," which effectively deprived them of their civil rights. They could thus find no employment, nor could they complete their studies in any institution of higher learning, whether public or private. Such an edict, forbidding people to learn, has no historical precedent and is a purely Russian invention. Along with the closure of the schools, he condemned several tens of students to the mines in Siberia, to hard labor, and to forced enlistment in Asian garrisons. Among their number were minor sons of the noblest Lithuanian households. Some twenty of these, teachers and university graduates suspected of Polish nationalism, were banished to lifelong, inner exile in the depths of Russia. Among so many exiles, only one has, to date, managed to extricate himself from Russia.

All of the writers who make reference to this persecution of Lithuania agree that, in the affair of the students of Wilno there was something mystical and mysterious. The mystical, gentle, yet unshaken character of Tomasz Zan, the leader of the youths; the religious resignation, brotherly concord and love among the young prisoners; the divine wrath, which evidently fell upon the persecutors, all left deep impressions upon those who were either witnesses to or participants in these events; described, they seem to transport the Reader into ancient times: the ages of faith and miracle.

He who is well aware of the events of those days will bear witness, that the historical scenes and the characterisations of the people taking part in them have been sketched by the author conscientiously, with nothing added and with no exaggeration. And why, after all, should the author wish to add or exaggerate anything? So as to rekindle in the breasts of his countrymen hatred of their enemies? Or to arouse pity among the peoples of Europe? For what are all of the cruelties of those times compared to what the Polish nation is now suffering, and upon which Europe looks with indifferent eye! The author's only wish is to store up for his nation a faithful record of recent Lithuanian history: he does not need to terrify his countrymen with hideous portraits of their enemies, whom they have known for centuries; and to the merciful nations of Europe, who shed their tears over Poland just as the wretched women of Jerusalem did over Christ, our nation shall speak only with the words of the Saviour: "Daughters of Jerusalem, weep not for me, but for yourselves."

## LITHUANIA
PROLOGUE

IN WILNO, NEAR OSTROBRAMSKA STREET, IN THE BASILIAN MONASTERY /TRANSFORMED INTO A STATE PRISON/—A PRISONER'S CELL

> *But beware of men. For they will deliver you up in councils, and they will scourge you in their synagogues.* Matthew, X: 17
> *And you shall be brought before governors, and before kings for my sake, for a testimony to them and to the Gentiles.* Matthew, X: 18
> *And you shall be hated by all men for my name's sake: but he that shall persevere unto the end, he shall be saved.* Matthew, X: 22.

/A prisoner, leaning against a window, sleeping/

GUARDIAN ANGEL.
    Alas, thou no good, heartless child!
    Such force has the incessant care
    Of thy sweet earthly mother mild,
    Her works on earth, in heaven her prayer,
    That thou hast lived a youth secure
    From tempting itch and deed impure:
    Just like that angel of the lawn
    That daily blooms, and all the night
    Bedecks her children with a crown
    Of scent to beat back worm and blight.

    I, now and then, at her request
    And with permission divine
    Have urged my wings, my footsteps pressed
    Unto that frail demesne of thine
    To take my post beside thy bed
    And gaze upon thy sleeping head.

    While thou rocked on the lap of night,
    Above thy fierce, impassioned dreams
    I stood there, like a lily white

Bends over a muddy, moiling stream.
Thy soul would fill me with disgust
At times, so it seethed with thought and sense,
Yet still I sought the good out, just
Like, in ant-hills, grains of incense.

As soon as I should glimpse a thought
Of goodness, I'd take up thy soul,
And hand in hand, I, soaring, brought
Thee to eternity, where whole
And bright shines God's good universe,
And I would sing to thee such verse
As earthly children seldom hear
When sleep overcomes them, to forget
On rising. I played chanticleer
To future greatness, goodness, yet
Thou heard'st the music of the spheres
As if it were bawdy tavern cheers.

Then I, a spirit pure, who dwell
Among angelic ranks in heaven
Took on the forms of beasts in hell
To scare, and strengthen thee: harsh leaven,
Didactics strict of a gentle Lord —
Which like a hangman's scourge thou bore!
Then in thy soul awoke unease.
With angry pride thy breast did swell
As if thou'd drunk deep of the well
Of ignorance — to the very lees!
And memories of the higher spheres
Were sucked into thy depths, as glades
Of leaves and blossoms disappear
In caverns, borne on dark cascades.

At this I wept such bitter tears!
Covering my face with trembling hands —
Although I wished, I didn't dare
Turn back toward the starry strands,

So that I shouldn't meet her there,
Thy mother, and have to reply
When asked what sort of news I bear,
"How goes it with that son of mine?"

PRISONER /*awakes after troubled sleep and looks through the window: early morning*/.
Still moon, when you arise, who asks of you
Whence you come; when you toss before you stars,
Which of them might your future ways construe!
"The sun's gone down," call the astronomers
From their high towers, but why's the sun gone down?
No one replies. Dark shades enwrap the globe,
The people sleep. But why? The wisemen frown
And shrug. They sleep, and wake, like blindmen grope
Through shadows thicker than the fumes of night —
They trudge on, dead eyes fixed upon the ground,
While just like guardsmen, Darkness shifts with Light,
But where's the officer that appoints their rounds?

And dream — that silent world, mysterious!
The soul's life — ah! now, there's a research theme!
Who'll take its measure? Who will time its pulse?
Asleep, man's gripped in terror; he wakes — and laughs off the dream.
The wisemen say "dream is but life recalled."
Cursed wisemen, all!

Can I not distinguish dream from memory?
Maybe they'll tell me next that this prison
Is but a dream vision.
They label tortures dreams and passion
Imagination —
Fools, who scrounge imagination's shards
From poets, and proceed to preach to bards!
I've plumbed her depth, gauged both height and expanse,
And know that beyond her lies — vatic trance.
Day sooner will be night, and torture passion
Than dreams mere memories — or imagination.

*/He lies down, then starts up again and goes to the window/*

Can't sleep. Such dreams deceive me and distress:
And never let me rest!

*/Drowses/*

NIGHT SPIRITS.
Black down, soft down, lay here — his head to press.
Let's sing — but soft! — cause him yet no distress.

SPIRIT FROM THE LEFT.
A sad night here in jail, but the festive town is gay:
Music resounds from hall and table;
Minstrels warble at the board where cup by cup is laid;
Bright comets flash through byways sable —
Comets with blue eyes gleaming, each trails a golden braid.

*/The prisoner falls asleep/*

And he who struggles with frantic oar
Over these swelling billows, will fall asleep on the wave
And wake to find himself on our shore.

ANGEL.
We've asked the Lord to press
Thee in thy foeman's hands:
Solitude feeds the soul.
Here, in thy loneliness,
As if on desert sands,
Think on thy destined role.

CHORUS OF NIGHT SPIRITS.
God torments us by day, but in the nighttime we play:
Late at night, when the fat get fatter
The empty still more vain, and lusty songs more gay:
When Satan tunes the strings and piles the platter.

The pew's still warm where this one sat at Mass,
A wreath of noble thought her brow adorns:
Her crown the Snake will wither like dry grass —
His grace the Leech will drain before the morn.

Let's sing over the sleeper, sons of night!
We'll serve him until he our slave becomes.
Bore through his heart, seep through his inner sight:
He'll be ours yet — ah! may his sleep be long!

*ANGEL.*
   On earth, in heaven, prayers are raised for thee —
   Soon from these tyrants thou shalt be set free.

*PRISONER /Stirs and considers/.*
   Ah, you who dare torment your fellow men,
   Smiling by day and gorging through the night,
   Can you recall one dream, however slight?
   And if you can, say: can you comprehend?

*/Nods off again/*

*ANGEL.*
   We've come to tell thee, that thou shalt go free.

*PRISONER /Roused/.*
   I shall go free? Where did I hear those words?
   Someone said — no, — a dream... are they the Lord's?

*/Slumbers anew/*

*ANGELS.*
   Let us take care to guard his thought.
   'Tis there the battle will be fought.

*SPIRITS FROM THE LEFT.*
   Double the legions for attack!

*SPIRITS FROM THE RIGHT.*
   Double the ranks to beat them back!
   Shall bad thought win, or good thought vanquish?
   Tomorrow speech and deed will show.
   One moment of this battle's anguish
   Spells this man's fate, for ever more.

*PRISONER.*
   I shall be free — yes! But whence is this news?
   For what a Russian pardon means, I know.
   They'll free me from these fetters and rank mews,
   And then, by exile, wrap chains round my soul!
   Wandering amidst foreign mobs and enemies,
   A bard — who there will understand my chant?

   Harsh rhyming nonsense, tattered by the breeze.
   They've torn my only weapon from my hands.
   No, not quite. But they've broken it, beaten it blunt.
   Alive, but for my Fatherland, a corpse.
   My thought will fester in such shadows dun,
   Like diamonds deep in rockbeds dull and coarse.

*/He rises and writes the following on one wall with a piece of coal/:*

D. O. M.
GUSTAVUS
OBIIT M. D. CCC. XXIII
CALENDIS NOVEMBRIS

*/and on the facing wall/:*

HIC NATUS EST
CONRADUS
M. D. CCC. XXIII
CALENDIS NOVEMBRIS

*/He leans against the wall and falls asleep/*

*SPIRIT.*
    Ah, mortal! If thou only knew thy power!
    When but a thought, like a spark in the mist
    Shines in thy mind unseen, great stormclouds lour
    To pour forth gentle rain or savage tempest.
    If but thou knew, that as each thought alights
    There gather round in silence, and stand by
    Like storm-hounds, angels both sooty and bright:
    — Wilt dash to hell, or flash out in the sky? —
    Yet thou, like a steep cloud, fliest on aloof,
    Knowing not where thou art borne, nor what thou do.
    Ah, mortals! Each of you might, imprisoned, alone,
    By thought and faith overturn the stoutest throne!

## ACT I
### SCENE I

/A CORRIDOR—GUARDSMEN WITH CARBINES STAND NEARBY—A FEW YOUNG PRISONERS, WITH CANDLES, LEAVE THEIR CELLS—MIDNIGHT/

JAKUB.
　　Well, what? — Can we meet?

ADOLF.
　　　　　　The guardsmen are drunk:
　　The corporal's ours.

JAKUB.
　　　　　　What's the time?

ADOLF.
　　　　　　Just midnight.

JAKUB.
　　If the shift should catch us, the corporal's done.

ADOLF.
　　Just snuff your candle so that the light
　　Won't flash in the window. The guards are fools!
　　The shift'll have to knock both long and hard,
　　Find their keys, exchange their passwords with the guard,
　　Then they must march down a long corridor —
　　They won't hear anything except our snores.

/Other prisoners exit their cells, meet them/

ŻEGOTA.
　　Good evening.

KONRAD.
　　　　　　You're here!

FOREFATHERS' EVE

FR. LWOWICZ
>You're here!

SOBOLEWSKI.
>I am too.

FREJEND.
> Know what? Żegota, let's go to your cell.
> Our sacred congregation's got a new
> Novice — with a stove —there, we'll be hot as hell.
> Besides, they say travel broadens the mind.

SOBOLEWSKI.
> Żegota! How've you been? So you're here too!

ŻEGOTA.
> Too many to fit in that cell of mine.

FREJEND.
> We'll go to Konrad's cell, that's what we'll do.
> It's farthest — right next to the church's wall.
> From there you can't hear anything — nor song, nor cry.
> And I'd like to talk loud and sing tonight —
> They'll think it's coming from the choir stalls.
> Tomorrow's Christmas Day, my friends, and so
> I've got a couple bottles…

JAKUB.
>Does the corporal know?

FREJEND.
> He likes a snort himself, the honest soul.
> What's more important, like us, he's a Pole.
> One of the Grande Armée, a Legionnaire,
> A silk purse the Tsar refashioned a sow's ear.
> He's a good Catholic, and won't berate
> His charges if they wish to celebrate
> On Christmas Eve.

JAKUB.
           But if the Russians learn...

/They go into Konrad's cell, start a fire in the stove, and light their candles. Konrad's cell as it was in the Prologue./

FR. LWOWICZ
    How did you get here, Żegota? And when?

ŻEGOTA.
    Today. They plucked me out of my own barn.

FR. LWOWICZ
    You were a farmer, too?

ŻEGOTA.
           A born one, friend!
    Could you but see my oxen and my sheep!
    They call me the best yeoman in the land
    — Who at one time couldn't tell hay from wheat!

JAKUB.
    They took you by surprise?

ŻEGOTA.
                I understand
    That for some time now, an investigation's
    Been going on in Wilno. My house lies
    Close to the road — I've seen the coaches hasten
    And heard at night the bell that terrifies —
    The post-chaise — boding evil like the croak
    Of a raven. Sometimes, sitting down to eat
    Somebody'd ring their wineglass as a joke:
    The girls would shiver, old folks jump to their feet,
    As if they had heard the Feldjäger's bell.
    But who're they chasing? I don't know. For what?
    As yet I've never conspired in any plot.
    I think the government just wants to fill

Their pockets. Once they squeeze from us a fine,
They'll let us go.

*TOMASZ.*
                    That's what you're hoping for?

*ŻEGOTA.*
    What else? We've not committed any crime!
    They can't just send us to Siberia?
    You're all so quiet... What's wrong? What's the score?
    How come you're being so mysterious?

*TOMASZ.*
    The reason's just arrived here from Warsaw:
    Novosiltsov. You know the Senator:
    Fell out of favour with the Emperor
    For drinking through the loot such as they'd fleeced
    Before, getting in debt, and pining poor —
    And since in Poland he found not the least
    Bit of conspiracy (though, no denying,
    It wasn't that he failed for lack of trying),
    He's come to cast his lot in a new land,
    In Lithuania, and with him, brought
    His whole company of stoolies and spies.
    Now, so that he might rob with a free hand
    And find favour anew in the Tsar's eyes,
    He has to think up non-existent plots
    To ready more lambs for the Tsarist knife.

*ŻEGOTA.*
    We'll prove our innocence —

*TOMASZ.*
                    Don't bet your life.
    Both the investigation and the trial
    Are secret. The defendant never learns
    What he's accused of, and, in the meanwhile,
    The judge, who's supposed to hear our defence,

Responding to each charge in even turns,
Already contemplates the punishment
Of those who've no right to be innocent.
One last chance's left us, sad though it may be:
Some of us must make a self-sacrifice,
Shouldering the burden of the blame alone.
It's only right the blow should fall on me,
Who was your chief: the role is mine by rights.
Now, pick some others of us to be thrown
To the lions with me — but only such
As might not weigh down dear hearts overmuch:
Orphans and oldsters and unmarried men,
So that those needed more might live again.

ŻEGOTA.
It's come to that?

JAKUB.
                The poor chap's set to cry.
He didn't know he'd said his last goodbye.

FREJEND.
Our Jacek had to leave his wife about
To give birth, and he's not crying!

FELIKS KÓŁAKOWSKI.
                              That I doubt.
He's got a lot to weep for. Listen here:
If it's to be a son, I'll read his stars.
Give me your hand. You know, I'm quite the seer,
Among my other talents. By the scars
Here in your flesh I see: if he matures
Into a good and honest man, he's sure
To meet with Russian justice, *id est* chains:
Tossed in this hole, where Daddy yet remains!
Won't that be touching?

ŻEGOTA.
                    How long have you been here?

FREJEND.
    How might we know? No calendars, no letters,
    What's worse, who knows how long we've yet to sit here.

SUZIN.
    My window hangings are two wooden curtains.
    It's day? It's night? I never can be certain...

FREJEND.
    Ask good old Tomasz, sorrow's Patriarch.
    The biggest pike was first snared in the net:
    He greeted our arrival, and will yet
    Be here when we've passed on. It's him that knows
    Who's here, from whence they came, and even when.

SUZIN.
    O, blast my eyes! So you are Tomasz, then?
    I didn't recognise you! Come, your hand!
    We met once, but had no chance to grow close:
    You were packed round by such a mob of friends
    Back then — the friendship of no other man
    Was so sought after. You can't have known me
    In such a crowd, but oh, I knew you well:
    Knew what you did and suffered to keep us free.
    And now my chest has a real reason to swell
    When, dying, I'll recall, I wept with you.

FREJEND.
    O God, again the tears begin to brew!
    Look here — even when he walked the streets unfettered
    There on old Tomasz' brow, in shining letters
    Was writ: *This one is for the clink*. Today
    He loves the jail better than his home.
    Outside, he lived like cryptogamic mushrooms
    That wilt in sunlight. Then when he was thrown

In prison, where we sunflowers grow pale
And choke, he spreads, he positively blooms!
He's benefited from this modish spa
That keeps you healthy, helps you watch your weight
By putting next to nothing on your plate.

ŻEGOTA /to Tomasz/.
  They starved you?

FREJEND.
                    O, they gave him something to gnaw.
  If you'd but seen it! My invention quails
  At its description. Just set it alight,
  And all the cell's vermin croak in one night.

ŻEGOTA.
  How could you eat it!

TOMASZ.
                    I didn't — for a week.
  And then I tried it. Fainted dead away!
  Tried it again, and felt such pricks and pains
  As poisoned men are said to feel — I lay
  Unconscious for a good couple of weeks.
  There was no doctor by to list the names
  Of all the sicknesses I suffered through.
  At last I woke, and, with my strength renewed,
  I slurp it up now like my favourite stew!

FREJEND /With forced gaiety/.
  Hey! Outside they don't know what they are missing!
  The lockup's got the only gourmet kitchen
  That seasons horrors by mere repetition.
  The devil sits in muck. Go ask him why:
  "Because I'm used to it," he will reply.

JAKUB.
  But to get used to it!

FREJEND.
                    Yes, that's the key.

JAKUB.
  I've been here eight months, by the notches scored,
  And long for home no less…

FREJEND.
                        And yet no more?
  Tomasz has got so used, that one fresh breeze
  Would knock him dizzy to his knees!
  He hardly moves ten feet beyond his bunk
  And has got so unused to breathing air
  That, if they drove him out of jail, he'd fare
  Quite well, saving on alcohol and wine:
  One sip of air and he's already drunk!

TOMASZ.
  I'd sooner starve and moulder under ground
  Than see you fellows prison-mates of mine.
  I'd sooner take their blows, ah, let them pound!
  Or, worse — let them question me a second time.
  Devils! They're digging us a common grave!

FREJEND.
  Is it for us you're shedding bitter tears?
  As if you had a reason! Look at me:
  So what if I should live a hundred years?
  Ha! I'm a soldier, and if there's a war,
  I'm good at making Russian shishkabob,
  But set me free in peacetime? Why? What for?
  To curse at Russians through my muffled gob?
  Drag on a useless life, then die, and rot?
  Out there I'd waste away an age's time
  Like cheap gunpowder, or second-rate wine.
  Here, corked up tightly, rammed in tight with tow,
  The bottle's full, the powder's set to burst.
  Uncork the bottle out there, and I'd go

Flat like a champagne magnum opened first
And then neglected, or like powder fizzle
In a damp pan out in a steady drizzle.
But, send me to Siberia in chains
And let my brother Lithuanians
Take one look at my unbent, crackling frame,
They'll say: "Dear Lord, a noble lad like him!
Just wait, you bloody Tsar!" And thus their thin
Expiring ember-hate will burst to flame!
Tomasz, with happy heart I'd go to hang
If, by my death, you'd live a moment more.
Chaps like me serve the Fatherland in dying,
We're good for nothing else. I'd die a score
Of times to resurrect you from the dead —
You, or else Konrad, the gloomy bard
Who, like a gypsy reads her tarot cards,
Sings us the future.

/To Konrad/

I believe you're great
'Cause Tomasz told me so. And I love you,
Because you're like a bottle of wine too:
You pour out song and feeling, make us high
With hope and faith while you spill yourself dry.

/Wiping his tears, he takes Konrad's hand/
/To Tomasz and Konrad/

You know I love you. But one can love and yet
Not cry. So, brothers, let us dry our tears,
'Cause if I set to sobbing, damn it, I fear
Tea won't get made, and our crumbs will get wet.

/He makes tea. A moment of silence/

FR. LWOWICZ
    He's right. This is no way to greet a friend.
    Tears at harvest homes bring bad luck. Now, come:
    Have we not hours enough to hold our tongue?

JAKUB.
    Are there no news from town?

ALL.
                            News?

FR. LWOWICZ
                         No news, then?

ADOLF.
    Jan went in for questioning today. An hour
    He was in town — but from his looks
    You see he's in no mood for talking. Sour
    And silent.

SOME OF THE PRISONERS.
                Come on, Jan, what news?

JAN SOBOLEWSKI.
                            They took
    Full twenty carloads to Siberia
    Today. Well, that's your news. None of it good.

ŻEGOTA.
    Who did they take? Our men?

JAN.
                    Students from Żmudź.

ALL.
    Off to Siberia?

*JAN.*
                Like a parade!
"As seen by thousands!"

*SEVERAL.*
                         Carted off for good…

*JAN.*
   Saw it myself.

*JAKUB.*
                With your own eyes, you say?
   My brother, too? Did they take everyone?

*JAN.*
   Everyone there — yes, every mother's son.
   Saw it myself. While on my way back "home."
   I asked the corporal for a rest. We'd come
   To the church. I stood there in the portico
   Behind a column. Mass was being sung
   Inside; then, suddenly, the congregation
   Rushed outside and took up a station
   Near the court house. What was going on?
   I looked back in the freshly emptied nave:
   The priest and server were yet in the apse,
   The sacring bell was rung, and then a rasp
   From across the street made me turn around —
   The rusty jailyard gates screeched 'cross the ground:
   Soldiers, with guns and drums, a double row,
   Between them: transport wagons. Then, a knave
   Swung up into the saddle. You would know
   From his scowl that he was an important man.
   About to lead a triumph in his van:
   A northern triumph for a northern Tsar
   Who triumphs over children.
                        Then he barked,
   A signal sounded on the drum, and all
   — I saw them —
   The prisoners were led from the council hall.

Little boys! Broken, heads shaved every one,
Just like recruits. And at each back, a gun.

Poor lads! The youngest was no more than ten:
He whimpered that the heavy fetters rankled
His feet, and pointed at his bloody ankle:
The iron had eaten halfway to the bone.
The toff on horseback canters up, looks down,
"What's this?" he frowns, in righteous consternation.
"It weighs ten pounds. Ten pounds is regulation!"

I recognised Janczewski, though disfigured,
Thinned, wasted, and yet, strangely transfigured.

A year ago he was a carefree child.
Now, gazing through the bars, like from some wild
And lonely cliff — a Caesar! — and his eye,
Proud, calm, contemptuous of the drabs, and dry —
As if he wanted to cheer up his mates,
And with a bitter smile, but sweet, he bade
Farewell to the onlookers, as if to say
"It doesn't really hurt."
                      He looked my way,
And, seeing not the corporal holding me
By sleeve's-end, he assumed that I was free.
He smiled and blew a kiss, nodded his head
To bid farewell and send felicitations.
Eyes turned our way. The corporal lost patience
And tried to jerk me out of the crowd's sight.
But no, I wouldn't let him! I just stood tight
There by the column, watching every move
And the deportment of the prisoner.
He noticed that his chains had caused a stir
Of pity in the crowd, and so he smiled
And kicked contemptuously, as if to say
"They're not so heavy." Whips cracked, horses pulled,
And they were off. He doffed his cap, and cried
Three times, "Poland hath not perished yet!" While

His wagon vanished in the rout, I stood
There marking his black hat wave from his hand
Like a black flag of mourning, flapping in the van
Of a funeral march. His shaven crown
From which the hair was torn by violence,
That head, proud and unshamed, from a distance
Could still be seen, against the thick background
Of black hats, bruiting forth his innocence,
Vivid and thrilling, as a dolphin leaps
Above the swelling sea. This image keeps
Itself forever in my eye — that head,
That hand — as o'er this thorny road I tread;
For compass-like, to virtue it points the way.
Ah, God in Heaven, should I ever forget
Them, forget me as well on that last day!

*FR. LWOWICZ*
   Amen for you.

*EACH OF THE PRISONERS.*
               And us. Without regret.

*JAN SOBOLEWSKI.*
   Then more wagons drew up, in a long line,
   Devouring one by one those left behind
   By the first transport. As I looked around
   At those standing in the tightly-packed crowd,
   And at the soldiers, I saw, to my shock
   That their faces, as well, were white as chalk.
   Like corpses! and such a dead silence reigned
   That I heard every clink of every chain.

   It's odd — all sense how wrong the judgments are,
   Yet all keep quiet, they so fear the Tsar.
   They had to carry out the last poor soul:
   It seemed he fought — but no, he just couldn't go
   On his own legs. He tottered on the brink
   Of fainting, with each step he seemed to sink;

At last, his legs gave up, and he fell down
The steps and lay there, stretched out on the ground.
'Twas Wasilewski. He had been confined
With us here till they took him out one time
For questioning, and gave him such a whacking
That colour in his cheeks was always lacking
From that day forth. And then a soldier ran
Up to him, picked him up with one big hand
To help him to the wagon (on the sly
He used his other to wipe his own eyes dry).
Now, Wasilewski didn't faint, or sag,
Or droop, he just fell outright on the flags.
There on the soldier's breast, his arms around
His neck, he looked like one just taken down
From the cross. His eyes were a horrible sight —
Round and wide-open, and completely white.
The crowd as well opened wide their eyes and mouths
And from a thousand breasts there then rushed out
A common sigh — a deep, underground moan
As if it seeped out from beneath gravestones.
Then it was stifled by an officer
Who shouted, "Arms! Now, forward march!" a whirr
Of drumsticks and then thunder — on the street
The people's pity trampled 'neath the feet
Of horses, and the wagons spurted past
Like lightning. There was no one in the last,
It seemed — until we saw an arm a-flap —
Bruised, torn, and corpse-like, through straw and gaps
Between the bars. And there it rattled still
As if it were bidding everyone farewell.
They drove the wagons into the weeping press
Of people, and before they could suppress
Their sorrow with a regulation whip,
The wagon had to halt before the steps
Where I stood — and at that moment, rang a bell.
I turned about and looked, and I could tell
That it was Elevation — the priest lifted high
The Body and Blood of Christ, and, with a sigh

    I prayed: O Lord, who before Pilate stood
    And for man's saving spilled Thy blameless blood,
    Accept this children's blood by Moscow shent.
    Not quite so holy, but just as innocent!

/long pause/

JÓZEF.
    I've read of wars in ancient, savage times —
    How less like wars they seemed, and more like crimes:
    How enemies would take the harvest whole,
    Bind it to trees and burn both to charcoal.
    Wiser the Tsar, and deeper, Poland bleeds:
    He tears the ripe corn and treads flat the seeds.
    Satan himself teaches the Tsar these ways —

KÓŁAKOWSKI.
    And wreaths his pupil's brows with first-prize bays!

/pause/

FR. LWOWICZ.
    Brothers, perhaps that prisoner hasn't died.
    God only knows, Who brings all things to light.
    I, as a priest, will pray for him, and you
    Should say a prayer for the martyr's rest, too.
    Who knows? Tomorrow, we might share his fate.

ADOLF.
    Remember Ksawery, who blew his pate
    Apart rather than fall into their web.

FREJEND.
    Łebski! Who lingered with us 'round the wine,
    But come the gall — he's gone, with hasty step!

FR. LWOWICZ
    Prayers for him too would not be out of line.

*JANKOWSKI.*
>You know, this faith of yours is worthless, priest.
>Say what you will — that I'm worse than a beast,
>A Turk, a Tatar, a thief, spy, or bandit,
>Austrian, Prussian, or even Russian, damn it —
>But God's ire, if such thing be, creeps still afar.
>They're dead, we're here, and smiling lives the Tsar!

*FREJEND.*
>You've taken the words out of my mouth, my friend,
>And with them all the sin, so thanks again.
>Ho! Hold on a second, let me catch my breath
>And clean my head of tearful tales of death.
>Now, Feliks, come and make your brothers laugh.
>You could make Hell seem like a sauna bath!

*SEVERAL.*
>That's right! Come on, old Feliks, make us laugh —
>He's got a voice — Frejend, pour him a draught.

*ŻEGOTA.*
>Hold, friends. My clan's sat in the House of Lords,
>And though I'm a newcomer, a few words
>From me, perhaps, would not be out of place,
>Since Józef speaks of seeds, for in that case,
>A yeoman such as I who's farmed the land
>Can speak of seeds like one who understands.
>Now, if the Tsar must filch seed, fruit and stamen,
>Prices will soar indeed, but fear no famine:
>Though he may stamp it down in Russian muck,
>Still, as old Antoni says, for him worse luck.

*ONE OF THE PRISONERS.*
>Antoni who?

*ŻEGOTA.*
>>Gorecki. Don't you know
>His fable? It's the truth!

*SEVERAL.*
>What? How's it go?

*ŻEGOTA.*
>When God kicked Adam out of Paradise,
>He didn't wish to see him die of need,
>And so He had His angels spill some seed
>Along the road, there, where his downcast eyes
>Couldn't fail to notice them. Anon, the man
>Chanced on them, wondered, shrugged, and then walked past,
>Knowing not the jewels he weighed in his dull hand.
>And so day turned to deepest night. At last,
>The devil, in his wisdom, worked it out:
>"It's not for nothing the Lord cast about
>These grains — they must possess some hidden power.
>I'd better hide them then, this very hour,
>Lest Adam profit." And so, with his horns
>He dug a trench and placed therein the corn,
>Spat on them, and covered them up with dirt,
>Stamped on them with his hooves, glad to have hurt
>Men once more by frustrating the Lord's plans.
>Of course, he laughed too soon, for when Spring came
>Up came the shoots, the flowers, the heads of grain
>Bursting with golden food on every hand.
>Oh, you who rule the wide world from the north,
>Who think wiles wisdom, call your ire power,
>Though faith and freedom your taiga devour,
>You sow God's judgement — wait till it shoots forth!

*JAKUB.*
>Bravo, Antoni! Your wisdom will find
>A meet reward — one more year in the mines.

*FREJEND.*
>That's good — and yet I'll turn to you again
>My Feliks — poetry's for thinkers,
>And I've too dull a head. Come on, my friend,
>Let's have a song. A sprightly one, for drinkers!

*/Pours him some wine/*

JANKOWSKI.
  Since Lwowicz would have us pray for the dead,
  I'll sing him this sort of rosary instead.

*/Sings/*

  Sing it out, if suchlike thee pleases,
      Mary and Jesus!
  Pray for it, until Hades freezes,
      Mary and Jesus!
  I'll still doubt that God even sees us,
      Mary and Jesus!
  Till Russia's Tsar by the neck He seizes,
      Mary and Jesus!
  And Novosiltsov's life He outsqueezes,
      Mary and Jesus!
  I'll still doubt the Lord ever heeds us,
      Mary and Jesus!

KONRAD.
  Hey!
  Don't dare pronounce those names while in your cups!
  My faith's been… misplaced, and I've given up
  The litanies and telling rosaries,
  But you won't spit on those names — not on Mary's!

CORPORAL */Approaches Konrad/*.
  It's good that you still bank on that one name!
  The gambler who's burnt through his purse at games
  Is not lost yet, if even one coin he guards
  Preserved from hazard, and kept safe from cards.
  He'll find it on a happy day, God willing,
  Invest it, and before death, from that shilling
  Will grow a capital by far exceeding
  Whatever he lost before, wheeling and dealing.
  That name's no joke, I tell you. Back in Spain,

Ah, long before the Tsar soiled my good name
By cramming me in this bloody uniform,
I was in Dąbrowski's Legions, before
I served in Sobolewski's company —

SOBOLEWSKI.
    He was my brother!

CORPORAL.
                    May he rest in peace!
Ah! What a soldier! Five balls took him down,
Five wounds — just like the Lord. Well then, one day,
Your brother led us into Lamego town,
And there we met up with those *chiens français:*
This one rolls dice, and that one rolls a girl;
Another's howling — 'cause you know the French—
No sooner drunk than they begin to twirl
Their tongues round songs that give off such a stench!
Shame on such old men! See, young as I was,
I was the only one among them blushed.
Deeper and deeper, on and on they pushed,
From swinish tales they moved on to the saints,
Right through the calendar, and each fool paints
These holy men and women scarlet red,
Then they began beneath their feet to tread
The Blessed Virgin. That's when I got up
And, with fists clenched, I roared at them, "Shut up!"
You know, sir, I was in the Sodality.
Defence of Mary's honour is for me
A sacred duty. All the singing stopped:
Nobody fancied this fist in his chops.

*/Konrad muses, others begin talking among themselves/*

But here's the moral of my tale. At last,
We all lay down to sleep after the quarrel,
All of us good and tired. And then, just past
Midnight, a bugler speeds up on his sorrel.

"To arms!" We're up and reaching for our caps,
But only I'd a perch for one — those chaps
That sang so lustily the night before
Were strewn about, besmeared in their own gore:
Each Frenchman's head sliced off, neat as you please,
Like flower pods clipt, full of poppyseeds.
Then, in my hat, a paper caught my eye:
*Vivat Polonus, unus defensor Mariae.*
Who wrote it, and who put it there? I'd give
A lot to learn that — but by Her name, I live.

ONE OF THE PRISONERS.
   Feliks, you've got to sing. Pour him some tea
   Or wine.

FELIKS.
       Since you perforce would have me gay,
   I'll sing a merry song, though my heart's breaking.
   My brothers force on me the undertaking.

/Sings/

   Whatever the penalties are,
       Siberian mines or chains,
   A faithful subject I shall remain
       And I shall work for the Tsar.

   While breaking the ore from the spar,
       I'll think: from these veins and cracks
   I'm scratching out iron to make the axe
       That'll strike off the head of the Tsar.


   While living in exile afar,
       I'll marry some Khan's daughter,
   And our son, half-Roman and half-Tatar
       Will play Brutus to the Tsar.

And banished at last to Tashkent,
    I'll plough up garden and field,
And the only crop my land will yield
    Will be strong, tough-sinewed hemp,

That someone will spin into yarn
    And bind it round with a string
And plait me oh such a pretty thing:
    A stiff necktie for the Tsar.

CHORUS.
  We'll play Brutus to the Tsar, hurrar!
  We'll play Brutus to the Tsar!

SUZIN.
  But what's with Konrad? Sitting near the wall
  As if he's telling over his sins to take
  Into the priest at the confessional!
  He didn't hear you sing... Konrad! For God's sake —
  Look: now he's pale, and now he flashes red.
  Is he sick?

FELIKS.
          No, this was to be expected.
  Oh, we know Konrad! Midnight belongs to him.
  Now Feliks will be quiet, and we'll hear
  A better song. Frejend must now begin
  To play his old tune on the flute, and we
  Will be a chorus for him, if need be.
  But we need music: Frejend, soft, but clear!

JÓZEF /Looking at Konrad/.
  Brothers! His spirit's left his body now
  And wanders far away, amongst the stars,
  Meeting with kindred spirits, a phantom crowd
  Who bring to him prophecies from afar —
  Like pollen from distant blooms. Look at his eyes:
  How strongly do they smoulder beneath the lids,

> Like campfires by a silent army lit
> And then abandoned under the night skies
> As they move off for a surprise attack...
> Before they quite burn out, they will be back.

*/Frejend tries different notes on his flute/*

KONRAD */Sings/.*
> My song was in her grave, already cold,
>> Then she smelt blood, and, like a ghoul
> She rises from the earth, enthralled,
>> Desiring blood to drink, for blood she drools.
>>> Yes! vengeance, vengeance,
>>>> vengeance on our enemies!
>>> With or without God's sanction,
>>>> as the Lord shall please!

> And my Song says: I shall go out tonight
>> Upon my countrymen to chew —
> Whomever with these fangs I bite
>> Perforce becomes a vengeful vampire, too!
>>> Yes! vengeance, vengeance,
>>>> vengeance on our enemies!
>>> With or without God's sanction,
>>>> as the Lord shall please!

> Then shall we go as one our thirst to slake
>> Upon the foes who us enslave,
> And through their hearts we'll drive a stake
>> That they might never rise from out the grave.
>>> Yes! vengeance, vengeance, vengeance
>>>> on our enemies!
>>> With or without God's sanction,
>>>> as the Lord shall please!

> We'll even unto Hell hound his black sprite
>> Crush him beneath us, thick astraddle;
> As long as he can feel, we'll bite,

As long as life breathes in him, shall we throttle.
　　　　　Yes! vengeance, vengeance,
　　　　　　　　vengeance on our enemies!
　　　　　With or without God's sanction,
　　　　　　　　as the Lord shall please!

FR. LWOWICZ.
　　For God's sake stop! That's the song of a pagan!

CORPORAL.
　　Look at his eyes! That's the song of a Satan!

/All stop singing/

KONRAD /to the accompaniment of the flute/.
　　I rise! Above the cliff's summit, I fly,
　　　　Now, far above the vulgar crowds,
　　　　　　'Midst those who prophesy
　　Where the future's dirty clouds
　　I cleave with sword-like eye.
　　My arms like tempests the mists tearing,
　　Until I soar through sunlight, glaring
　　Upon the Sibyl's scroll, wherein the fates of the world
　　　　　　Are writ, below me —
　　Look! all the things to be, and years in ranks
　　Lie unfurled!
　　Look how they flee —
　　　　Like little birds swept by the eagle's shade
　　　　　　My eagle-shadow sighting!
　　Look at them diving down toward the glades,
　　　　Fearing my talon-blades.
　　See how they toward the covert hie,
　　　　Ha! After them! my falcon eye! —
　　　　　　My eye of lightning,
　　After them, talons! Seize them, tear and pry!
　　But what's this? What bird before me spreads his plumes,
　　　　Shielding them all, me with his glances daring?
　　His sable wings like a great stormcloud flaring

    Wide, and long, as a rainbow looms
        Blotting out all of heaven?

A giant kite — who art thou, who art thou, raven?
Who art thou? — I'm an eagle — he stares —
Who art thou? — I wield the fire of Heaven! —
His eyes cloud mine with smoke, as he stares,
        And my thoughts tangle —

*SEVERAL OF THE PRISONERS.*
    What's he saying — What — What is it? — Look how pale!

*/They grab Konrad/*

    Calm down!...

*KONRAD.*
    Hold! Hold!! I've taken his measure —
    Hold on! I'll unwrangle
    My thoughts, I'll finish my song — finish —

*/He staggers/*

*FR. LWOWICZ.*
    Enough of these songs!

*OTHERS.*
            Enough!

*CORPORAL.*
            Yes, God love us!
Hear that? The guard's changing.
            They're right above us.
Put out the lights — back to your cells!

ONE OF THE PRISONERS.
                    They've opened the gate —
Konrad's fainted — let him be — alone, at his own grate!
/All escape/

## SCENE II
## IMPROVISATION

KONRAD /*after a long silence*/.
  Solitude.
  "The people." Ha! Do I sing for the crowd?
  Show me the man who's grasped
  My song's thoughts whole —
  Unblinded by the sun-flash of its soul!
  Wretched is he who jabbers for the rout:
  Tongue belies voice, voice belies thought,
  Thought springs from soul, then is broken, caught
  In words, swallowed by words brooding, aquiver,
  Like the earth above a secret river.
  From topsoil trembling, can men sound the stream's depths?
  Or whence it's rushing — can they even guess?

  Feeling courses in the soul, catches fire, radiates
  Like the blood in its dark narrows, rushing along;
  And just how much blush one can tell on my face,
  So much feeling can be pulled from the depths of my song.

  O my song, you're a star past the world's farthest bounds.
  Earthly eyes, even fluttering on wings of ground glass,
  Think to soar to you, but merely hop off the ground.
  And even if they reach your Milky Way at last
      They've learned to glimpse your sun's bright treasure,
      But flag at calculation, scope and measure.

  My songs, you have no need of human eyes —
      Flow through the recesses of my soul,
      Shine at the zenith of her starry pole,
  Like underground rivers — like stars of the night skies.
  Thou God, thou Nature! I would have you hear —
  Such a song as mine is worthy of Your ear.
          A master, I!
      A master, I stretch forth my hands,
      Stretch forth unto the heavens, and place my hands

Upon the stars, as if upon the crystal wheels
    Of a harmonium, and roll
      Now softly, swiftly now, stars, with my soul.
    A million tones, and of these myriads
      Each I coax forth, and am aware of all,
      Binding, sundering, chords, triads,
Spilling out rainbow mists and thunder peals!

I take my hands away and lift them up
Over the world's edge — and the wheels stop.
    The spheres are silent. I sing alone.
      Long, drawn-out, like the wind's deep tone;
      I hear my songs engulf the race of man:
      They moan in mourning, scream in rage,
      Accompanied by age on age
And each note a seraphic firebrand!
    It's in my ear, it's in my eye,
      Just like the whistling wind that sweeps
      The billowed waves across the deep,
      The burly clouds across the sky.
Worthy of God, such versification!
This song, this great song, this Song-Creation.
Such song is strength — causality —
Such song is immortality!
I feel the Eternal — the Eternal I've wrought —
What greater thing might'st Thou have done, O God?
See how I pull these thoughts out of my Being —
    Incarnate them in words, they fly,
    Scattered about the vaults of sky,
    Jostling and playing, shining, reeling;
    Though far away, I feel them still,
    Delighting in their perfect graces.
    My palms explore them — spherical —
    And in my thoughts their orbits trace.
    How I love you, my bardic offspring!
    My contemplations, O, my stars!
    My rushing winds, my feelings!

I stand amongst you like a patriarch,
    My children all, partaking of my being!

How I contemn you bards, rhyme-fitters,
You wisemen and prophets inspired,
Whom all the world loves and admires.
If you could stand here 'midst your mewling litters,
Basking in the applause and praise of men,
If you could feel them well-won and profound,
And see the shine of adulation's rays
Sparkling upon your tinfoil diadems,
With all the hymns and decorations
Drooled out by ages, pinned on by generations,
Still you wouldn't feel the happiness, the might
That I feel on this lonely night
When I sing in myself,
Sing for my very self.
Yes! Tonight I feel — tonight I'm strong, and wise.
I've never felt as I feel now.
I'm at my zenith, my strength swells in size —
Am I almighty, or just overproud?
— Tonight I'll know. This moment is my fate.
Tonight I flex the sinews of my soul —
    This is my Samson hour, my weight
Is pressed against the columns of my prison.
I'll cast my flesh aside, and when I've risen
    On spirit wings, I'll soar
Out of the sluggish round where star and planet roll,
To where Created borders on Creator.

I have them, yes, I have — I have such wings;
They suffice — I stretch them out from east to west,
The left on Past, the right on Future rests:
I glide on rays of sentiment, to Thee!
    And I shall gaze upon Thy feelings.
O Thou! All-feeling heart that beats on high,
I'm here! I've come! What strength is mine, you see:
    So far on my own wings I've climbed,

Yet I'm a man — and there on earth my body rests apart;
It's there I've lived — my Fatherland — and there remains my heart.

But my love there, in the world,
That love did not dote on a single man
Like worm on flower curled:
Nor on one generation or one clan.
I love my nation whole! And I have pressed
All of her past and future sons and daughters
Here to my breast
Just like a friend, a lover, husband, father:
I wish to raise her, happy, from the ground,
And with her the entire world astound!
And yet I lack the means. That's why I've come:
Armed with the total governance of my thought,
That thought, which tore Thy thunder from the sky,
Spelled out the grooves in which Thy planets run,
Parted Thy seas and through their valleys pried.
I've more: might which cannot be bestowed or bought:
That feeling, which within itself lies cloaked
Volcano-like — these words of mine, its smoke.
I didn't suck this power from the fruit
Of Eden's apple-tree, nor did I root
Through books for it. From no story,
From no mathematician's worry,
From no spell have I this glory.
I was born but to create:
From the springs where Thou drawest strength,
Thus do I draw power thence.
Thou didst not have to beg Thy might
Nor dost Thou fear to lose it — nor do I.
Didst Thou bestow it on me — this eye, sharp and strong,
Or did I seize it myself? Does it belong
To me as Thine doth? In my powers' wax,
When I gaze at the moiling tracks
Of cloud and hear the flights
Of minute, migrant birds a-wing,
And net them with my lime-like sight,

No matter how they struggle, moan, or sing,
Until I will them free, until I flinch,
No wind of Thine can push them on an inch!
I swell my soul, and stop the comet with my stare,
And until I turn my eyes away, it hangs
Sputtering in the air.
  Only man — contemptible,
   Tarnished, puny... immortal...
Serves me not, knows me not — neither Me nor Thee.
That's why I've crossed Thy sapphire portal.
The sway that I have over stone and sod
I want to have over the human soul.
I've galaxies and sparrows at my nod —
  I must have man beneath my control.
  Not by Sword — for swords are brittle.
  Not with Song — they grow too slowly.
  Not with Lore — e'er late, e'er little;
  Not with Marvel—far too showy.
I want to wield the Heart that burns in me.
I want to rule as Thou dost — always, secretly:
  What I will — let them but understand,
  Do it directly, and count them blest
  With each task, and should they protest,
  Then let them suffer for it, and be damned!
Let people be to me as word and thought:
Bricks of song-structures to be willed and wrought!
  Such is, they say, Thy governance!
My mind is clear: Thou knowest I do not prate —
If Thou wouldst give me equal influence
Upon the souls of men, I would create
My nation as a living hymn —
And better scales than Thine would I employ —
Thy song is grim,
    And mine would be a hymn of joy!

Give me souls'-rule! How I contemn this shed
The mob calls "world" and has grown used to praise it;
How can it be that I have not as yet

Attempted with my mighty hand to raze it?
And yet I feel that, should I tense my will,
Screw it down tight,
Then, burst it forth, I might snuff out one hundred stars
And another hundred light,
For I'm immortal! And in creation's round
There are such others — but I've never found
A greater. O Thou, greatest by far
Here in the heavens! It is Thee I've sought
Here at the cosmic axis,
I who stand greatest in the earthly vale.
I haven't met Thee yet; that Thou dost exist
I sense, I know — let us meet! Let me feel
Thy exaltation!
'Tis rule I want; such power is my lot —
Give it to me, or but point out the road
That leads to this my fated destination!
There have been prophets — soul-rulers, I know —
They've done great things, well, so can I!
I want to rule as Thou dost, from on high,
And as Thou dost, I want to rule the soul.

/long silence/
/with irony/

Thou art silent? Silent! Now I've plumbed Thy depths.
I know what Thou art, what sort of rule Thou'st kept.
Thou art love? A liar Thee so named!
Thou art nothing but a brain.
Cold thinking, not the heart, divines Thy ways;
Cold thinking, not the heart, Thy might displays.
  Only he who worms through calfskin,
  And metal, number, corpse devours,
  Only such a one can win
  A sputter of Thy awesome powers:
Such as poison, powder, mist,
Such as flashes, smoke and gale,
Such as law and faith's betrayal,

> For wiseacres and half-wits.
> Thou'st given the mind all the world's glory;
> The heart: eternal Purgatory.
> Into my shortest life, Thou'st crammed
> The strongest feelings of any man!

/silence/

> What is my feeling?
>         Ah — only a spark.
> What is my life?
>         Ah — a flash in the dark.
> What are they now, tomorrow's thunderbolts?
>         Only a spark.
> And the ages, which before me lie unrolled?
>         A flash in the dark.
> From what is man, this microcosm, born?
>         From but a spark.
> What's death, which tears through thought's fine web, in scorn?
>         A moment of dark.
> What was He, whilst He held all in His breast?
>         Only a spark.
> When He'll consume it, what of timelessness?
>         A flash in the dark.

*VOICE FROM THE LEFT.*
> Up in the saddle!
> Now I'll bestraddle
> His soul.
> How near the goal!
> Giddap! Giddap!

*VOICE FROM THE RIGHT.*
> *(simultaneous with above)*
> Stop them, stop!
> Just listen to him rave!
> He plunges on, foam-flecked;
> We must deflect

>   Them,
>   Protect him,
>   Save!

KONRAD.
>   A moment, a spark, but when it lengthens, ignites —
>       It creates and it smites.
>   On, boldly, boldly! Lengthen this moment, stretch it tight;
>   On, boldly, boldly! Kindle the spark, ignite —
>   Now — good, yes! Again my gauntlet I throw Thee.
>   Once more, as a friend, my bared soul I show Thee.
>   Th'art silent?! With Satan Thou'st deigned to grapple —
>       Now I call Thee forth to battle!
>   Contemn me not — though exalted, I'm not alone:
>   On earth I'm brothered to an awesome nation.
>   I've armies and dominions, powers and thrones,
>       And if I choose to blaspheme,
>   I'll grip with Thee more bloodily than did Satan!
>   I fight at hearts'-point, where he could but scheme.
>   I've suffered, loved; torture and love my leaven;
>   For when Thou'd torn from me my happiness
>   Against my own breast I bloodied my fist,
>       And shook it not at Heaven.

VOICE.
>   I change the frothing bay
>   Into a bird of prey.
>   With eagle's wing,
>   Soaring on high!

VOICE.
>   Ah, bright comet!
>   What rage drives thee
>   Into the plumbless pit!

KONRAD.
>   Now my nation is incarnate in my soul:
>       My body's swallowed her spirit whole —

    I and the Fatherland am the same.
    My name is Million, for the millions' dole
    I love as my own pain.
    I look upon my Fatherland
       As a son sees his father strapped to the wheel.
    I feel the sufferings of my land
       As a pregnant mother her child's woe must feel.
    I suffer, rave — whilst Thou, wise and gay,
        Reignest on
        Constrainest Thy pawns
        And still they croon, Th'art never wrong!
Now listen, if it's true what, with a faith
As loving and receptive as a son's
I heard, that Thou didst so well love the world
That for Thy love Thou didst this muddy ball create,
And that Thou lovest it with paternal love,
Even plucking twinned beasts from the flood that whirled
In Noah's days; if Thy heart's greater than a beast's,
Birthing blindly, stifling before the race is run, —
If in Thy realm kindness is not anarchy;
If when the millions scream out "Help!" to Thee
Thou dost not measure profit against loss —
If love on this earth be a generation
Natural, needful, not miscalculation,

*VOICE.*

    From eagle to hydra!
    I'll tear out his eyes, jab
    Him on to more
    Storming!
    More smoking, more
    Burning!
    Howl! Thunder!

*VOICE.*

    From such a bright sun
    Falls this cometing blunder.
    Thy road's end, I wonder?

Endless,
Ah, on, on and on!

KONRAD.
   Th'art silent! Behold my cleft heart, open wide!
   Now, give me power! Just its baser part,
   A crumb of what on earth was won by pride,
   And with it, how much happiness I'll fashion!
   Th'art silent! If Thou'lt not give to my heart,
   Give to my intellect! Of all the nations
   Of men and spirits, Thou well knowest I stand
   First among all, and Thou knowest I know Thee
   Better than all Thine archangelic band!
   I'm worth it — split Thy rule in half with me!
   If what I say's mistaken, speak up. No?!
   Th'art silent — there's Thy seal set — I've not lied!
   Th'art silent still, and trusting in Thy might.
   Yet know: feeling consumes what can't be pried
   Open by thought — behold my bonfire: Feeling,
   I stoke it, bank it that it burn more bright,
   My iron will in its red-hot core steeling
   Like a charge seething in a cannon's maw.

VOICE.
   Shoulder arm, aim...

VOICE.
   Sorrow, madness restrain!

KONRAD.
   Respond! I take aim at Your very nature,
   And if I can't completely devastate Your
   Substance entire, I'll shake to the foundations
   Your realm, howling throughout all of creation,
   To every generation, that You are
   Not the world's Father but...

*VOICE OF THE DEVIL.*
                          It's Tsar!

*/Konrad stands a moment, totters, and falls/*

*FIRST SPIRIT FROM THE LEFT SIDE.*
   Grab him! Snatch him!

*SECOND.*
            He's still breathing!

*FIRST.*
                              So?
   Throttle him!

*SPIRIT FROM THE RIGHT SIDE.*
               Back! They're praying for his soul.

*SPIRIT FROM THE LEFT SIDE.*
   You see? They beat us back!

*FIRST.*
                     You stupid beast!
   You and your stupid prompting! He'd've died
   Had you but let him simmer in his pride,
   And right now we'd've been sitting down to feast.
   A moment longer! Ah! To smell that meat
   Beneath my nose, and be forbidden to eat!
   To see the blood that swells there in his mouth
   Yet with my tongue forbidden to lap it out!
   You stupid sprite! To let him off the line!

*SECOND.*
   He'll come back when I whistle.

*FIRST.*
                       Get behind me!
   I've half a mind to skewer you right now,

>   Twist you a thousand years upon these horns,
>   Then jam you tight in Satan's very maw!

SECOND.
>   Will you now? Oh, you'll make me cry! Waah! Waah!
>   Like a kid scolded by a half-brained aunt.

/cries/

>   Mama! Mama! Well then, it's horns you want?

/strikes him with his horns/

>   How's that for a skewer? Ran you right clean through.
>   Bravo, old horns o' mine!

FIRST.
>                   Sacrédieu!

SECOND /hits him/.
>   Here, have another!

FIRST.
>                   Hold it! Can't you hear?

/A knocking; keys turn in the lock/

SECOND.
>   Come on, let's hide! A monkey's drawing near.

## SCENE III

/ENTER: THE CORPORAL, THE BERNARDIN BROTHER PIOTR, AND A PRISONER/

*FR. PIOTR.*
In the Name of the Father, the Son, the Holy Spirit.

*PRISONER.*
He's fainted for sure. Konrad! — He can't hear it.

*FR. PIOTR.*
Peace to this house, and to the sinner, peace!

*PRISONER.*
Good Lord, he's had it! Look at him gnash his teeth!
He's very sick — look at him toss and foam!

*CORPORAL.*
Good Sir, go now, and leave us three alone.

*PRISONER.*
For God's sake — he needs more than empty prayer!
Lift him from the ground — let's get him in bed,
Father Piotr!

*FR. PIOTR.*
        No, don't touch him. Leave him there.

*PRISONER.*
Here — at least take this pillow for his head.
Ah, I know what's going on with him. Sometimes
This fury falls on him, he sings, and then
He babbles, faints — it looks bad at the time,
But in the morning, he'll be strong as ten.
But who told you he had a fit tonight?

CORPORAL.
>   Please — just sit there quietly, if you don't mind.
>   Let brother Piotr pray now over your mate,
>   'Cause I know, something... awful's... happened here.
>   When the watch passed, I heard a hellish row
>   Within the cell. I peeped in through the grate
>   And what I saw, that's not fit for your ear.
>   I up and ran to find this friend of mine,
>   Good Father Piotr. Look at your friend now —
>   It wasn't good before, and it's still bad.

PRISONER.
>   I'm out of my depth. I think I'm going mad!

CORPORAL.
>   Mad? Ah, you learned gentlemen, watch out!
>   Saws in your head and wisdom on your tongue,
>   Yet see this learned head roll in the dung.
>   See the wild foam that fills the lettered mouth!
>   I heard him sing, but couldn't comprehend
>   The words, but what I saw there in his eyes,
>   And there above his brow... Believe me, friend,
>   This man's in trouble. In my younger days
>   I was a legionnaire, and I've attacked
>   Fortress and monastery, barricades ...
>   I've seen more people die in my long life
>   Than you've read books. Lord, don't think that a boast!
>   But when you see a man give up the ghost
>   You learn a lot. I've watched in Warsaw's Prague
>   Priests have their throats cut as if they were dogs;
>   In Spain I've seen them tossed from battlements,
>   And mothers with their living wombs wide rent,
>   And children squirming on a Cossack's pike,
>   Frenchmen drop dead along their winter's hike
>   From Moscow, Turks run through like sworded sheaths,
>   And I know how to tell a martyr's death
>   From that of thieves and bandits, Russians, Turks.
>   I've seen men face the death squad with a smirk,

Refusing handkerchiefs to shield their sight —
Yet when they were cut down, I saw the worm
Of terror that they'd kept battened down tight
During their life, exit the corpse and squirm
About them in the dust. And that's a fear
Greater than any that a coward feels
When bullets start to chase him to the rear.
You've only got to look at that cold brow
To see the soul in mortal terror, how
It flops about in fits, it foams, it reels,
Contemning pain, yet suffering just so.
And for its crimes, the prize: eternal woe.
Upon the dead man's face, this final vision
Is stamped hard, like a military commission,
From which you read how he will be received
There in the next world: his rank and degree;
Whether from God's canteen he'll draw his ration,
Or whether he'll be front-lined to damnation.
And so, neither this fellow's song, nor his look
Boded aught good — nor does this turn he took.
Go back then, to your cell. I shall abide
Here with the sick man at the Father's side.

/Exit Prisoner/

KONRAD.
    The gulf — a thousand years — empty — ha, give me more!
    A thousand more — ten thousand — I'll endure!
    Prayer? — Prayer's not good for anything down here —
    Was there such an abyss here all the while?
    I didn't know — there was...

CORPORAL.
                        He's sobbing! D'you hear?

FR. PIOTR.
    My son, you rest upon a heart that loves you.

/to the Corporal/

    Go out into the corridor and steer
    All men away while I am still in here.

KONRAD /starts up/
    No! — He hasn't robbed me of my eagle's eye —
    I see, even from here, though dark, though deep —
    I see you, Rollison — my brother — speak!
    You, here in prison? Is it you I spy
    All bloodied, beaten? So God heard not your prayer
    Either! You seek a knife, you try your worst
    To brain yourself — you're in despair
    Too! "Help" you call! But though your cheeks may burst
    No help will come from Him, and none from me.
    And yet, I've got that eye of power, wait — let's see:
    Maybe I can kill you with my stare... No good...
    And yet at least I can show you the road
    To death — look there — that window! Jump! The spasm
    Of death done with, we'll fly into the chasm
    Together! The eternal chasm... Worth
    Far more than all the glory of the earth —
    No brothers there, or mothers, nations — tyrants —
    Come here.

FR. PIOTR.
    I know you by your venom, hellish siren!
    You, wiliest of Satans! You again!
    You've found another empty house, reptile;
    Crawled in his mouth to your own destruction!
    In the Lord's Name, I'll fashion you a bridle.
    *Exorciso* ...

SPIRIT.
            Stop! Not another word!
    I'll come out —

*FR. PIOTR.*
>Only when it please the Lord.
The Lord is Judah's Lion — victory
Belongs to Him! You foolish lion hunter!
Setting out nets for such a prey. Now see:
Into the toils you set yourself you blunder!
God's tripped you up in this sinner's mouth. Now I
Will measure you, liar, a blow severe:
You must respond to my questions, whate'er
I ask, and you are not allowed to lie.

*SPIRIT.*
>*Parle-moi donc français, mon pauvre capucin,*
>*J'ai pu dans le grand monde oublier mon latin.*
>*Mais étant saint, tu dois avoir le don des langues —*
>*Vielleicht sprechen Sie deutsch, was murmeln so bang —*
>*Co to jest, — Cavalleros, rispondero Io.*

*FR. PIOTR.*
>You'll chatter true, foul parrot, even so!
>You speak through him.

*SPIRIT.*
>*C'est juste, dans ce jeu, nous sommes de moitié,*
>*Il est savant, et moi, diable de mon métier.*
>*J'étais son précepteur et je m'en glorifie,*
>*En sais-tu plus que nous? parle — je te défie.*

*FR. PIOTR.*
>In the Name of the Father, the Son, the Holy Spirit.

*SPIRIT.*
>Ah, anything but that, priest — I can't bear it!
>No, no, sweet Daddy — can you be a Satan
>To so torment me?

*FR. PIOTR.*
>Your name?

SPIRIT.
                    Lucrece, Leviathan,
     Voltaire, Alter Fritz, Legio sum.
FR. PIOTR.
          What is it that you saw?

SPIRIT.
              The beast.

FR. PIOTR.
              And where?

SPIRIT.
                  In Rome.

FR. PIOTR.
          He heeds me not. So, back to prayer.

/prays/

SPIRIT.
          I'm listening! I'm listening!

FR. PIOTR.
                  Where'd you see
     The prisoner?

SPIRIT.
                  In Rome.
FR. PIOTR.
                  You lie to me.

SPIRIT.
     No, Father — I swear — On my sweet whorish bride,
     My black-skinned lover, who sighs so sweetly!
     You know her name perhaps, dear Father? Pride.
     Ah, you're no gossip!

FR. PIOTR /to himself/.
                        Spirits at variance —
    I must humble myself in penitence.

SPIRIT.
    No need, I'm coming out, no ands or buts!
    To speak the truth, I don't like it in here.

    This soul's all porcupiny, and, I fear
    I've put it on all wrong: prick-side to guts!

/the Priest prays/

    'Cause you're a master, you are! You're no dope!
    Those Roman asses ought to make *you* Pope.
    Instead, they make of dullness the façade
    And hide you deep inside the apse, like —

FR. PIOTR.
                                    Stop!
    Tyrant and flatterer, both base and proud,
    You fawn at my feet to snap at my breast.

SPIRIT /laughing, mocking/
    Ha! You've stopped praying. Let's go then, from the top!
    If you could only see the way your hand
    Thumps round! Just like a bear swatting his chest
    To kill a flea! But — I'm at your command.

    Enough of this. It's time to play the seer.
    You know what they say about you in the town?

/the Priest prays/

    What Poland will be like in two hundred years?
    Why the prior won't support you in the least?
    Or what, in Revelations, means "the beast?"
    He's silent, on he flails, I can't bear his eyes…

Tell me, my priestling, why do you torment me?
What have I done, that you so cruelly rend me?
Am I the king of demons? I'm a pawn!
You smite me for my master's deeds? That's wrong.
I'm slave to orders that I must obey.
I must do as I'm told. I have no say —
Do you think that I'm Satan's right hand man?
*Landrat, Gubernator, Kreishauptmann —*
That's more the style: an unimportant clerk.
They say "Grab that soul, lock him down deep and dark,"
And I come with a warrant for arrest.
Granted, that soul feels some... unpleasantness
In the process, but how am I to blame?
I'm just a tool. I have to check the name
Stamped on the devil's writ, and then apprise
Him of the fact he's overstepped the laws,
And while I sink into his side these claws,
Oft, with my tail, I have to wipe my eyes

/sighs/

Of tears! Yes! Ah, what torture to have a heart!
To torture him, and feel that torture's smart!
Believe me, it's the truth, priest. I'm not shamming.

/the Priest prays/

You know who they'll beat tomorrow, just like Haman?

FR. PIOTR.
*In nomine Patris et Filii et Spiritus Sancti, Amen.*
*Ego te exorciso, spiritus immunde —*

SPIRIT.
Stop — priest — I'm talking — I'm coming — hey!

*FR. PIOTR.*
Where is that prisoner, the unfortunate,
About to kill his soul? What's this — you balk?
*Exorciso te...*

*SPIRIT.*
                All right! I'll talk!
I must.

*FR. PIOTR.*
                Whom did you see?

*SPIRIT.*
                              A reprobate.

*FR. PIOTR.*
      Where?

*SPIRIT.*
                In another monastery.

*FR. PIOTR.*
                    Where?

*SPIRIT.*
St Dominic's. But Father, what's the use?
He's damned, and he belongs to me by law!

*FR. PIOTR.*
     You lie.

*SPIRIT.*
                He's dead.

*FR. PIOTR.*
                  You lie.

SPIRIT.
>                        That's what I saw!
> At least, he's sick.

FR. PIOTR.
> *Exorciso te —*

SPIRIT.
> I speak, I sing, what would you have me say?
> Just stop the binding prayers! How can I speak?
> You've choked the breath right out of me! I'm weak...

FR. PIOTR.
> The truth!

SPIRIT.
>        The sinner's sick, mad, so forlorn,
>        He's sure to break his neck tomorrow morn!

FR. PIOTR.
>        You lie!

SPIRIT.
>                Go ask my Uncle Beelzebub!
>        And rake his soul, not mine, against the rub!

FR. PIOTR.
> How can I save him?

SPIRIT.
>                I'll see your damnation!
> I won't tell!

FR. PIOTR.
>                *Exorciso —*

SPIRIT.
>                        — With consolation!

*FR. PIOTR.*
    Good, but of what sort? Speak clearly this time.

*SPIRIT.*
    I can't, I'm hoarse...

*FR. PIOTR.*
        Speak!

*SPIRIT.*
            My lord and my king!
    Let me rest!

*FR. PIOTR.*
        Speak!

*SPIRIT.*
            I won't!

*FR. PIOTR.*
                Speak!

*SPIRIT.*
                    Ah — bread — wine —

*FR. PIOTR.*
    Thy Body and Blood, Lord! Now I understand.
    Now help me, Lord Jesus, to fulfil Thy command.

    /to the Spirit/

    Now, take your anger, and all your torments,
    And whence you first entered, now exit him, thence!

/the Spirit is driven out/

KONRAD.
> You lift me up? — who... Take care, lest you tumble
> Into this same abyss! He gives his hand,
> And we fly upwards — through the scented breeze,
> Bird-like, I soar, and shine with the sun's rays —
> Who gave his hand? An angel, or a man?
> Who dared descend among the hellish rubble
>
> Where I had landed, senseless and forgot?
> Contemning men, the angels I knew not!

FR. PIOTR.
> Pray now, smitten by the Lord's awesome hand.
> The mouth which spat upon His Majesty
> The evil spirit soiled and travestied
> With words of foolishness — the worst torment
> For wise men. May they count towards your penance,
> And be forgotten.

KONRAD.
>          They're carved here in adamant.

FR. PIOTR.
> Sinner, may you never read them again,
> And may the Lord of you never demand
> Their meaning. Wrapped in rags torn and unclean,
> Chased from her throne, just like a sinful queen,
> Your reason, dressed in penitential weeds
> Before the church-porch, barefoot, if she pleads
> With true repentance, she'll again be dight
> In royal robes that never glowed so bright.
> He's fallen asleep.

/he kneels/

> Merciful Lord!

/falls to his face, lies cross-wise/

> Thy servant's nothing but a wraith
> Worn thin with age and labour, and with sin.
> Make this young man the servant of Thy faith —
> Let him take my place; I'll change mine with him:
> He'll sing Thy praises, I'll pay his sins' price.
> Through Christ our Lord, accept the sacrifice!

/he prays/
/From behind the wall, in the nearby church, we hear the Christmas carol "The Angels to the Shepherds Said". To the same melody, the Choir of Angels begins to sing above Fr. Piotr/

CHOIR OF ANGELS /voices of children/.
> Peace unto this lowly house,
> And unto the sinner, peace.
> Servant humble, servant mild,
> Thou'st raised up in this house of pride
> Peace, and sin's release:
> Peace unto this lowly house.

FIRST ARCHANGEL /to the melody 'God is our Refuge'/.
> Lord God, his transgressions are bloody red,

SECOND ARCHANGEL.
> Yet for him, see: Thy angels prayers extending:

FIRST ARCHANGEL.
> Lord, trample stubborn-necked sinners instead;
> Spare them who sin, Thy ways not comprehending.

ANGEL.
> When with the star of hope I sped
> To shine above Bethlehem,
> The angels sang above the shed
> Where Christ new-born was lain.
> And yet the wise men saw nothing
> Of us, nor rulers heard us sing.
> 'Twas shepherds saw our starry fleet

    And raced unto the stable,
    Where Heaven's wisdom they did greet,
    Laughing in His rude cradle.
    Such did the Sovereign Babe agnize:
    The simple, poor, small, and misprised.

*FIRST ARCHANGEL.*
    When curiosity and scheming pride
    Infected angels pure, the righteous flame
    Of God's ire flung them down from Heaven's height.
    Today, whole troops of wise men in their train
    Plummet down headlong, in thick sheets, like rain.

*CHOIR OF ANGELS.*
    The Lord to humble souls reveals
    What He from souls puffed-up conceals.
    Have pity on the sons of earth!
    He too o'erstaked his petty worth —
    Have pity on the sons of earth!

*SECOND ARCHANGEL.*
    'Twas not for wisdom that he pried
    Into Thy ways, nor out of empty pride:

*FIRST ARCHANGEL.*
    He knew Thee not, he praised Thee not, great God!
    He loved Thee not, dear Lord, nor feared Thy rod!

*SECOND ARCHANGEL.*
    Yet he held chaste the name of Thy blest Mother —
    He loved his nation, Lord, he loved his brothers.

*ANGEL.*
    A golden cross is fixed upon
    The crowns of kings; on wise men's chests
    It shines as brilliant as the dawn.
    And there's the rub: outside it rests,

And never takes root in their breasts.
Enlighten them, dear Saviour!

CHOIR OF ANGELS.
Ah, how we love the race of man!
How closely do we press upon
Their paces, always close at hand,
Though kings and wise men oft do shun
Us, simple folk give us welcome.
For them we sing, dear Saviour!
CHOIR OF ARCHANGELS.
Lift up this head, and it shall reach the skies.
Then, at the foot of the Cross will it fall,

Beside which, all the world in homage lies
Praising Thy justice, and mercy, Lord of all!

BOTH CHOIRS.
Peace unto simplicity!
Peace, to noble humility!
Servant humble, servant mild,
Thou'st raised up in this house of pride
Peace to this sinful, orphaned child.

## SCENE IV.

/A VILLAGE HOME NEAR LWÓW. A BEDROOM—EWA, A YOUNG GIRL, RUSHES IN, FIXES THE FLOWERS BEFORE THE ICON OF THE MOST BLESSED VIRGIN, KNEELS DOWN AND PRAYS. ENTER MARCELINA/

MARCELINA.
What — still at prayer! It's midnight. Go to bed.

EWA.
I've prayed for the Fatherland, as I've been taught;
I've said my prayers for Mama and for Dad.
Now let us pray for those who've been forgot —
Though they're so far away, yet all the same
They're children of one mother, our Poland.
That traveller — the Lithuanian —
Who stopped here at the house today, he came
Straight from the Russian zone. The tales he told
Of what they do there made my blood run cold.
Tsar Herod's locked up the youth of the nation
Hoping to wipe out a whole generation.
These stories made my father very sad.
He went out walking in the fields, and still
Hasn't come back; my mother sent the lad
To have a Mass said — many have been killed
By that bad man — I'll say a special prayer
For him who wrote these poems.

/pointing to a book/

For he's there
Suffering in prison along with the rest
Of the young men, according to our guest.
I've read these poems — some are beautiful —
Before the Blessed Maid again, I'll kneel
And pray for him — who knows if there's a soul
Alive besides me to pray for his weal?

/exit Marcelina/

*/Ewa prays and drowses/*

ANGEL.
   Softly now, quietly let us descend.

CHOIR OF ANGELS.
   Like gentle sleep upon our kindred soul,
   And bathe the gentle sprite in happy dreams,
   Washing her face in starry beams,
   Singing and plaiting a dancing garland
   Above our purest, quiet darling.
   Her lily hands caressing, weaving,
   Her gentle brow to rose-blush breathing,
   Her starry-golden braids resolving,
   Ourselves in fragrant beams dissolving,
   Winding ourselves a living cincture
   Round breast and temples, a scented tincture
   Blooming, an angelic garland
   For our purest, silent darling.

EWA */Vision/*.
   This rain so sweet and calm and fresh, like dew —
   Yet whence falls it? Behold the heavens blue,
   The cloudless blue!
   Green drops like lovely grasses, lush
   Rose, lily garlands plush
   Wind me about — Ah, such a fragrant breath
   This dream wafts me — may I so dream till death!
   Rose sun-bright, silky,
   Lily most pure, milky!
   Not of this earth are you — you bloom on high,
   Narcissus, winking with your snowy eye,
   And you, azure forget-me-nots,
   As pure as new-born infants' thoughts;
   I know you, my flowers, in my garden blooming,
   Watered by me and culled in dusky gloaming,
   Plaited to crown the Blessed Mother's head
   That on the icon watches over my bed.

I see — the Blessed Mother! — brilliant
With glory, as she takes up in her hand,
Looking at me the while, the humble garland,
And gives it to the Babe, who, laughing, throws
At me narcissus, lily, rose —
How they have swelled in beauty at His touch!
How many there are now! How much
More lovely as they spin,
Each searching for his twin,
    My darlings,
Twining new garlands!
How lovely it is here, like paradise!
How happy I am here, my God, my Christ!
May this garland ever wind me round!
May I die, by rose and lily bound,
Gazing in the white narcissus' eyes.
That rose, that rose is alive!
A spirit dwells inside —
She lightly bobs her lovely head
And what a fire beats there! How red
The living blush, just like the early dawning
She laughs, and cool green leaves burst from her smile.
And there, deep in her cheerful smile's heart,
Two lips of coral spread apart.
She's saying something — but how quietly, how calmly —
What is it, rose, you whisper me the while?
Too quiet, sad — is that the voice of mourning?
You're sad at being from the garden torn,
Your native soil? I plucked you not for fun,
But to present you at the Virgin's throne.
I watered you with tears after confession
Just yesterday — what do you whisper me?
From out your lips, so coral-dark
Your words fly forth like living things,
Spark upon spark —
What is this light, the song you sing?
What is your behest?

*ROSE.*
>   Press me to your breast.

*ANGELS.*
>   Now the angelic garland parts.

*ROSE.*
>   I spread my wings, unbind my brow.

*ANGELS.*
>   We fly back home with joyful hearts.

*ROSE.*
>   And I'll abide with her till dawn,
>   Wreathing her heart like a rose-crown,
>   Like the apostle who did rest
>   His head upon the Saviour's breast.

## SCENE V.
*/FR. PIOTR'S CELL/*

*FR. PIOTR. prays, spread cross-wise on the floor/.*
    Lord, what am I worth in Thy sight?
    Dust, not a mite.
    Yet should I but confess my worthlessness,
    Then grantest Thou converse with Thy holiness.

*/Vision/*

    A tyrant rises — Herod! — Lord, all young Poland
    Is given over into Herod's hand.
    What do I see? — the arms, long and white, of a cross road
    Extending far — farther than sight — through snow
    And wasteland, northward! where they deliver
    Their sad cargo, like a river:
    This river flows under an iron gate,
    That one falls over a cliff, precipitate
    Into an abyss; that one feeds the sea.
    Look: along these roads a crowd of wagons speed
    Like clouds by the wind pushed
    In one direction rushed —
    Lord! each carries a child
    Of ours; children, dear Lord!
    Each by a tyrant's sword
    Prodded into exile!
    And can it be that Thou hast sealed their fate?
    A generation wiped whole from the slate?
    But look! — one child's escaped — and he shall bring
    Salvation to his nation suffering!
    Of foreign mother — heroic blood of yore —
    And his name shall be forty-four.
    O Lord! Wilt Thou this child's advent not hasten,
    To cheer my people chastened?
    No — the people shall suffer — I see the rout
    That drags along to judgement my Nation bound —
    All Europe tears and drags him, mocks,

"To the Tribune!"— innocent, to the stocks.
There at the bench, mugs heartless, handless, sit:
His judges!
"Gaul!" cry the people, "the trial! Get on with it!"
Gaul finds no sin in him, and yet begrudges
The verdict — washes his hands
While the kings cry out, "Death is our demand!
Torture and death! May his blood be upon
Us and our sons!
Crucify the Son of Mary; give us Barabbas!
Crucify him, for he's knocked Caesar's crown in the dust!
Crucify him, or thou prove thyself Tsar's enemy!"
Gaul gives him up, they drag him back,
And on his blameless brow
Bloodied and bruised, they jam a mocking, piercing crown.
Then they display him to the world for all nations to see
While Gaul cries out: "Behold the nation, independent, free!"

Ah, Lord — and now I see the cross. How long
Must he bear it! Have mercy on Thy son!
Bestow on him Thy strength, lest he should die
Along the road — as deep and long and wide
As Europe, so his cross, fashioned of three
Desiccated nations, as if from trees
Of hardest gnarl — now, on this penance-throne
My Nation's raised. I hear Thy servant groan,
While Mother Freedom stands below and weeps,
"I thirst" — Austria vinegar, and Prussia
Gall offers — Look! and now a Russian
Leaps forth and stabs him — blameless blood
Flows out my Nation's side in a salvific flood.
What have you done, most stupid, brutal knave!
Yet he alone repents, and shall be saved.

O, my beloved! "My God!" he cries to Thee,
Hanging his head, "Why hast Thou abandoned me?
It is finished!"

/We hear the Choir of Angels; a distant Easter hymn, at the end of which, "Alleluia! Alleluia!"/

Upward and upward! To Heaven he flies!
And from his feet, his snowy shroud
Drops down, and spreads out, far and wide
Over the earth, and wraps it round about —
His pupils three a starry trinity,
His punctured palm aloft for all to see.

Who is this man? — Thy deputy on earth,
I know him — since his very birth.
But how he's grown! His soul — how grand!
He's blind — an angel leads him by the hand.
A fearsome sight: three faces — look!
He has three brows.
Above him, like a baldachin, a book,
A book mysterious shades his head,
And on three capitals he rests his foot.
Three corners of the world shiver in dread
When he takes voice; I hear a voice like thunder
From on high, like the skies riven asunder:
"Behold the visible vicar of peace
Upon the earth!
On glory he'll found and bid increase
His holy church!
Above all kings and peoples he is set,
Upon three crowns, himself sans coronet:
Labour of labours, his life's requital,
People of peoples, his only title:
Of foreign mother, heroic blood of yore,
And his name is forty-four.
Glory! Glory! Glory!"

/he falls asleep/

*ANGELS /descend visibly/.*
    He sleeps — come now, let us take up his soul
    Just like a babe from out a cradle of gold —
    Wrap him around in cloaks of the dawn's light
    And to the third heaven let us take flight.
    We'll lay the baby on our Father's breast.
    He'll nestle there in joy, by his Father caressed,
    And then, before the Morning Prayers begin,
    We'll bear him back to clay, and tuck him in,
    Just like a babe, in a cradle of gold.

## SCENE VI.

/A SPLENDID BEDROOM—THE SENATOR TOSSES AND TURNS ON THE BED—TWO DEVILS ABOVE HIS HEAD/.

**DEVIL 1.**
    He got drunk and can't fall asleep,
    And I've been waiting a long time.
    Damn you, stop your tossing, creep!
    What's the quilt stuffed with, porcupines?

**DEVIL 2.**
    Sift some poppy on his eyes.

**DEVIL 1.**
    He sleeps! Ha, now's my time to play.

**DEVIL 2.**
    Swoop down on'm, like a bird of prey.

**BOTH.**
    Drag his soul off to Hell's furnace —
    Bind him tight in serpent-harness.

**BEELZEBUB.**
    Clear out!

**BOTH.**
               And who the hell are you?

**BEELZEBUB.**
    Scare off my game, and straightaway you'll know!

**DEVIL 1.**
    But when the bastard's fast asleep,
    His dreams are mine to warp and weave?

BEELZEBUB.
> But should he see the night, the flames
> That await him, the unending pain,
> He could take fright at suchlike scenes.
> Tomorrow, he'll recall his dreams,
> He might start to believe again,
> And bustle off his soul to shrive.
> For some time yet, he'll be alive...

DEVIL 2 /bearing his claws/.
> Aw, let us have a little fun!
> You're scared of losing such a beast?
> When he shall to confession run
> I'll shave my horns — and become a priest!

BEELZEBUB.
> I tell you — scare him overmuch,
> And he'll recall the frights he's seen;
> He'll finish by deceiving us:
> You'll let the toiling bird go free.

DEVIL 1 /points to the sleeper/.
> Aw, come on! This little one
> Is truly my best-beloved son!
> He'll sleep with no torment at all?
> If you're squeamish, he'll feel my claw.

BEELZEBUB.
> You blackguard! Cease the dull derision.
> The Tsar himself signed my commission!

DEVIL 1.
> *Pardon, mon chef.* To what extent
> Then, may we his foul soul torment?

BEELZEBUB.
> Well, you may puff him up with pride,
> Then drag him down; with shame deride

Him, snatch him from the heights of fame
And drag through filth his once-proud name.
Set him on high, then mock him well,
But not a single peep of Hell!

/he flies off/

DEVIL 1.
So, now his soul's within my claws —
Ha! How you shiver, little louse!

DEVIL 2.
First take him gently in your paws,
Just like a cat plays with a mouse.

SENATOR /Vision, while he sleeps/.
A parchment — to me — a rescript from the Tsar!
In his own hand — ha, ha! — one hundred thousand!
Medal — sash — Slave, pin it here — a Prince's cross!
Ah! — Ah! Grand Marshal! How they'll kiss my hand
And croak with jealousy!

/he turns/

Ah — there they are —
Tsar's antechamber — they're all at a loss —
How they hate me! Yet how low they bow!
Marshal — Grand Contrôleur — they know me now!
Sweet, jealous whispers!
All round me, whispers!
In the Tsar's grace, Tsar's grace, Tsar's grace!
May whispers such as this ever swirl me round.
May I die thus, ears tickled by the sound!
All bow down low,
I'm the very soul
Of the gathering!
So jealous! And I lift my nose up high,

O, what delight! Such joy, I'm fit to die
From their slavering!

*/he tosses/*

The Tsar! — Ah! His Imperial Majesty
Enters and — Does he look askance at me?
Wrinkling his brows?! Ah, gracious lord, I lack
The power of speech — I sweat, shiver with cold —
The Marshal — what's this?! On me he turns his back?
What? Him too?! Senators, ministers, the whole
Lot of them? Now I die and rot from shame!
And worms of mockery burrow through my name!
Jokes and pasquilles, bons mots — and now I'm left
Alone — cast out — abandoned and bereft —
The chamberlain — Look how the rascal snarls!
That smile of his has crept into my maw
Just like a spider!

*/spits/*

          What's that buzzing sound?
A pun, a pun! — like a bluebottle round
My nose!
It goes

*/he flails about his nose/*

Like a pesky wasp.
Epigrams, jokes and allusions I hear
Chirping like crickets, crawling about my ears.
My ears! My ears!

*/digs in his ears with his finger/*

Junkers hooting now like tawny owls,
Dames rustling here and there like rattlesnakes

    Chirping, buzzing, laughter, howls:
    He's lost his place! his place! his place!

*/falls out of bed to the ground/*

DEVILS */descend visibly/*.
    And now, let us the rabid soul unchain
    Like a mad dog from out a filthy kennel.
    But not entirely — let half remain
    There in his body's muck, for then he'll
    Still feel the pain! Come, stretch him on the rack
    From here unto the world's farthest ends,
    Where Hell's frontier meets with the bad conscience.
    That's where we'll chain him by the nose
    And beat him till the rooster crows
    At which time, we must drag him back
    And bind him, bloodied, to his corpse again
    Just like a mad dog in a filthy kennel.

## SCENE VII.

/A WARSAW SALON. SEVERAL GREAT OFFICIALS, SEVERAL GREAT LITERATI, SEVERAL LADIES OF HIGH SOCIETY, SEVERAL GENERALS AND STAFF OFFICERS, ALL DRINKING TEA AT A TABLE, INCOGNITO — NEAR THE DOORS, SEVERAL YOUNG PEOPLE AND TWO POLES OF THE OLD SCHOOL. THOSE STANDING THERE CONVERSE ANIMATEDLY — THE COMPANY AT THE TABLE ARE SPEAKING FRENCH; THOSE AT THE DOOR SPEAK POLISH/.

### At the doors.

ZENON NIEMOJEWSKI /to Adolf/.
So it's the same story in Lithuania, then?

ADOLF.
Worse — they're spilling blood there. Killing men.

NIEMOJEWSKI.
Blood? Killing?

ADOLF.
        Not on the battlefield.
In dungeons. Bludgeons are the arms they wield.

/they speak more softly/

### At the table.

COUNT.
So, were there many soldiers at the ball?

FRENCHMAN.
No — as boring as church, I heard. An empty hall.

LADY.
No, it was full!

COUNT.
        And gay?

LADY.
                    Descriptions fail!

KAMMERJUNKER.
    The service was boorish, though there was a mass
    Of livery — I couldn't get a glass
    Of wine, not to mention a spoon of paté.

LADY 1.
    No grouping for the dance — everything goes!
    All English routs: blue ribs and swollen toes.

LADY 2.
    But it was an impromptu celebration…

CHAMBERLAIN.
    No, it was formal — here's my invitation.

/he flourishes his invitation; all nod/

LADY 1.
    So much the worse! Mixed styles, salons, mixed groups;
    Thus, how might one evaluate the costumes?

LADY 2.
    Ever since Novosiltsov left Warsaw
    There hasn't been a single tasteful ball.
    At his evenings, everyone knows his part —
    His groupings are a very work of art!

/laughter among the men/

LADY 1.
    Laugh, Gentlemen, as merrily as you may —
    Our Warsaw needs just such a man, I say!

### *At the doors.*

ONE OF THE YOUNG MEN.
  Cichowski's freed?

ADOLF.
                    I know Cichowski well.
  I've just been with him — wanted to establish
  What news in Lithuania should be published.

ZENON NIEMOJEWSKI.
  We ought to stick together. Otherwise
  Each dies alone; our deaths will be in vain.

YOUNG WOMAN /standing near them/.
  Dear Lord, how could he endure so much pain!

/they converse/

### *At the table.*

GENERAL /to Literatus/.
  Come on, declaim for us! We beg you — please!

LITERATUS.
  I don't know it by heart.

GENERAL.
                    Perhaps, but look:
  You've got it with you. Isn't that your book
  There, peeking out the pocket of your vest?
  The ladies want to hear.

LITERATUS.
                    Oh, it'd be best
  To hold one's peace in their presence. I know
  They have more poetry in French by rote
  Than I by half...

GENERAL /to one of the Ladies/.
>I beg you, just don't laugh!

LADY.
>He'll read? In Polish? Ah — *langue malheureuse!*
>I understand it somewhat... but not in verse...

GENERAL /to Officer/.
>That's harsh, but she's not all that wrong, if you please.

/pointing to the Literatus/
>He's written a thousand lines on planting peas.

/to Literatus/
>Go on then, read! If you don't stoop to bore,

/points to another Literatus/

>Look at that rhymer standing by the door.
>He's got no scruples. Do us all a favour.
>Look how he smiles and winks — he fairly slavers
>Over the thought. He's opened wide his mouth,
>Ready to sing, like a three day old trout.

LITERATUS /to himself/.
>They're moving off —

/to the General/

>My poems are too long.

GENERAL /to the Officer/.
>Before he reconsiders, let's be gone!

YOUNG WOMAN /moving from the younger group, by the door, to the table/.
>So horrid! So horrid! Listen, sirs —

/to Adolf/

> Tell them about Cichowski — what you told me.

HIGH-RANKING OFFICER.
> What is it you say? Is Cichowski free?

COUNT.
> After so many years clapped in the stir!

CHAMBERLAIN.
> And I thought he was clapped inside his grave.

/to himself/

> Even to hear such talk is not quite safe —
> But to leave in mid account would be gauche...

/exit/

COUNT.
> They let him go? Strange...

ADOLF.
> He was innocent.

MASTER OF CEREMONIES.
> Who speaks of guilt? No, something different's
> Behind this. Prisoners get all too close
> To the state's secrets, locked up behind bars.
> The state's got its own goals and searches far
> Into the future, weighs each consequence,
> Considers every angle; thus, my friends,
> Often when somebody's let out of prison
> It's not the judge's, but the state's, decision.
> Such is the logic of officialdom.
> But you're from Lithuania, and so

These things are new to you. You'd like to know
As much about the Tsar's imperium
As your own barnyard!

KAMMERJUNKER.
                    Where is it you're from?
From Lithuania? Upon my soul!
You speak our language like a very Pole!
And here I'm thinking everyone up there
Is Russian! I know far more, I declare,
Of China than of Wilno. I once read
In the *Constitutionel* about you gents,
But nothing since that time... at least not in French ...

GIRL /to Adolf/.
Please tell us, sir: this touches the whole nation.

OLD POLE.
I know the old Cichowscy: generations
Born and raised in Galicia. I heard
They'd grabbed the son. They're my distant kin.
I haven't seen him since... ah, years it's been!
But what's new there? They've tortured our fathers,
Ourselves, and now they lock up our toddlers!

ADOLF /as everyone gathers round/.
I knew him as a child — he was young then,
Carefree, alive, the handsomest of men,
The soul of every party. When he'd come,
You'd know it, because you'd see everyone
Gathered around him, laughing at his jokes.
He was a magnet! Not just older folks,
But younger people, and mere kids like me
Would rush to him. He'd take us on his knee
And laugh with us and play, so nice and mild,
You'd think he was himself a little child.
He was so pleasant, and so innocent...
We kids called him the "merry gentleman."

When I knew him, he had a fiancée,
And he would bring us presents now and then
From her. Then, just after his wedding day
He disappeared. No one saw him again.
But where could he have gone? This no one knew;
The police searched, but uncovered no clue.
Finally they said "He's killed himself. Drowned."
For evidence they brought his greatcoat, found
Muddy and wet down by the river side.
His wife confirmed it his; but everyone cried,
"How could it be — Cichowski? Suicide?!"
Among the mourners, this the single thought;
Nor tears nor quarrels any answer brought.
We cried some more, and gradually forgot.
Thus two years passed. And then, one evening,
When from the cloisters, the armed escorts bring
Transports to Belvedere for questioning,
Someone who looked on — was it happenstance,
Or one of those brave youths, who take the chance
Of getting nabbed themselves, and stand nearby
The courtyard wall and heave across a cry:
"Good prisoner, what's your name?" The night was clear,
The city silent, and among the cheer
Of tens of names, he heard "Cichowski!" cried,
And on the morrow he informed the bride.
She wrote, she flew, she begged, she went and came —
But she heard nothing more, except his name.
Three more years passed without another clue.
And then someone said — But where? But who? —
That, though they torture him sans intermission,
Still he lives on, and will sign no confession.
The rumours claimed he was deprived of sleep,
Force-fed with salty foods, then given no drink;
With opium drugged and terrified at night
With threats and horrors to jolt loose his mind;
To tears and laughter both provoking,
Yet he endured it all, unbroken.
And then some other prisoner would be thought on,

And Cichowski was once again forgotten.
But not, of course, by her.
Then, late one night, there's a knock at the door:
She opens it — who is it there that stands
Between two armed guards, one on either hand,
But him! They thrust her paper and a pen:
"It's him. Sign the receipt," they growl, and then
Just as they'd come, they scuttle off again
After a finger wagging and a threat:
"If you but breathe a word…! Now, watch your step!"
I heard that he was out, and set off straight
To see him. "No! They're watching at the gate!"
My friends warned me. All right. I'll go next day.
But "They're still watching his door. Stay away!"
And so they were. I waited one more week,
But he could have no visitors. Still too weak.
At last, one afternoon out for a ride
I met him walking in the countryside,
But couldn't recognise him, when my friend
Pointed him out. How he'd changed since then
When last I saw him! He had put on weight —
But healthy pounds they weren't. In jail he ate
The worst things out of hunger, and the air
Poisoned his constitution, all his hair
Fell out, his flaccid cheeks hung down like jowls,
And half a century's furrows creased his brows.
Nor did he know me. Didn't want to speak,
And looked at me with a dull eye and weak
When I told him my name. Just the sight
Of that eye told me more of the sleepless nights
He'd suffered there, and his torments by day,
Than tongue might in a month of Sundays say.
His eye was misted over with a film
Such as you see covering barred windows —
The colour of spider webs; a look within
Frustrating, but from the side, it glows
With colour like a rainbow. You could tell
Those eyes were starved of light in a dank cell:

All bloody rust and sparks and blackish stains...
One month passed, and I visited him again,
Thinking to help him his old life regain
And jog more pleasant memories, but he
Had been so long under club, lock and key,
So many tortures had he to endure,
So many talks with his own self, unsure
Whether the walls had ears, his one defence
Against incrimination — stubborn silence,
With only shadows for his company,
That, no month in the town, however gay
Could undo lessons rote-learned day by day
For fifteen years. He saw the sun's bright eye
As the unsleeping gaze of some great spy;
His servants — keepers, each guest an enemy.
When someone would drop by for conversation,
He'd think it was for an interrogation.
He'd turn around and so avert his gaze
That what his lips said not, nor should his eyes
Betray; withdrawing deep inside himself,
He'd concentrate his strength, so as not to tell
A word unweighed. You'd ask him any question —
He'd think himself again back in his prison,
Rush off as if he were still in his cell,
To cower in the corner, crying "I won't tell!
I don't know!" Ah, how many tears his wife
Poured out, convincing him that all was well!
How much it cost them, hours of such strife,
And his child's pleadings, too, to bring him round,
Assuring him that he was safe and sound!
I've heard that prisoners like to recount
Tales of their past imprisonment; I thought
That he might best retrieve from underground
Tales of the secret battles that he fought
Alongside Poland's other quiet heroes —
For you know that the flower of Poland grows
'Midst snows Siberian and prison shade —
And yet — such was the answer that he made:

That he'd forgotten his long-suffered woe,
His memory — a book lost long ago,
Buried beneath the ashes of Pompeii.
And should its author, risen from the clay,
Attempt to read it, it should be for naught:
The pages dim, the language near forgot.
He said, "Someday I'll have to ask the Lord.
He writes down all, and loses not a word."

/Adolf wipes away a tear/
/long silence/

YOUNG WOMAN /to the Literati/.
    Why doesn't one of you write about that?

COUNT.
    Old Niemcewicz, in his memoirs, perhaps.
    I'm told he crams therein all sorts of scraps.

LITERATUS 1.
    Ah, what a story!

LITERATUS 2.
                    Horrible!

KAMMERJUNKER.
                            Indeed.

LITERATUS 1.
    It's fine to listen to, yes — but to read?
    And how should one write about modern things?
    Heroes must be... heroes, gods, or kings —
    You can't ignore Aristotle, and then —
    Horace says to wait until...

*ONE OF THE YOUNG MEN.*
                                    Till when?
   Till fruit unpicked rots on neglected trees?
   Until, like old snuff, it won't raise a sneeze?

*LITERATUS 1.*
   The rules don't say.

*LITERATUS 2.*
                 A hundred years.

*LITERATUS 1.*
                         No, more!

*LITERATUS 3.*
   A thousand. A couple thousand —

*LITERATUS 4.*
                             By my score,
   The problem isn't that the matter's fresh —
   Too bad the content isn't... quite Polish.
   Our nation loves the *mores rustici* —
   Simplicity and hospitality,
   Despising violence and cruelty.
   We like village songs and peasant frolics.
   We Slavs like idylls. This is not bucolic!

*LITERATUS 1.*
   And then that torture with the salty food.
   For your readers, that's a trifle uncouth…
   Now, poetry should be a polished thing
   And there's no polish where there is no king:
   The court determines taste and sets the tone —
   We've no court. Ah, the glory that was Rome…

*MASTER OF CEREMONIES.*
   No court! — To me that comes as a surprise.
   Why, I'm the master of ceremonies!

COUNT /whispers to the Master of Ceremonies/.
   One word from you, my lord, and my wife's made
   The Deputy's Consort's First Chambermaid!

/aloud/

   There's no room for our kind at Court, alas!
   The sun shines only on the upper class.

SECOND COUNT /freshly patented, not long ago just a bourgeois/.
   The peers defend the nation's liberties!
   Just look, my lords, at Britain, if you please.

   /A political quarrel erupts — the Young People move off/

FIRST YOUNG MAN.
   The scoundrels!

A*** G***
            If it weren't such a waste
   My fists would show them what to think of taste!

N***
   What good can we do here? Let's not fool around
   With those whom chance placed at the nation's crown.

WYSOCKI.
   Say rather: at the nation's crust. You know,
   Our nation's like a living volcano:
   The top is hard and cold, worthless and dried,
   But boiling, fiery lava seethes inside.
   One hundred years of cold won't cool its breath:
   Spit on the crust — come, we'll plunge to the depths.

## SCENE VIII.
### The HONOURABLE senator.

/WILNO — AN ANTESALON — TO THE RIGHT, DOORS LEADING TO THE INTERROGATION CHAMBER, INTO WHICH PRISONERS ARE ESCORTED, AND GIGANTIC STACKS OF PAPERS CAN BE SEEN — IN THE DEPTHS — DOORS LEADING TO THE SENATOR'S APARTMENT, WHENCE MUSIC IS HEARD — THE TIME: AFTER DINNER — AT THE WINDOW A SECRETARY BENDS OVER SOME PAPERS, FURTHER, A BIT TO THE LEFT, A TABLE AT WHICH SOME PEOPLE ARE PLAYING WHIST. NOVOSILTSOV IS DRINKING COFFEE; NEAR HIM CHAMBERLAIN BAIKOV, PELIKAN, AND THE DOCTOR — AT THE DOORS: GUARDS AND SEVERAL MOTIONLESS SERVANTS/

SENATOR /to the Chamberlain/.
 *Diable! quelle corvée!* — and we've already ate,
 *La princesse* lets us down — she isn't coming yet.
 At any rate, *en fait des dames*, old and stupid —
 To speak, *imaginez-vous*, of politics, at soup! It...
 *Je jure*, I won't have such *patriottes à ma table.*
 *Avec leur franc parler et leur ton détestable.*
 *Figurez-vous.* I'm talking of casinos, style,
 And my guests plead for this one's father, that one's child!
 "He's too old now, he's still young yet, Lord Senator!
 He's too weak to bear life in jail, Lord Senator!"
 This one wants to see his wife, that one wants a priest,
 Such pleasant conversation, *Diable*! for a feast.
 I'm finished here! To go mad *il y a de quoi,*
 I must escape Wilno for my beloved Warsaw.
 *Monseigneur* wrote me lately, *de revenir bientôt,*
 Says he's bored stiff there, and me? Among this dull lot,
 *Je n'en puis plus* —

DOCTOR /sidling up/.
                 You will recall, your Grace,
 That we've just started to build up our case.
 It's like a patient whom a doctor visits
 And makes his diagnosis. Many sit
 In jail, interrogations, but no results —
 We haven't as much as taken the pulse.

What have we found? Poems! *ce sont des maux légers,*
*Ce sont,* one might say, *des accidents passagers.*
But the conspiracy we've still to find.
Elusive...

SENATOR /insulted/.
    You must be out of your mind!
*Signor Dottore,* have you indigestion?
I am the one conducts investigation
Into this matter, *et, Docteur, vous osez*
To speak, in my very presence, in such a way?
We've still to find, say you, the conspiracy?
When was more formal police work ever seen?

/showing the papers/

    Look: charge sheets, voluntary confessions,
Heaps of evidence and testimony,
And you say, "Where is the conspiracy?"
You dare to bring my work thus into question?

DOCTOR.
    Pardon, your Grace, none doubt conspiracy
Is rampant, but...

SERVANT.
        My Lord, the man from Vanitch
Is here to speak with you about a bill.

SENATOR.
    A bill? What bill? From whom?

SERVANT.
        My lord, from Vanitch.
It seems you told him...

SENATOR.
                    Go, son of a bitch!
You see I'm busy!

DOCTOR /to the Servant/.
                      You dolt! Can't you see
His Grace the Senator is taking tea?

SECRETARY /getting up from his table/.
He says it's overdue. The invoice date...

SENATOR.
Send him my compliments. Ask him to wait.

SECRETARY.
He says if you don't settle, he may sue.

SENATOR.
Sue, will he? Well, he'll do what he must do...
Now that I think of it, we should arrest
Vanitch's son, as part of our inquest.

SECRETARY.
He's just a boy!

SENATOR.
           So what? So are the rest.
They're all of them just boys. But, search their hearts:
Fires are best tamped out when they're just sparks.

SECRETARY.
All right, yet Vanitch's son's in Moscow.

SENATOR.
Aha! An agent of the clubs. And now's
The time to smash the mould before it sets.

SECRETARY.
  The word is that he serves in the cadets.

SENATOR.
  That's just his cover. Really, he foments
  Insurrection against the crowned heads.

SECRETARY.
  He left here as a child!

SENATOR.
                    *Cet incendaire!*
  So that means he's got contacts here.

/to Secretary/

                  *Pas ton affaire,*
  *Comprends-tu?* Now, I need a warrant. You!
  Writ and a wagon before the day is through!
  Old Vanitch has no reason to be scared
  If his son's *témoignage soit volontaire*...

DOCTOR.
  And that's just what I had the honour to
  Suggest, your Grace: the plot's a very stew
  Of all ages and ranks — a deadly thing
  All set in motion by a hidden spring
  That...

SENATOR /insulted/.
  Hidden?!

DOCTOR.
              ...until your Grace deigned to bring
  What was in darkness wrapped, unto the light.

/to himself/

To talk with such a devil is a fright!
Yet how to break these silken chains? That I might!

PELIKAN /to Senator/.
What is your Grace's pleasure for Rollison?

SENA`TOR.
Who?

PELIKAN.
The one they beat during interrogation.

SENATOR.
*Eh bien?*

PELIKAN.
He's in bad shape.

SENATOR.
So he was trounced?

PELIKAN.
I saw the strokes, but I didn't keep count.
Botwinko questioned him.

BAIKOV.
Ha, ha! Botwinko!
He doesn't let up soon. What do you think? O—
I bet he beat him till his joints were sundered.
*Parions*, that he dealt him at least three hundred.

SENATOR /surprised/.
*Trois cents coups et vivant? trois cents coups, le coquin,*
*Trois cents coups sans mourir — quel dos de jacobin!*
I thought that back in Russia *la vertu cutanée*
*Surpasse tout* — that rascal has *une peau mieux tannée!*
*Je n'y conçois rien! — Ha! mon ami, vous pigez?*

*/turning to a fellow at the whist table,
who's waiting for his companion/*

These Poles will run us out of the skin trade!
*Un honnête soldat en serait mort aix fois!*
*Quel rebelle —*

*/moves up to the table/*

    I've got for you un *homme de bois*—
He takes three hundred swipes — or maybe five?
A boy, from Botwinko — and he's alive!

*/to Pelikan/*

Did he confess?

PELIKAN.
     Not quite. He merely states
Through gritted teeth, he won't betray his mates.
But we've scraped something from these odds and ends:
For example, that these students are his friends.

SENATOR.
 *C'est juste*: how stubborn!

DOCTOR.
       It's just as I've said:
All of our youth are addled in the head,
From what they read. O — ancient history!
That this drives them all mad, who doesn't see?

SENATOR */gaily/*.
 *Vous n'aimez pas l'histoire — ha, ha, un satirique*
*Aurait dit,* that you're afraid *devenir historique.*

DOCTOR.
>    I'm not against all history, my dear sirs:
>    Let them read of kings, and great ministers...

SENATOR.
>    C'est juste.

DOCTOR /gladdened/.
>                   That's my opinion! Tell the truth,
>    But truths such as will not corrupt the youth.
>    Why babble on so, of republicans,
>    Those Spartans, Romans, and Athenians!

PELIKAN /to one of his companions, pointing at the Doctor/.
>    Just look at that one sucking up to favour!
>    How hard he licks! He relishes the flavour.

/moving up to the Doctor/

>    See here. Now's not the proper time, it seems,
>    To bore the Senator with schoolhouse schemes.

SERVANT /to the Senator/.
>    Your Eminence, they're here again: those women
>    Who come here every day. Shall I let them in?
>    One's blind, the other —

SENATOR.
>                   Blind? What is her name?

SERVANT.
>    Rollison.

PELIKAN.
>    She's the mother of that same
>    Boy we've been talking of.

SERVANT.
           She's here every day —

DOCTOR.
    Dear Lord!

SENATOR.
        And Lord be with her, send her away!

SERVANT.
    We've tried, but she won't go. She hangs about,
    Just sits there at the steps and howls. We've tried
    To put her under arrest, but — she's blind —
    One of the guards was beaten by the crowd.
    So — let her in?

SENATOR.
               Ach! You incompetent...!
    Yes, let her in, and lead her up the stairs.
    But only half-way up...You comprehend?
    Then — send her back down — along with all her cares,

/makes a shoving gesture/

    That she may never more clutter our stoop.

/Second Servant enters, and hands a letter to Baikov/

    What are you waiting for? A combat troop
    For reinforcements?

BAIKOV.
            *Elle porte une lettre.*

/hands him the letter/

SENATOR.
    Who wrote it for her?

BAIKOV.
>                    *La princesse, peut-être.*

SENATOR /reads/.
>    The princess! What business is this for her!
>    Damn it, let her in! *Avec quelle chaleur...!*

/Enter two Ladies and Fr. Piotr/

PELIKAN /to Baikov/.
>    There's the old witch — *la mère de ce fripon.*

SENATOR.
>    Welcome! Which of you is Mrs. Rollison?

MRS. ROLLISON.
>    — That's me! — My son, your Grace...

SENATOR.
>                                    Yes, yes, anon.
>    Madame has a letter of introduction,
>    But why have so many of you come?

SECOND WOMAN.
>    We're only two.

SENATOR /to Second Woman/.
>                    But why have I the honour
>    Of greeting you at my poor hearth as well?

SECOND WOMAN.
>    She can't see, and ...

SENATOR.
>                        Can't see, but she can smell?
>    For every single day she seems to wander
>    Here without any problem.

SECOND WOMAN.
                              Because I lead
   Her here. She's all alone, and old, and sick.

MRS. ROLLISON.
   O God...!

SENATOR.
                  Hush!

/to Second Woman/

                     Who are you?

SECOND WOMAN.
                              My name is Kmit.

SENATOR.
   You'd better keep watch over your own fold
   At home, than worry about stranger's sons.
   For your own lads are under suspicion.

MRS. KMIT /pales/.
   How can that be, your Grace!

SENATOR /laughing/.
   Ha, ha! If you could only see your face!

MRS. ROLLISON.
   Your Grace, have mercy! I'm a poor widow!
   I heard... they killed him! O dear God, my child!
   And then, the good Father here told me, no —
   He lives, and yet they beat him all the while.
   They beat him — torturers — they beat my son.

/she weeps/

*SENATOR.*
   Who? Where? Damn it, speak clearly, old woman!

*MRS. ROLLISON.*
   Who? My boy, my child! Lord, I'm a poor widow...
   Ah! Bear and raise a child, and watch him grow...
   My Jaś was teaching others now, you know —
   Ask anyone, how well he studied, taught —
   And every month, from his lean pay, he brought
   Me food and kept a roof over my head.
   I'm blind, he's my eyes. Without him, I'm dead!

*SENATOR.*
   Who said that he's been beaten? How'd you hear?
   Who talked?!

*MRS. ROLLISON.*
            Nobody. I've a mother's ear.
   And now I'm blind — so my entire soul
   Is in my hearing — Yesterday, I know
   They took him to the courthouse, and I heard —

*SENATOR.*
   They let her in?!

*MRS. ROLLISON.*
            Ah no — the soldiers turned
   Me from the door, and cast me from the yard.
   I sat there near the wall, and pressed ear hard
   Against the stones and listened there till dawn.
   You know, at night it's quiet in the town,
   And there I sat and listened, all night long
   And heard — like God above — the goings-on.
   I heard his voice — believe me, I'm not raving —
   I heard his voice, as if from out the grave!
   My hearing pierced those walls, deeper inside
   It plumbed the depths than can the sharpest eye.
   I heard them torture him!

SENATOR.
                    You're babbling nonsense!
    There are, Madame, many men there, perchance?

MRS. ROLLISON.
    You think that I can't recognise my child's
    Voice when he calls? Lord, even in the wilds
    The mother ewe picks out her bleating lamb
    Among so many sounds — among thousands
    In the same flock! And what a voice
    It was, your Grace — and that it was my boy's!
    Had you heard it, you wouldn't sleep for days!

SENATOR.
    He must be well then, if he so lustily brays.

MRS. ROLLISON /falls to her knees/.
    If you've got a human heart...

/The salon doors open—music is heard—a Young Woman rushes in, dressed for a ball/

YOUNG WOMAN.
                    Monsieur le Sénateur—
    Oh! je vous interromps, on va chanter le choeur
    De "Don Juan," et puis le concerto de Herz.

SENATOR.
    Herz! choeur! We were just talking about hearts.
    Vous venez à propos, vous belle comme un coeur.
    Moment sentimental! il pleut ici des coeurs.

/to Baikov/

    If *le grand-duc Michel* had heard that pun,
    *Ma foi*! — I'd soon be skipping up a rung!

/to the Young Woman/

*J'y suis — dans un moment.*

MRS. ROLLISON.
                        Your Grace, don't toss
  Us in despair—

/she grabs the hem of the Young Woman's dress/

YOUNG WOMAN.
                        *Faites-lui donc grâce!*

SENATOR.
  *Diable*! I don't know what she wants, in the least!

MRS. ROLLISON.
  To see my son.

SENATOR /with emphasis/.
                    The Tsar says no.

FR. PIOTR.
                        A priest!

MRS. ROLLISON.
  If not me, him then. My boy wants a priest.
  Maybe he's dying. If pity won't move
  Your heart, may fear of Hell the stronger prove!

SENATOR.
  *C'est drôle!* — and now they're crying on the streets
  Which of the prisoners would see a priest?
  Who told you that?

MRS. ROLLISON /pointing at Fr. Piotr/.
                    Who? Honest Father Piotr.
  For weeks now he's been begging of the porter
  Permission to enter my son's cell,
  But he won't let him.

SENATOR /glancing quickly at the Priest/.
                    So he's the one? Well
Then, Honest Father Piotr, this I'll grant.
For our anointed Tsar's a righteous man —
He won't forbid a priest access. In fact,
He sends his own to call the lost sheep back.
No one values religion more than he —

/sighs/

   Ah, youth without morals — what a tragedy...
   If they would only listen... So, farewell.

MRS. ROLLISON /to the Young Woman/.
   Ah, good young lady, by the five sweet blessures
   Of our Lord's Body, be my intercessor!
   My son's a young lad — he's been kept a year
   In a cold, dark dungeon, and his only cheer's
   Been bread and water.

YOUNG WOMAN
                *Est-il possible?*

SENATOR /embarrassed/.
   What's that you say? He's been there a full year?
   *Imaginez!* How is it I don't hear
   About such things?

/to Pelikan/

            You! Find me the people
   Responsible for this aberration,
   And we'll soon see who gets the slender rations!

/to Mrs. Rollison/

   *Soyez tranquille* — come back again at one.

*KMIT.*
>Don't cry — He didn't know about your son.
>Now that he knows, perhaps he'll set him free.

*MRS. ROLLISON /overjoyed/.*
>He didn't know? He wants to? There, you see!
>God bless him! I've always said he cannot be
>As cruel as people say — for God made him
>A man no different from the common ilk:
>He too was born of woman, drank mother's milk.
>They laughed at me — but who's right in the end?

/to the Senator/

>You didn't know! — and those rascals pretend
>To be your helpers — keeping you in the dark!
>You're hemmed in by such liars! You should talk
>To us more — we'd give you the naked truth,
>All that these brutes hide from your eyes —

*SENATOR /laughing/.*
>                    Forsooth!
>We'll talk of that some other time. Today I'm pressed —
>Now, if you'd be so kind, tell the Princess
>That all that's in my might, I'll do for her.

/politely/

>Adieu, Madame Kmit — I'll do my all. Adieu.

/to Fr. Piotr/

>You stick around. We must exchange a word.

/to the Young Woman/

>*J'y suis dans un moment.*

/Exeunt all save those who were present at the start of the scene/

SENATOR /after a pause, to the Servants/.
                      You rogues! You curs!
Is that the sort of order you clowns keep
There at the door? I'll skin you all like sheep,
You brutes! I'll teach you service!

/to one of the Servants/

                      After her!

/to Pelikan/

No, I'll entrust this business to you, sir.
As soon as she's left the Princess's side,
Take her a prison-pass, see her inside
As if she were to see her son. And then,
Clap her into a cell and lock her in
Alone, under four locks. You stupid curs!
*C'est trop!* — We'll soon shape up this troop of yours!

/grabs a chair/

SERVANT /trembling/.
  Your Excellency bade us let her in —

SENATOR /quickly, violently/.
  What's that?! You dare say such a thing?
  You learned to speak like that here in Poland!
  Well, I'll set you to rights! Take him in hand,
  And off to the Politzmeister with him:
  One hundred lashes and four weeks of thin
  Rations: bread and water.

PELIKAN.
                  Careful, your Grace!
We don't want word of Rollison's beating

  Bruited about, to become a common thing —
  So that it doesn't blow up in our face;
  We don't want our good works and best intents
  Perverted to the Tsar by malcontents.
  Before this matter should become... aerated,
  It's best to have the whole thing liquidated.

DOCTOR.
  I've held a like opinion for some time.
  Rollison's not been quite right in the mind,
  Beating against the window like a bird
  Caged; poor soul, the window's barred...

PELIKAN.
         ...and I've heard
  His lungs have become consumptive in there —
  What he seems to need, your Grace, is fresh air.
  Have them ungrate his window, if you please.
  His cell's on the third floor, where there's a breeze...

SENATOR.
  To send such witches in while I'm at tea!
  Thy don't give me a moment's rest —

DOCTOR.
         You see,
  That's just what I've had the honour to say:
  Forget these legal headaches. Let them be
  For a while and rest — *Ça mine la santé.*

SENATOR /calmly/.
  *Eh, mon docteur,* above all we must work,
  Then think of tummies — I can't afford to shirk.
  This stirs the bile, which *fait la digestion.*
  After supper, I can *voir donner la question,*
  When duty calls; — *en prenant son café,*
  Now, that's the time to watch *autos-da-fé.*

PELIKAN /pushing the Doctor out of the way/.
　Now, if that Rollison should... die today,
　What should we do, then?

SENATOR.
　　　　　　　　　Toss him in the clay.
　Even if you'd like to embalm him, we can pay.
　A propos balsam, Baikov, you'd do worse
　Than use some yourself — you look like a corpse,
　And you're about to marry, isn't that right?
　Did you all know he's got a fiancée?

/Doors open on the left, a Servant enters, the Senator points to the doors/

　In there. She's pretty. Dressed in red and white.
　Tsk, tsk, young bridegroom! *Avec un teint si délabré,*
　You should get married like Tiberius — *à Capré.*
　What strength of will it must've cost that *déesse*
　To rein her stubborn lips into a "yes!"

BAIKOV.
　Ha! Strength of will? *Parions*, that in a year
　I'll divorce her, toss her out on her rear
　And every twelvemonth thence I'll warm my hide
　Against the pink flesh of some new young bride.
　It takes much less persuasion than you think
　To lead these fillies to water, and have them drink.
　They like to brag about the administration,
　Sneer at their jealous kin, and meet the Tsar —
　Ask Father if he's witnessed hesitation
　When such a morsel stands at the altar!

SENATOR. *A propos* Father —

/to the Priest/
　　　　　　　　　Come here, my black cherub!
　Look — *quelle figure!* He has *l'air d'un poète* —

Have you ever seen *un regard aussi bête*?
Give him some rum — Drink! — that'll warm you up.

FR. PIOTR.
I don't drink.

SENATOR.
          Drink!

FR. PIOTR.
          I'm a friar.

SENATOR.
I'll tell you what you are: you're a damned liar!
To tell tall tales of other peoples' sons!
It's you that ran and squealed to Rollison?

FR. PIOTR.
It's me.

SENATOR /to Secretary/.
          Write that down in the protocol.

/to the Priest/

And how did you find out about it all?
Well? You won't talk in front of a witness?
He saw your pen, and now he won't confess.
Where is your cloister?

FR. PIOTR.
          I'm a Bernardin.

SENATOR.
But you've got kin at the Dominicans?
Because that's where you'll find Rollison's cell.
Speak up! How did you know? Who told you? Well?
Listen — I'll have you talk! I'll make you dance!!

>   Do you know, priest, what sort of penance
>   I can give sinners such as you? Now, monk,
>   In the name of the Tsar — unbind your tongue!

/to the Secretary/

>   Write it down that the priest spoke not a word.

/to the Priest/

>   Listen here, priest. If you do serve the Lord
>   You ought to somewhat know theology.
>   You know all earthly power comes from God —
>   Now, power questions you. Open your gob!
>   It's as if God were quizzing you, not me.

/the Priest remains silent/

>   You know that I can snip off stubborn heads?
>   Then we'll see if your prior can raise the dead!

FR. PIOTR.
>   Not all do homage, who are lying prone.
>   God sometimes sits a devil on the throne.

SENATOR.
>   And if I have you hung for that, today,
>   Tomorrow, you know what the Tsar will say?
>   "Eh, Senator — another little fling?"
>   But as you swung, poor bastard, still you'll swing!
>   Come close — I'll question you one final time.
>   Who was it told you about these monkeyshines?
>   Ha? Still you're silent — it wasn't God, eh?
>   An angel? A devil?

FR. PIOTR.
>                   That's what you say.

SENATOR /enflamed/.
"You?" "You?!" That's how you address me?

DOCTOR.
You peasant priest! Call him "your Excellency!"

/to Pelikan/

A country parson! Teach the boor to speak!
Then let him turn to you his other cheek.

/makes a slapping motion with his hand/

PELIKAN /slaps the Priest/.
You ass! You've insulted his Excellency!

FR. PIOTR.
Father! Forgive. He knows not what he does.

/to the Doctor/

The straw that broke the camel's back, that was.
Today you'll stand before the Lord.

SENATOR.
                    What's that?

BAIKOV.
He's clowning! Here, let's give him another
And let him prophesy some more.

/strikes him/

FR. PIOTR.
                    Ah, brother,
You follow his example! That you'll rue —
And follow still: your days are numbered, too.

SENATOR.
    Send for Botwinko! and detain the monk.
    I'll stick around myself to watch the fun.
    Now we shall see how long he'll play the dummy.
    He's in somebody's pay.

DOCTOR.
                    Just as I've humbly
    Suggested, your Grace: these conspiracies
    Are machinations of Prince Czartoryski's.

SENATOR /grabbing a chair/.
    What's that you say about the Prince, my friend?
    Impossible —

/to himself/

              Yet, who knows? Maybe ten
    Years of proceedings, before Prince Adam
    Gets out of jail if I have a go at him.

/to the Doctor/

    How do you know?

DOCTOR.
                    I've watched him for some years.

SENATOR.
    Yet you said nothing?

DOCTOR.
                  I did, but I fear
    Your Excellency didn't care to mind it —
    I told you that someone big was behind it.

SENATOR.
    Someone! Someone! But the Prince?

*DOCTOR.*
> The trail
> I've found of letters, complaints and confessions
> Will lead you to him, and him straight to jail.

*SENATOR.*
> The Prince's letters?

*DOCTOR.*
> Among the letters, some
> Speak of the Prince and what he has begun:
> Many professors are in on it too.
> Lelewel's the main link in a long chain.

*SENATOR /to himself/.*
> If only there were proof that it was true!
> If only there was somehow we could blame
> Him and... If only just the shadow of a doubt...
> I've sometimes heard such rumours tossed about:
> "It was the Prince who shoved aside the senator."
> Well, now's the time to even up the score —
> We'll see who shoves, and who gets shown the door!

*/to the Doctor/*

> C'mere! — *que je vous embrasse*! That's something else:
> I knew at once it wasn't just these whelps!
> I knew at once it was the Prince's work!

*DOCTOR /confidentially/.*
> Who ever could keep your Grace in the dark?

*SENATOR /seriously/.*
> Although I knew about this from the start,
> I swear to you — this hand upon this heart —
> That if these accusations are borne out,
> *Ecoutez*, and we do upend the lout,
> I'll have your pension by a full half raised,

Your rank will take a leap! You'll end your days
　　　A subprefect fat with sequestered lands,
　　　A nice star on your chest...Why, who can say?
　　　The Tsar pays well — you leave it in my hands.

DOCTOR.
　　　This matter cost me quite a lot, you know.
　　　I have my spies to pay, and my pay is low —
　　　But God save the Tsar! All for the commonweal!

SENATOR /taking him by the arm/.
　　*Mon cher*, take my secretary, break the seal
　　On these documents.

/to the Doctor/

　　　　　　　　We'll set all to rights
　　　Before the rooster greets the dawning light.

/to himself/

　　　Wait — I do all the work, sift through each story,
　　　And he's the one to grab — like that! — the glory?

/thinks/
/whispers to the Secretary/

　　　Arrest the doctor, with the evidence.

/to Baikov entering/

　　　This is a matter of great importance.
　　　I've just found out the doctor is a traitor.
　　　I squeezed some things from him just now, and later
　　　We'll glean some more still through interrogation.

/Pelikan, understanding the Senator's plans,
bows low to the Doctor before leading him out/

DOCTOR /to himself/.
> He pushed me off once, ho ho, Pelikan!
> Now when I push you down, rise again — if you can.

/to the Senator/

> I'll be right back.

SENATOR /carelessly/.
> I'll be leaving at eight.

DOCTOR /glancing at his watch/.
> What? Twelve o'clock? Is my watch running late?

SENATOR.
> It's five o'clock.

DOCTOR.
> Five? Blazes and thunder!
> The hour hand's on twelve, and from the same number
> The minute hand's not even moved a hair.

FR. PIOTR.
> And from that place it never more shall roll
> Around again. Brother, think of your soul.

DOCTOR.
> What's he babbling about?

PELIKAN.
> Just more hot air.
> More empty prophecies from the old fake.
> Look how his eyes are shining — like a snake!

FR. PIOTR.
> Brother, the Lord speaks through the oddest signs.

PELIKAN.
  That friar looks more guilty all the time.

/The doors on the left open; enter a mob of gaily dressed women, officials, guests—and with them, music/

GOVERNOR'S WIFE.
  May we?

SOVIETNIK'S WIFE.
    C'est indigne!

GOVERNOR'S WIFE.
          Ah, mon cher sénateur,
  We're waiting, sending for you...

SOVIETNIK'S WIFE.
          Vraiment, c'est un malheur.

ALL /together/.
  And now we've come ourselves.

SENATOR.
          Ah! So grand a ball?

LADY.
  Why, we could dance right here! It's a large hall.

/they rise and set themselves to dance/

SENATOR.
  Pardon, mille pardons j'étais très occupé!
  Que vois-je, un menuet ? parfaitement groupé!
  Cela m'a rappelé les jours de ma jeunesse!

PRINCESS.
  Ce n'est qu'une surprise.

SENATOR.
> Est-ce vous, ma déesse!
> Que j'aime cette danse, une surprise? Ah! dieux!

PRINCESS.
> Vous danserez, j'espère.

SENATOR.
> Certes, et de mon mieux.

/*The minuet from Don Juan is played — on the left stand the Russian Officials, male and female — to the right, some Young People — several Old Men dressed in the Polish style and several Young Women. — In the centre, the minuet. The Senator dances with Baikov's fiancée, Baikov dances with the Princess*/.

### The ball
### Choral scene
### From the right side

LADY.
> Look how the old toad twirls and sweats.
> I hope he breaks his bloody neck.

/to the Senator/

> How lively and how light you dance!
> *Il crévera dans l'instant.*

YOUNG MAN.
> Look how he fawns on them — so gay!
> Last night he murdered, and today
> He dances, dandles palms, and winks,
> Jumping about like a caged lynx.

LADY.
> Just yesterday he thought it good
> To spill — drop by drop — blameless blood,

Today he will his claws retract
And snuggle up like a tame cat.

### *From the left side*

KOLLESKIJ REGESTRATOR.
    The Senator has joined the dance,
    See? Come on, Sovietnik, let's go!

SOVIETNIK.
    But don't you think it would be gauche
    Should I, with such as you be, prance?

REGESTRATOR.
    We'll find she-partners for the ball!

SOVIETNIK.
    That wasn't what I meant at all.
    I'd rather dance all by myself
    Than next to you. Now, go to Hell.

REGESTRATOR.
    What's that for?!

SOVIETNIK.
            I'm Sovietnik, see?

REGESTRATOR.
    And I am a Staff Officer's Son!

SOVIETNIK.
    Right! And I would never dance with one
    Of such an abysmal degree.

/to the Colonel/

    The Senator has joined the dance.
    See? Come on, Colonel, let's go!

COLONEL /pointing at Regestrator/.
   What was that waif who pestered you so?

SOVIETNIK.
   Kolleskij Regestrator! Kin
   To some officer.

COLONEL.
               Jacobins!
   It almost seems like we're in France!

LADY /to Senator/.
   How lively and how light you dance!

SOVIETNIK /angrily/.
   They've mixed up the official ranks!

LADY.
   *Il crévera dans l'instant!*

### Left side (chorus)

LAIDES.
   *Aha! Quelle grace! et quelle beauté!*

GENTLEMEN.
   What splendour! Never seen the like!

### Right side (chorus)

GENTLEMEN.
   I've never seen such rogues, I say!
   Would that a thunderbolt would strike!

SENATOR /dancing, to the Governor's Wife/.
   I'd like to get to know, Madame,
   The subprefect. It seems he has

A daughter and a lovely wife,
But he's so jealous!

GOVERNOR /racing to the Senator's side/.
                    A simple man
Your Grace — leave it all in our hands.

/approaches the Subprefect/

Good evening, Sir. And where's your wife?

SUBPREFECT.
    Sitting at home.

GOVERNOR.
              And — your daughters?

SUBPREFECT.
    I've only one.

GOVERNOR.
              You should have brought her.

SUBPREFECT.
    No!

GOVERNOR'S WIFE.
        Where's your wife and daughter?

SUBPREFECT.
    Home.

GOVERNOR.
    Does your wife know the Senator?

SUBPREFECT.
    My wife is for myself alone.

*GOVERNOR'S WIFE.*
>I stopped by your house yesterday,
>To take your daughter out, to savour
>A bit of the high life at court.

*SUBPREFECT.*
>I know how to value the favour,
>And yet at home it's best she stay.

*GOVERNOR.*
>But look, old chap: the Senator
>Needs girls to pair the minuet.

*SUBPREFECT.*
>It hasn't gotten that bad yet
>That I can't find a pair for her
>When the time comes.

*GOVERNOR'S WIFE.*
>                    It's said she's gay,
>And that at dances she's divine.
>The Senator oft entertains —

*SUBPREFECT.*
>More than one girl at the same time.

### *Left side (chorus)*

The music! Dancing! Wine! The food!
Everything's splendid here, in sum!

### *Right side (chorus)*

At breakfast, these bastards drink blood,
And after dinner, rum.

SOVIETNIK /points at Senator/.
>  He flays them with his toes, it's true —
>  But such a flaying's good for you.

SUBPREFECT.
>  Our boys rot behind prison walls
>  And they make us come dance at balls.

RUSSIAN OFFICER /to Bestuzhev/.
>  It's no wonder they hate us so:
>  For full one hundred years, they've seen
>  From Moscow into Poland flow
>  Such a sewage-laden stream.

STUDENT /to Officer/.
>  Look! Look at Baikov! How he romps!
>  What a sad figure does he cut —
>  Like toad through cesspool, so he jumps;
>  Look how he bellies out his gut!
>  Baring his fangs — my ears! Horror!
>  He's not going to try a song?
>  Ah! Listen to the rascal roar!

/Baikov sings/

STUDENT /to Baikov/.
>  Mon Général, quelle chanson!

BAIKOV /sings Béranger's song/.
>  *Quel honneur, quel bonheur!*
>  *Ah, monsieur le sénateur!*
>  *Je suis votre humble serviteur, etc.*

STUDENT.
>  Général, ce sont vos paroles ?

BAIKOV.
>  Oui.

STUDENT.
   *Je vous en fais compliment.*

ONE OF THE OFFICERS /laughing/.
   *Ces complets son vraiment fort drôles,*
   *Quel ton satirique et plaisant!*

YOUNG MAN.
   *Pour votre muse sans rivale*
   *Je vous ferais académicien.*

BAIKOV /whispers, pointing at the Princess/.
   *Cornard, le sénateur sera!*

SENATOR /whispers, pointing at Baikov's fiancée/.
   *Va, va, je te coifferai bien.*

MAIDEN /dancing, to her mother/.
   O God, he's ugly! And so old!

MOTHER /from the right side/.
   If that's how you feel, cut him cold.

SOVIETNIK'S WIFE /from the right side/.
   My little daughter's in the pink!

SUBPREFECT.
   How all these rogues of rum do stink!

SECOND SOVIETNIK'S WIFE /to her daughter, standing beside her/.
   My dear Zosieńku, lift your eyes:
   Maybe the Senator will waltz up.

SUBPREFECT.
   My wife! My daughter! If he tries,
   I'll stick this knife in his fat gut!

*/He lays his hand on his ornamental scimitar/*

### Left side (chorus)

*Aha! Quelle grace! et quelle beauté!*
What splendour! Never seen the like!

Right side (chorus).
I've never seen such rogues, I say!
Would that a thunderbolt would strike!

### From the right side, among the young men.

JUSTYN POL /to Bestuzhev, pointing at the Senator/.
    I'd like to break his bloody nose,
    Or stab his fat gut with my knife.

BESTUZHEV.
    And so you'd take one rascal's life.
    But all the others? What of those?
    They'll group together in petition
    To close your universities
    As Jacobin nests of sedition,
    And thus eat up your youth with ease.

JUSTYN POL.
    Perhaps, but with his dying throes
    He'd pay for all the blood he's shed.

BESTUZHEV.
    The Tsar's kennels are all well stocked.
    What cares he if one mutt lies dead?

POL.
    How my fist itches! Let me go!

BESTUZHEV.
    And let the wolf eat the whole flock?

*POL.*
   One little fillip in the face.

*BESTUZHEV.*
   No!
   It's not the time, it's not the place.

*POL.*
   Ah, rogues and rascals! Excrement!

*BESTUZHEV.*
   Come now, outside. You're much too hot.

*POL /moving towards the doors/.*
   Will they never see punishment?
   Will no one ever avenge us?

*FR. PIOTR.*
                              — God!

*/Suddenly, the mood changes; we hear the Commendatore's aria/*

*DANCERS.*
   What's with the music?

*GUESTS.*
                         Ugh — such gloom!

*SOMEONE /by the window/.*
   Look how dark it's got in the room.
   Look! Thunderclouds — there'll be a storm.

*/Closes the window — we hear thunder afar off/*

*SENATOR.*
   Why don't they play?

MUSIC DIRECTOR.
              The score's mixed up.

SENATOR.
  What? Idiots! Get my gendarmes!

DIRECTOR.
  We were to perform different cuts
  From Mozart's operas, different tunes...
  And ...

SENATOR.
          Well? *Arrangez donc. Mesdames...*

MRS. ROLLISON /behind the door, in a horrid voice/.
  Stop! Let me in! Let go my hand!

SECRETARY.
  The old blind woman!

SERVANT /terrified/.
                See her hop
  About the stairs — stop her now! Stop!

OTHER SERVANTS.
  How? She has the strength of a giant!

MRS. ROLLISON.
  Vampire! Bloodsucker! Where's the tyrant?

ONE OF THE SERVANTS /attempting to restrain her — she knocks one of them down/.
  Look how she felled him! She must be possessed!

/They run off/

MRS. ROLLISON.
>   Where are you?! I'll knock the brains out of your head
>   Just like you did to my son! My son's dead!
>   Tossed though a window! Have you no conscience?
>   My son was out of a high window thrown,
>   And bashed to death upon the cobblestones.
>   Hey, you bloodsucker! Fattened on a child's
>   Gore! Where are you, you old crocodile?
>   Lapping the blood of so many innocents!
>   I'll tear you into pieces, that I will,
>   Who shoved my dear son off a windowsill!
>   My only son! My one support! My only eyes—
>   This devil lives, and God looks on? And Christ?

FR. PIOTR.
>   Do not blaspheme! Your son lives, though gravely hurt.

MRS. ROLLISON.
>   What? My son lives? He lives? Who spoke those words?
>   Father, can it be true? — I heard them yell
>   "He's fallen!" And ran to where they said he fell,
>   But they'd already borne the corpse away:
>   The body of my son! If I but could
>   See, but I'm blind! And yet, I smelt his blood,
>   God is my witness, the blood of my son.
>   And here I smell it too, splashed on someone —
>   Still dripping from the hangman's hands!

/She moves straight toward the Senator, who tries to skip away from her — Mrs. Rollison faints to the ground — Fr. Piotr and the Subprefect go over to her—a loud thunderbolt is heard/.

ALL /terrified/.
>   The Word became flesh!

SOMEONE.
>                    That struck here.

FR. PIOTR.
                              No.

ANOTHER /looking through the window/.
                                        See?
   Close by — it struck the university.

SENATOR /coming up to the window/.
   The doctor's window!

ONE OF THE ONLOOKERS.
   Hear how the women scream!

SOMEONE ON THE STREET /laughs/.
   Ha! The devil took him!

/Enter Pelikan, confused/

SENATOR.
                  Our doctor?!

PELIKAN.
                                 It seems...
   Dead from a lightning bolt... a phenomenon
   Worthy to be carved up by the physics dons —
   The house ringed fully round by ten lightning rods,
   And yet it struck him dead. An act of...
   It struck him in the farthest room, his study.
   Touched nothing else but him, and harmed nobody —
   Melted some silver rubles, near the Doctor's
   Head, in a closet... they were the conductor...

SUBPREFECT.
   Russian rubles are dangerous, I see.

SENATOR /to the Ladies/.
   *Quoi? Mesdames! Dancez!* One, two, three!

/notices those helping Mrs. Rollison/

>Take her away, take her — help the poor dear —
>Take her away!

FR. PIOTR.
>    To her son?

SENATOR.
>            Anywhere
>You like!

FR. PIOTR.
>    Her son's not dead, although he fell—
>Permit me to see him.

SENATOR.
>            Go! Go to Hell!

/to himself/

>The doctor dead, *ah! Ah! C'est inconcevable*!
>The priest foretold it him — *ah ! C'est diable!*

/To the guests/

>Why are you so upset? You know it's spring —
>And spring means clouds, clouds storms, and storms lightning!
>That's not odd. That's the most natural thing —

SOVIETNIK'S WIFE /to her husband/.
>Say what you want, yet fear is always fear.
>I don't want to be under the same roof
>With you all — didn't I say "keep aloof"
>From the interrogation of those kids?
>I kept my mouth shut when you beat the Yids
>(Though they were innocent), now what d'you think
>Of the Doctor and that bolt of lightning?

SOVIETNIK.
   I think you're stupid.

SOVIETNIK'S WIFE.
                    Well, I'm out of here!

/Another peal of thunder — everyone runs for cover, first left, then right. There remain the Senator, Pelikan and Fr. Piotr/.

SENATOR /watching his guests leave/.
   That goddamned windbag never gave me rest,
   And still, though dead, he drives away my guests!

/to Pelikan/

   *Voyez* how that priest stares — *voyez quel oeil hagard;*
   It's a strange coincidence, *un singulier hasard.*
   Tell me then, Father — do you know such spells
   To move the clouds and blast a man to hell?

/The Priest remains silent/

   To speak the truth, the doctor was at fault.
   Too eager. Too "above and beyond the call."
   *On aurait fort à dire* — a warning of God's wrath:
   "See that you keep to the straight and narrow path!"
   Well what, priest? Silent? How he hangs the nose...
   But I'll let him go — *il dirait bien des choses!...*

/falls into thought/

PELIKAN.
   Ha, ha! But if it's God's wrath, you'll agree
   That bolt was better aimed at you and me!

FR. PIOTR.
   Since you move the matter of the culpable
   I'll tell you two —

SENATOR /with interest/.
>                         Prophecies?!

FR. PIOTR.
>                                   Parables.
> One summer's day, oppressed by blinding heat,
> A group of travellers left the dusty street
> To rest beneath the shade of an old wall.
> Among them was a bandit. Shortly, all
> Had fallen asleep. Now, while the bandit snored,
> There came to him an angel of the Lord
> Who warned him: "Rise! The wall's about to crumble!"
> No sooner did he stand, but the earth rumbled,
> The wall fell, and killed them all there on the spot.
> The bandit folded hands, gave thanks to God
> For sparing him; then spake the angel grave:
> "God showed thee no mercy, that thou art saved;
> Thy sins are foul in the Almighty's eye —
> A much more shameful death art thou to die."
> The other goes like this: Once, long ago,
> A Roman general did overthrow
> In battle a powerful foreign lord.
> He had his legionnaires put to the sword
> All of the officers and troops and slaves;
> Only the king's life did he deign to save
> From the slaughter, along with the prefects
> And colonels. The king laughed: "See — he respects,
> Though beaten in battle, our untarnished ranks —
> We'll have to send the general our thanks."
> The stupid man! Their guard overheard,
> While he was serving them, these foolish words
> And said, "Although indeed he's spared your life
> He's only done so to drag you in chains
> Behind his chariot when he regains
> Rome. He's already got the Senate's vote
> To lead a triumph. So, I wouldn't gloat:
> The triumph ended, all the people shown
> Just what a king his might has overthrown,

He'll hand you over, too, unto the knife."
The king roared, "Slave!
Thou knowest what thy lord's thinking?
Humph!" And with that he turned back to his drinking...

SENATOR /bored/.
    *Il bat la compagne*... Father, I won't delay you
    Longer — but should I see you again, I'll flay you
    So, that even Rollison's sharp-nosed old mother
    Won't be able to tell one pulp from the other.

/The Senator moves toward his rooms with Pelikan. Fr. Piotr moves toward the door and there meets Konrad, being led to interrogation by two Soldiers. Seeing the Priest, he stops and looks at him closely./

KONRAD.
    That's odd — I've never seen that priest before.
    And yet, I seem to know him. I'm as sure
    As if he were my brother. Once, I dreamed...
    Yes — now I do remember where I've seen
    That very face, those very eyes of his...
    His was the hand that plucked me from the abyss.

/to the Priest/

    Father, though we don't know each other well
    — At least you don't know me — please, deign accept
    The thanks of one who in his conscience knows
    The grace poured out on him while his reason slept.
    Friends are always well met, even such as those
    Seen in dreams only, when so many foes
    Surround us. Take this ring, Father, and sell it —
    Give half to the poor, half for the suffering souls
    In Purgatory. Well I know their dole,
    If Purgatory be imprisonment —
    And who knows if I'll ever hear Mass again.

FR. PIOTR.
>    You will, and for the offering bestowed
>    Take this warning: a long and unknown road
>    Awaits you; you'll find yourself hemmed about
>    By a mob of the great, the rich, the proud...
>    Seek out a man who's more expert than me.
>    He'll greet you first in the Lord's Name. You'll know
>    Him by that. Listen to him ...

KONRAD /*looking at him closely*/.
>                     Can it be... ?!
>    Wait... for God's sake!

FR. PIOTR.
>                Can't. Farewell. I must go.

KONRAD.
>    One word!

SOLDIER.
>        That's enough! Each one his own road!

## SCENE IX
## FOREFATHERS' EVE
*/A chapel in the distance—a cemetery/.*

GUŚLARZ.
   Now all the crowd is filing in
   To church, and Dziady will begin.
   The night is deep, it's time to go.

WOMAN.
   I'll stay here, guślarz, even so,
   Here in this darkling cemetery —
   There's only one soul I would see:
   The one that, long ago, appeared
   Among the spirits, in the year
   That I was married — suddenly —
   Pale and bloody, silently
   Measuring me with a wild eye.

GUŚLARZ.
   It's possible he hadn't died —
   That's why he wouldn't answer me,
   Despite my strongest conjuring.
   For it is possible, you know,
   To conjure, on Forefathers' Eve,
   The spirits of the living, too.
   The dust remains at cards, in fight,
   Or at the table; all the same,
   The living spirit thence takes flight
   When it is conjured by its name,
   Appearing like a shadow thin.
   As long as its time hasn't come
   Though, it can't speak — it stands there, dumb.

WOMAN.
   That breast-wound, though — what did it mean?

*GUŚLARZ.*
>That wound was deep — it touched his soul.

*WOMAN.*
>I'll lose my way here, all alone.

*GUŚLARZ.*
>I can remain behind as well
>With you here. They can work the spells
>Without me. There's another old
>Guślarz among them. Hear the hymn?
>They've gathered all, and now begins
>The conjuring with the incense
>And with the wreath, to call the souls
>That are buffeted in the air.
>Look — see those thousand sparkles there —
>That look like thickly falling stars?
>Those fiery chains of brightness are
>The souls of airy spirits. Come!
>See how they shine above the dome
>Of the church, under the black sky —
>Like flocks of pigeons, when they fly
>Above a fire that's burning
>In a city's midst — their white wings
>Reflect the flames' vermilion glow
>Like flights of stars that errant go.

*WOMAN.*
>His spirit won't be among theirs!

*GUŚLARZ.*
>Now, see the flash that bursts forth there
>From out the chapel. By the fire
>They conjure those spirits most dire —
>Condemned souls. Out of graveyard pile
>And from the deep forgotten wilds
>They lure the bodies of the damned.
>The sprites will be passing by here.

Recall his figure, if you can —
You'll recognise him, if the drear
Troop is his company. Come here —
Hide with me in this hollow oak.
This tree, long ago, served to cloak
Old fortune tellers from the eyes
Of angry men. See the turf rise!
The graves are gaping — from the earth
The eerie blue flames now burst forth:
Pine-boards are burst, and cerements
Split wide, their ghastly inhabitants
Crawl forth — with pale heads and thin arms.
Instead of eyes, an ember burns
In both dry sockets — close your eyes
And hide within the tree — the glance
Of such damned spirits can entrance
From far off — but cannot harm me,
A guślarz... Ha!

WOMAN.
                    What do you see?

GUŚLARZ.
  That's a fresh corpse. His clothes are free
As yet from grave-mould. Such a mist
Of sulphur smokes from him like steam —
His forehead is as black as coal.
No eyes — in his eye-pits there gleam
Two white hot, molten coins of gold,
And at the centre of each, flits
A devil turning somersaults,
A-crackle like a lightning-bolt.
He's running this way, gnashing teeth,
And milling with his hands as if
Each were a sieve, and he would sift
Something — can you hear him screech?

*SPECTRE.*
>Where's the church?
>— Where's the church where the people praise God?
>Where's the church? Won't you show me, man?
>See these ducats here in my skull, ah! Are they hot!
>Molten silver is searing my hands.
>Pour some out, pour some out for the orphaned and old
>For the imprisoned and widowéd;
>Pour it out, scrape it off me, this silver and gold!
>Dig the ducats out of my head!
>You don't want to? Ha! On I must pour, on must roast
>Till that ghoul who ripped children apart
>Should at last give up his plumbless, gluttonous soul
>And I pour the ore straight in his heart.
>And then, for all time thence, I swear: as God lives
>Through his eyes and his ears, through each rift
>I will pour the hot ore, using him as a sieve,
>Pour it into him, out of him, sift!
>One day I'll sift, and tilt, and turn,
>But long I wait, and how I burn!

*/he runs off/*

*GUŚLARZ.*
>Ha!

*WOMAN.*
>What do you see?

*GUŚLARZ.*
>>Sh! So near—
>Another sprite comes running here,
>And what a hideous corpse is he!
>Freshly buried, pale and fat,
>Around his neck, a fresh cravat —
>Dressed for a wedding, so it seems.
>The worm's hardly touched this one at all —
>Only half-gnawed is each eyeball.

He's sprung away from chapel-side —
The devil leads him far astray
And will not let him get inside:
Like a girl on her wedding day,
The devil winks, and blows a kiss
At him, and so, the dazzled sprite
Lurches after the hellish miss
Like newlywed on wedding night.
With flailing arms does he make haste,
And stumbles into her embrace,
But just as he gets hold of her,
The ground gapes open at his feet
And mastiffs tear him from beneath,
Ah! Limb from limb! And then, each cur
Runs off with the disgusting meat.
The dogs are gone—now, a new wonder!
The corpse that had been torn asunder
And strewn about the churchyard wide
Now trembles, flops, and comes alive—
Each sundered piece of ghoulish meat
Drawing unto a ghastly heap.
The head hops hither like a frog
Propelled by the sulphurous fog
That blasts from out the nose; the chest
Crawls up more slowly to join the rest,
Just like a tortoise drags its shell.
The ripped-off fingers now, as well,
Like blindworms slither through the grass.
The palm there inchworms close; at last,
The corpse again stands whole, erect.
Again the maiden tilts her neck
Coquettishly, again the chase,
Again the horrible embrace,
Again the ground gapes, and the curs
Rip him apart, as at the first.
Ah God, I hope I never will
See that again!

*WOMAN.*
                You're scared?

*GUŚLARZ.*
                        I'm ill!
  Turtles and toads and graveyard worms —
  So many vermin one corpse churn!

*WOMAN.*
  He won't be among such as those!

*GUŚLARZ.*
  Listen! Now the third rooster crows.
  Forefathers' Eve is almost done —
  Our nation's ancient lays are sung
  And everyone moves off toward home.

*WOMAN.*
  It's over, and he didn't come!

*GUŚLARZ.*
  If his soul's in his body still,
  Pronounce his name but one more time,
  And I shall whisper one more spell
  On magic herb, in secret rhyme —
  His soul, slipped from his body's chains
  Will stand before your eyes again.

*WOMAN.*
  I said his name —

*GUŚLARZ.*
                He didn't hear it.
  I said the spell.

*WOMAN.*
              He's a dead spirit!

*GUŚLARZ.*
>Ah, woman! There might be another
>Cause — your lover must have changed
>Either the faith of his fathers,
>Or perhaps his given name.
>Look — the dawn. At this late hour
>All of our charms have lost their power.
>It seems your lover will not come.

*/They step out of the tree/*

>What's that?! There, on the horizon,
>From the west, from Giedymin's court,
>Among the thick and dusty clouds
>Kicked up by horse's hooves, a crowd
>Of armoured wagons hastens north
>As fast as straining steeds can run.
>Look there! At the head —

*WOMAN.*
>                    Ah! He's come!

*GUŚLARZ.*
>He sits alone, all dressed in black —
>He's racing towards us... now he's nigh!

*WOMAN.*
>He's passed — he took one brief look back,
>Ah — only once — but ah! that eye!

*GUŚLARZ.*
>Such gore was dripping from his chest,
>So many wounds are in that breast:
>His suffering is beyond words —
>He's wounded with a thousand swords,
>And each has pierced him to the soul.
>Perhaps his death will make him whole.

*WOMAN.*
>Who thrust him through with all those swords?

*GUŚLARZ.*
>Our nation's foreign overlords.

*WOMAN.*
>There was one wound between his eyes,
>One only, and of no great size.
>I thought it but a smudge at first.

*GUŚLARZ.*
>And that's the wound that pains him worst.
>I saw it, and its depths did sound:
>It is a self-inflicted wound,
>And even death won't ease its pain.

*WOMAN.*
>Ah! Make him whole, great God, again!

*END*

# FOREFATHERS' EVE

## PASSAGES

### *The Road to Russia*

Over the snow, towards ever wilder lands
The coach flies, like the wind over desert sands.
My eyes are like two falcons that were chased
Seaward by stormwinds; now hopelessly they soar
Above the foreign expanse — they seek a shore
Not there — they see only the barren waste,
With nowhere to rest; exhausted they fly
And know, they'll stoop, not to alight, but die.

Nor town, nor hillock here to cheer the heart;
No monument of nature or of art.
The land is flat, empty, unpopulated,
As if but yesterday it were created.
And yet, at times a mammoth is unearthed;
Washed here, perhaps, on the very Flood's waves
To bear witness to awed Muscovite knaves
That this land's aged with primordial birth,
And back before the Ark was even made,
These lands with Asia were involved in trade.
And after all, one might well read in book
Stolen, or borrowed forcefully from the West
That from this very land, so desolate
More than one nation its genesis took.
But as the flood receded from these plains,
Leaving no trace of those colossal rains,
So did those swarms abandon their demesne,
Leaving no trace of ever having been.
But far away, a lonely Alpine gorge

Bears witness to the passing of those hordes,
And further yet, on Roman monuments
One reads the record of their violence.

An open region, white and desolate,
A sheaf on which no pen has ever writ.
Is God's hand to illume the virgin scroll?
His characters — the honest human soul?
Inscribing here truth, faith, and holy peace;
That loving-kindness shall be mankind's law,
The trophies of the world: self-sacrifice?
Or will it be that God's most ancient foe
Shall come with sword, not pen, the page to stain,
Declaring man forever to be chained,
The trophies of the world: from quarter-draw?

Over the empty spaces white, the gale
Shrieks, lifting sheets of ice to hurl —
A sea of snow, unchanging in its pale,
Lifeless hue, swelling beneath the bitter swirl
Of wind, to freeze anew, as if petrified,
And always bleak, colossal, always white.
Sometimes a hurricane, gigantic, sheer
Sweeps down directly from the frigid pole,
With nothing to retard its fierce career
To the Black Sea, engulfing all in snow;
Sometimes it swallows the lone, straggling stage
Like the simoom, when Libyan sandstorms rage.
Though here and there, along the blinding miles
Of white, one sees a splash of black… A wall? A spur
Of rock? that seems the landfall of an isle —
It's just a lonely pine, or arctic fir.

But here and there, one sees a rough-cut fall
Of timber leant-to in haphazard dome,
A strange mass, which recalls a roof and walls,
With folk inside. This thing they call a "home."
And then, further on, thousands of these ricks

Are grouped together on the arctic plains
Like shakos fallen, from their smokestack strains
A wisp of steam against the cutting air;
A gleam of light anaemic here and there
Wanes in a window; hovels bunched in pairs,
With thin-planked fences circling them around,
And such a huddled mess they call a "town."

I've met the people: shoulders broad, a girth
Of chest expansive, napes sinewy, thick —
Just like the beasts and trees of Northern birth;
They're fresh and hale and strong; they're never sick,
And yet their faces are like their native lands:
An empty, open, and a wild expanse.
Their hearts are like deep buried volcanoes,
The fires of which have not leapt to their faces,
Nor in their lips and tongue the ardour glows,
Nor in their brows are found the cold, dark traces
Of lava-furrows, as in the countenance
Of Eastern man, or Western, with their scope
Of long historical experience,
Recording deeds and shocks, sorrow and hope,
So that they seem their nation's monuments.
The eyes of this tribe are just like their towns:
Widespread and clean; never a sudden rout
Of feeling in the soul forces its way out
Of startled pupil; mourning never drowns
Them long in musing, cogitation, doubt;
Seen from afar, they're splendid, full of grace,
But there inside — one finds but desert wastes.
Their bodies, weft of sturdy fabric, firm,
Are winter quarters for their soul: a worm,
That must mature in that cocoon's soft night
Before it sprout wings for the springtime flight.
And when the sun of liberty will arise,
What sort of wings will attempt the azure skies?
A splendid butterfly, a pied delight?
Or just a dirty moth, that shuns the light?

Straight through the desert wastes the highways shoot.
They grew there from no well-trod merchant paths,
Nor scuffed out by the plodding caravan's foot.
The finger of the Tsar decreed these swaths,
And if a Polish town lay in their way,
Or Polish castle challenged its ruled grade,
Their walls were broken down without delay
And with their rubble were the highways paved.
These highways can't be seen in winter snow,
But temperate seasons readily bring them forth.
Straight and eternal, speed they to the North,
Splitting the woods, as river torrents flow.

And who is it that travels them? Here gallop
A cavalry, with rime about their flanks,
And with caisson and cannon, endless ranks
Of infantry, who with monotonous wallop
Tramp obedient to the Tsar's *ukase*.
These march due west, to battle with the north,
While southward, to confront Caucasians
March others, although why, and whither sent forth
None of them know (but they know not to ask).
Here march the Mongols, puffy-cheeked, slant eyed;
There the blond peasant, far from his hearthside
In Lithuania, heartsore, plods to his task
Distasteful. With English rifles, Tartar bows,
And frozen sinew-strings, the Kalmuk goes.

Their officers? — Here in this coach, a Kraut
Hums something by Schiller (a sentimental air)
And thumps a straggling soldier's back; while there:
A Frenchman buzzes through his Gallic snout
A liberal ditty; the errant *philosophe*,
He's scheming ways to batten his career,
Now whispering into quartermaster's ear
To gypsy down the rations, skimming off
The half not spent on soldier's food — to line
Their pockets, half by half — So half this kine

Will starve? *There's more where they came from!* he scoffs,
And if they're clever, and mum, the grateful Tsar
Will reward their thrift, with rises, and a star...

And now a line of wagons thunders near;
The stream of soldiers, caissons and the sick
Are pushed off to the side; the wild career
Prompts even generals their steeds to prick
Aside, out of the way, and down the ranks
Subaltern thwacks subaltern 'cross the shanks.
Make room for the onrushing train! The slow
To move will find himself trampled below
The mangling hooves and wheels. Whence do they fly?
Who are they? Each man shifts aside his eye —
All curious — but none bold enough to ask —
The Tsar's police, about their Tsarist task,
In haste toward the capital they flash
On the Tsar's orders — Whom did he bid them catch?
"Perhaps from foreign parts they're hasting?
Perhaps the Prussian, French, or Saxon King's
Incurred the Tsar's displeasure?" (So he thinks,
The general) — "And off now to the clink
He goes! Or maybe even — saints above! —
It is none other than old Yermolov?
Who knows? That prisoner though, there in the straw,
What a flaming glance did his eye cast abroad!
That's some great soul — and following him, a train,
A regal crowd of his royal retainers,
Must be! Just look at their eyes! All so bold!
And yet — are they more than eighteen years old?
I thought they must be chamberlains at least,
Or generals, who at the Tsar's own feast
Would fill the very seats of honour — Did
I see correctly? Every one, a kid!
Where are they taking them? What does this mean?
They must be children of some suspect king..."
Thus did the brass trade gossip, in a hush,
While on the penal train flew, in a rush.

### Suburbs of the Capital

From afar, it's clear: this is the capital.
On both sides of the grand, proud boulevard
Stand rows of palaces. A kind of chapel
With dome and cross is here, and there stand guard
— Like hay ricks — statues wrapped in straw and snow;
And there, Corinthian columns in a row:
The Summer Palace, flat roofed, Italian,
Next to some Chinese kiosks, and there: Japan,
While further: aught of classic Catherine's doing —
Some freshly-aped Neoclassical ruin.
All orders present, buildings of all shapes,
Like beasts brought here from all the world's wild ranges;
Giraffes and bison, crocodiles and apes,
Exhibited in individual cages.
And — What is that? — Some child of their own nature,
One freak example of native architecture...
Such striking displays of the builder's skill!
So many stones wading the muddy swill!

In Rome, to build a theatre for Caesar,
Treasures were poured out in a golden flood.
These castles — of the lackeys of the Tsar —
Arose from a torrent of our tears and blood.
To fund these obelisks and orangeries,
They had to feign — how many conspiracies?
How many innocents had to be damned
To death, or exile, to confiscate our lands?
The blood of Litwa, the tears of the Ukraine,
The gold of Poland were all spent to buy
All that a Paris or London might contain,
All that the world of fashion might codify;
And magnums of champagne uncorked, in jets
Washed clean the parquet for the minuets.

But now it's empty. The summer being spent,
The courtly flies, buzzing after the scent

Of the Tsar's carcass, fly to him in town
Where he shall winter. Nothing spins around
The parquet but the winds. For where the Tsar
Is, there the vultures gather. — And the car
Speeds there as well. It's snowing, freezing cold;
The clock shows midday's already grown old;
The sun is now descending in the west;
The vault of heaven looms empty and vast;
No cloud, all's clear and quiet, colourless,
A grand transparency, that pale sky —
Just like a frozen voyager's dead eye.

The capital's before us. Up on high,
Above the city, strange structures seem to rise
Like castles in the clouds: pillars and stalls,
Arcades and buttresses, battlements and walls...
Like to the hanging gardens of Babylon:
Two hundred thousand chimneys smoking on
As many roofs — Straight up in columns flies
The smoke, Carrara white cozens the eyes
And here, like rubies, glow the leaping sparks.
Tree seems to bow to tree in swaying parks,
Forming arcades, curving, receding arcs;
False walls and rooftops shimmer in fairy shows
Just like that fabled city that arose
Quite suddenly, from out the sea's clear pane,
Or that one, glimpsed through sandy hurricane
In the Sahara — tempting despairing eyes,
Always so close, yet when drawn near — it flies.

The shackles punched off, open creak the gates,
Manhandled, numbered — in go the inmates.

### *Petersburg*

In the old days, of Rome, and ancient Greece,
The people grouped their dwellings round the fanes

Of gods, the springs of nymphs, or sacred trees,
Or in high mountains, fleeing foe-crossed plains.
In this way Rome was built, Sparta, and Athens.
In Gothic times, the shade of baron's keep
Was, in emergencies, a sure defence:
Above the peasants' huts loomed bastions steep.
Thus riverside towns grew into grand cities;
All by the hand of god or hero made —
Or sometimes, by necessities of trade,
Culture developed through slow centuries.

How did this Russian capital begin?
What was it drew these hordes of Eastern Slavs
To found this last of their icy enclaves
Here, torn from ocean's wave and northern Finn?
The earth here bears nor fruit nor wholesome grain,
The winds bring only snow and hailstorms shrill;
The sky too hot now, or too cold again —
Harsh and capricious, like a despot's will!
No peasant coveted this excrement
Dredged from the sea — it was the Tsar's command
That bade a city (not theirs, his) to stand
To his all-mighty whim a monument.

On shifting sands and marshes thick with mud
He bade them sink one hundred thousand piles,
Tread firm the muck with peasant bone and blood;
And thus, the ground made firm, an army toils
(Yoked, Moscow-style, to barrow, cart and ship)
Bearing great loads of wood and building stone
From distant lands, and the sea's bosom ripped;
Whole ages enslaved to build the Tsar's new home.

Now it is Paris that the Tsar recalls,
And so they raise some mock Parisian walls.
Once, on his journeys, he saw Amsterdam,
And so he floods the town again, and dam
And dyke are piled to regulate the flow.

In Rome, he hears, are palaces. And so
He has them built here too. Does Venice rest
In her lagoon, like some alluring siren
Lolling in waters lapping at her breast?
No sooner does his sceptre dredge the mire in
Canals and rios crisscrossed, far and near,
Replete with bridge, and boat, and gondolier.
So has he Venice, Paris, London made
Anew; there lacks but beauty, glory, trade.
Among architects, the saying goes:
*Man's hand built Rome, while Venice arose
By God's will*; such — but not of Peter's nation —
Say: *Sankt-Petersburg? Why, she was built by Satan.*

All of the streets down to the river run,
Like gorges splitting mountains: long and broad;
Gigantic buildings: these brick, those of stone.
Marble on mud stands — and on marble: mud;
All façades even, none than his neighbour higher,
Like ranks of recruits, soiled, but in parade attire.
So many signs screwed to so many walls!
So many tongues! So many quirky scrawls;
So multifarious the linguistic rabble,
One thinks oneself lost on the streets of Babel.
"Here resides Achmet, the Khirgizan Khan,
Senator for the Department of Poland."
There, one can "Learn from le Monsewer Jock
French lingo, as echte Parisians talk."
The "Tsar's Own Scullion" next "Vodkas and Wine,"
"Bass-Baritone" and "School Inspector." A sign
Reads: "Here lives Piacere Gioco, Italian,
Once Purveyor of Sausages and Scallions,
Now Welcoming all Girls of Good Repute
To Clean, Cheap Lodgings." Further on the route:
"Here lives the Reverend Pastor Denier,
Of Divers Tsarist Orders, Cavalier.
Today's Sermon: *By God's Omnipotent Grace,
Our Holy Tsar, the One Vicar of Christ,*

*Lord of our Conscience, Lodestone of the Faith.*
Followed By *Words of Most Prudent Advice*
*To Brother Calvinists and Lutherans*
*And Anabaptists and Socinians*
*To Heed the Clarion from Peter's Rock*
*(That is, the Holy Tsar, and His True Friend,*
*The Prussian King), to Gather, to the End*
*Of Sheepish Concord, in one Peaceful Flock."*
Here: "Dresses;" "Music" there, and "Swaddling Clouts;"
Here: "Children's Toys," and further on there: "Knouts."

Along the streets calash, coach and landau
Despite their size, and how fast they careen,
Because of sled-blades, race without a sound
Like images a lamp casts on a screen.
Between the seat-irons of an English coach,
The bearded coachman sits; his hand, his coats,
His hat and whiskers all encased in ice:
He cracks his whip and thunders; in a trice
The crowd of minor sledges hasten aside
(Before him, little boys on horses ride,
Sweeping the streets of riff-raff like a Northern gale,
Like ducks before a state ship under sail).
Pedestrians rush (the cold snips at their heels
And any other flesh-scrap that still feels);
Frozen their faces and eyes by frigid spatter,
They beat their hands and feet, their teeth a-chatter.
Each mouth that breathes sends up a cloud of steam
Straight, long and grey — it seems, looking at these
Thick smoking crowds, as if they're walking chimneys.
On both sides of the slush-flecked mob there goes
Two long, stately processions, like ice floes
On swollen rivers, or, on a holy day,
A pious cortege, behind the monstrance of gold;
Who are these multitudes on chilly parade,
Like a business of sables, inured to the cold?
This is the hour of modish promenade.
It's cold and windy? Who gives a fig for that?

This is the hour when strolling goes the ... Tsar,
Tsaritsa, and court, from chamberlain to cat:
Marshals and dames, officials, earls and dukes,
All boyars of first, second, and fourth Abzugs,
Like cards swept from a sharp's table in draves:
So many kings and queens (most of them knaves),
Both red and black, the full-faced and one-eyed,
All flutter down to join the flow, both sides
Of the bright street, to pace the paving stones.
First come the servile officers of the court:
This one in warm fur — though frozen to the bones —
His coat wide open (How else might he sport
His shivering bemedalled breast before
The envious eyes of all?) His own eyes seek
Only an equal, to whom he'd deign to speak;
He waddles more than strolls, he's grown so fat;
Behind him come some guardsmen: rakish hats,
All thin and straight as pike-staves, whose belts clasp
Waists thinner than any self-respecting wasp.
Then much more humbly slouched shuffle *chinovniks*,
With furtive glances seeking their own cliques
For bows obsequious, or the odd-lot sample
Of lower yet life-forms, whom they might trample.
Nearly bent double creep they by, each one;
Their spines so elastic — like a scorpion.
Among them, like pied butterflies, parade
The ladies, made up like a fashion plate;
So varied are the coats and hats and hoods,
So quickly flash their feet in furry boots,
As white as snow, as red as boiled crabs.
But now the court departs, a line of cabs
And carriages draw up, like sailing ships
That bar the small fry from the harbour slips.
The first have now gone, with whip-crack and whirr,
Drawing the foot-sore in their splendid wake
And more than one (with hack tubercular):
"How grand a stroll it was! For heaven's sake!

I saw the Tsar himself! And made a grave
Bow to the Junker — and talked with his knave!"

A few there were among the passers-by
Differing from them by clothing and by mien;
Who never on the gay crowds cast an eye,
Yet gazed around in wonder at the scene:
The walls and the façades and the foundations,
The iron fences and granite crenellations,
As if they weighed the tensile strength of each,
Searching between the bricks for a chance breach,
Then, letting their arms fall down in despair,
As if they thought: "A man don't have a prayer
To knock these down!" Eleven there were in all,
Then one remained, his smile bitter as gall;
He raised his fist, and beat the limestone wall
As if in striking one, he cursed them all.
And then he crossed his arms upon his chest,
His eyes upon the Tsar's palace fixed fast,
With piercing glance — stilettos two, his eyes —
A Samson he, among these Philistines.
Like Samson snatched by treason and enchained
Who, gripping the pillars, just begins to strain.
The sun went down, and on his silent brow
The shades of night fell — He, so still and proud,
You'd think that darkness, falling from the skies
First alights on him, and only thence it flies
To spread itself abroad, a gloomy shroud.

On the further side, across the street from him,
There was another man. He no pilgrim,
But seemed to be a native of the town,
Or one who's lived here long. He went around
Dispensing alms to all the poor. He called
Each one by name, and chatted with them all,
Asking them how their children were, their wives,
Turning none away. At last, alone, his eyes
Swept all the buildings and the palace there,

But looked not at them with that pilgrim's stare —
Still, as he rested on the granite kerb
That bordered the canal, without a word
He raised his both hands high into the air,
And on his face was stamped divine despair.
He seemed and angel from the realms of glory
Among the suffering souls of Purgatory,
Beholding nations whole in their torments,
And knowing their relief still ages hence;
Till freedom come — so many generations,
So many long years until their salvation.
He weeps on the canal-side, deep in woe,
Cries bitter tears lost in the dirty snow,
(Lost not to God — He gathers, counts each one,
And for each drop, pays back an ocean
Of sweetness).
          It grew late, and they stayed on
The two, alone, and distant. Before long,
Each man fixed his eyes upon the other.
The one from the right spoke first, calling, "Brother —
You stand there by yourself, sadly; maybe
You are a stranger here? What might you need?
Command me, friend, in God's most holy name —
I am a Christian, and a Pole. And fain
Would serve a fellow Lithuanian..."

The pilgrim, lost in solitary musing,
Started, and briskly shook his head, refusing
The proffered aid, then hurried away from there.
Next morning, though, when his mind again grew clear,
Remembering the stranger's kind advance,
He rued his brusqueness, swore, that if by chance
They'd meet again, he'd be the one to call
Out the first greeting — though he can't recall
Where, or when, before he might have met him...
There's something in his voice — Did he forget him,
Having known him once before? For so it seems
Deep in the pilgrim's soul... Perchance in dreams?

### The Statue of Peter the Great

Evening it was, a lightly falling rain,
Two youths, one greatcoat sheltering the twain;
The one — that pilgrim fresh come from the West,
The unknown victim of Tsarist violence;
The other — the Russian bard of greatest worth,
Whose songs are famous all throughout the North.
They stood there arm in arm. Of recent date
Their acquaintance — so soon grown best of mates.
Their lofty souls, all earthly obstacles
Far above — the summits of one Alpine range,
Though sundered by an angry flood that falls
Between them (yet they barely hear her rage),
Each to each bent in natural sympathy.
The Pilgrim gazed at the colossal rock
Upon which Peter's horse reared, lost in thought.
And then the Russian bard whispered, softly:

"To the First of Tsars, for his wondrous deeds
The Second Tsaritsa built this monument.
The Tsar, already poured in bronze, a giant
Astride the back of his giant bronze steed,
Awaited but direction for his ride.
For Peter couldn't rest on his own turf,
His Fatherland not sufficiently wide —
So land was sent for, beyond the Northern surf.
A granite hill from Finland thus was torn,
And at Her orders, on the cold waves borne
To humbly fall here, at her imperial throne.
The hill prepared, the Tsar of bronze now flies —
The stallion leaps upon the massive stone,
Rears from the shore, and strikes out at the skies
Bearing the togaed "Caesar," knout and all.

"Not thus, in ancient Rome, did there uprise
Aurelius' bronze — that man of all beloved —
Who first won fame by banishing the spies

And all informers from the state removed!
Then, when he'd crushed the parasites at home
And routed on the Rhine and the Pactol
Those hordes, whose fierce invasions threatened Rome
Did he return to the peaceful Capitol.
His brow is beautiful, noble and kind.
Upon it shines a fatherly concern;
His sober hand is raised up, in a sign
Of blessing to his people, as he turns
Now left, now right, while with his other hand
He grips the reins in sure control and firm.
The stallion fierce, so pliant to his command,
It's obvious that his lord was crowded round
By an adoring populace, who cheered:
"Behold Caesar! Our Father's drawing near!"
And so he does, restraining the steed's bound
To gently ford the living stream of praise,
Including all in his parental glance.
The horse, though fiery, proud-maned, fain to prance,
Yet seems aware (as he his vim restrains)
That on his back he bears the Best-Beloved,
So nothing spooks him: children crowd and shove
To draw close to their father: still calmly, straight
And proud he steps. Such a stately, even gait,
So loved this man of the commonality,
His road ends surely, at immortality!

"Peter here, gives the stallion the reins.
How many backs were trampled in the brawl
To spring atop the perch from which he strains
For — where now? Your eye waits for them to fall,
The maddened steed, who champs his bit to froth,
The rider, who controls the stallion not;
For one whole century the fall's been stayed.
They stand there, like a frozen stone cascade
Upon a bitter shore where cold winds blow.
But — should the sun of freedom chance to glow?

And this land's warmed beneath a western breeze?
What then, with this cascade of tyrannies?"

### *A Review of the Troops*

A large parade ground, or the Baiting Ring
As some call it, for here the Tsar mistreats
His dogs before he sets them at the beasts.
The more refined, polite, call it the Tiring
Room; here the Tsar sizes his uniforms
Before he arms with guns and pikes his swarms
To teach his neighbour monarchs meet prostrations.
No mincing coquette tries out more gyrations
Before her mirror and the minuet
Than does the Tsar each day, at martinet.
Some call the grounds the Locust Incubator —
For here the Tsar coddles the bitter eggs
From which will hatch the military plagues
That turn the lands they light on to lunar craters.
Still others name it the Surgeon's Whetstone,
For here the Tsar will all his lancets whet
Before he leans above the patient's bed
And Europe feels him probe unto the bone;
Before he thinks to cauterise the wound
From loss of blood, both shah and sultan swoon,
And blood is let from out Sarmatian hearts.
So much for kennel and medicinal arts.
In prosaic Russian Officialese,
It's simply the Review Ground, if you please.

It's ten o'clock: review time's coming soon —
the grounds are ringed now by a curious mob
Like to black shores surrounding a white lake
Where terns assemble; now and then a drake
Flies low across its surface: a dragoon
Hastens to butt back with his lance's knob
The more impertinent gawker; leather thongs

Whip down across the backs of the bolder throngs;
And he who, like a frog in spongy fen
Stuck out his snout, retracts it once again.
A distant thunder, dull and uniform,
Like heavy hammers, or flails in the dry corn:
The regimental guide it is: the drums.
Behind them, long as steppelands, the ranks come,
Many and varied, yet all of the same make,
In green that deepens black against the snow;
The columns like to mighty rivers flow
And empty upon the grounds, that plumbless lake.

And now, O Muse! bestow on me the lips
Of Homer (times one hundred!) and in them, tongues
Parisian — bons mots, metaphors and quips —
And don't stop there! One hundred accountants'
Pens, that I might describe the adjutants,
The colonels, the officers, the rows
Of rank-and-file-press-ganged-upon heroes.

And yet such heroes, like peas in a pod
So similar man to man, and squad to squad,
Like stabled horses munching in a barn,
Or tied in sheaves homogenous sprigs of corn,
Or shoots of hemp while in the fields it grows,
Or lines in books, or even-cut furrows…
So many similes, I could drone on…
O! Like dialogue in a Petersburg salon.
I could name one disparity, in a pinch:
Some Muscovites there were, five, or six inch
Taller than others; on their caps they've got
Brass disks with letters (like a large bald spot):
The grenadiers. There were three squads of those,
Each sporting whiskers beneath every nose.
Behind them stand the smaller fry in rows
Like cucumbers behind tomato stalks;
At further sorting my untrained mind balks.

A sharp zoologist's eye is what it takes
To sort the genus of so many snakes.

The trumpets sound, and now the cavalry
Makes its entrance: ulans, hussars, dragoons
In kolpaks, shakos (with and without plumes)
So rich a runway of millinery
Is hardly seen beyond the modish racks
Of upscale shops — upon the riders' backs
And chests is shining armour, whose purpose
Can't be — but seems like — a gleaming tea service;
Their horses' polls are carapaced as well —
As sharp as hooks they gleam. The regiments
So varied in their dress and arms, all intents
At classifying them are vain. It's best
To sort them by their mounts. It's just in
Fashion, this new tactic, and very Russian.
For as to worth, as Zhomini writes, of course
It's not about the rider, but the horse.
This fact is well known in the eastern marches
Of our old Republic — guardsmen's chargers
Can be had for the price of a mere three souls,
While an officer's mount will cost one fourfold;
For such a horse one must toss in a scribe,
A lutenist, and an acrobat beside;
In tougher times, you need to add a cook.
Official nags and mares, such as you'd look
Suspicious in the mouth, and even such
As pull sick-wagons still can be worth much
As antes in a hand; and mares, of course
Can be had cheap: for as little as two whores.

But back to the squadrons. First a heavy-sized
Black horse came trotting, the next was anglicized;
After them came two bays, the fifth, cremello,
The next again chestnut, and grey his fellow,
Just like a mouse; behind him a stalwart
Mount, followed by middling, again a swart

Stallion came prancing with a bobbed tail;
Upon his brow the twelfth had a star, pale
As a bald spot. The last was black as a crow.
The artillery was the next to show:
Forty-eight cannon, caissons more than twice
That number — so, two hundred met my eyes
Or more, or less, an educated guess
Is all that I could manage in that press
Of curious mobbing gawkers looking on.
'Twould need an eye like yours, Napoleon,
To sum up a more accurate register,
Or yours, you clever Russian quartermaster
— Not for the cavalry, but for the caissons —
You know how much you've filched from the powder rations…

So now the ground is thick with greatcoats green.
Just like a meadow in its April sheen,
While here and there the caissons' bulks are seen
Like muddy beetles wallowing in cack
Or field lice with their dunnish-colored back.
A tow-cart, with a cannon set astride her
That looks for all the world like a black spider.

Each of these spiders has four legs in front
And just as many legs there to the rear.
These limbs are otherwise known as cannoneers
And bombardiers. And when the cannon's shunt
Off to the side at rest, the legs detach,
Each pair goes wandering on its chosen path;
Unlimbed, the fatal torso just sits there,
Balloon-like, and seems to hover in the air.
But when the cannon, from its peaceful drowse
Is suddenly by some command aroused,
Like a tarantula, when someone blows
A puff of air at her arachnid nose,
Each pair of front legs — or cannoneers — hies
Close to rub about her mouth, as flies
Work off some irritation, when they've stuck

Their mug into some pile of noxious muck,
And then it frets with legs there in the rear
(Each termed, as we've just noted, "bombardier");
She bucks her arse, and then, all legs wide spread,
Spews forth her noxious venom of hot lead.

Then suddenly, the ranks are still, and silent:
They look: a fleet of landlocked, horseback admirals,
A crowd of adjutants, a mess of generals
Before, behind — the Tsar himself in front.
A strange crew this — bright, motley, flashy, pied,
Beribboned, like mediaeval fools they ride,
O'erhung with keys and pins and other trash:
This one a blue, and that has a gold sash —
So many crosses, medals, icons, what-on's
Before and aft, more than they've clasps and buttons.

Each one resplendent — but with borrowed light
Reflecting splendour falling from his eyes
(The Tsar's); a swarm they are of fireflies
That gad about on balmy St. John's Night,
But when the Spring of the Tsar's favour's past,
These insects, one by one, lose all their flash;
They don't migrate to some more clement clime,
But in what Russian muck they bide their time
Buried, who knows? The general, breasting fire
Basks in the warmth of the Tsar's smiling eyes,
But should those eyes cloud over with royal ire,
The general pales, and — sometimes — up and dies.

Some stoics may be found among the hangers-
On; and while they too feel the Tsar's anger,
Those splendid souls, they neither waste nor wane,
Nor end it quickly, pistol-shot to brain,
But to their country dachas emigrating,
Begin to write — now to the chamberlain,
Now to the Tsaritsa's ladies-in-waiting;
Those who have a more liberal savour

Write to the coachman 'til they're back in favour.
You toss a dog through window into street:
He's bought it; now, a cat lands on his feet
And licks his paws — no worse off than he'd been,
And starts to sniff him out a way back in.
Out in the sticks, he plays the Jacobin;
Called back, he's Tory... Is it nine lives? or ten?

The Tsar was in a uniform of green
And on his collar was a golden trim.
The Tsar un-uniformed is never seen.
The uniform is the Tsar's second skin.
The Tsar is born a soldier, a soldier rots;
No sooner does he outgrow swaddling cloths
Than — as befits the brat who would be Tsar —
They diaper him up in tiny hussar
Britches, and with toy sword is cinct about.
No rattle for his fat hands: a wee knout.
Before he learns to speak, he plays at wars.
His books of ABC all bear the scars
Of sabre-tracings; as he learns to skip
To dance-tunes, why, his metronome's the whip.
While armies made of tin amuse small boys,
Real soldiers are the Tsarlet's living toys:
They Face Left! and Face Right! and should they flub,
These flesh-and-blood tin soldiers feel his club.
Thus is the future Tsar to Empery raised,
And thus by Europe feared, by Europe praised —
Well did Krasicki opine, in the old days:
"The wise man made a speech of great renown;
The dolt was unimpressed, and knocked him down."

Long live the memory of Peter the Great!
'Twas he thought up how best to educate
Tsars for the throne and set them on the path
To greatness, the political polymath!
"I'll Europeanise Russia! Look here —
Shorten your kaftans, boyars! Cut your beards!"

His word is law; those who refused to wear
French frocks learned why the French feared Robespierre;
His word is law; those who saw *that* grew pale
With terror, and beards fell like thick brown hail.
'Twas Peter introduced drums, bayonets
And dungeons, and academies for cadets,
'Twas Peter introduced the minuet
And kidnapped partners to complete the set;
'Twas Peter introduced the customs shed,
And forged great chains to seal off the roadstead.
He founded senate, ranks, and dignitaries,
A liquor-tax, stool-pigeons, and canaries,
'Twas Peter shaved the peasant, scrubbed him clean,
Gave him a gun and uniform of green,
While Europe looked on in rapt fascination:
"Peter the Great's invented civilisation!"
So well had Peter built, indeed it's true,
That his successors had little else to do:
Send brother despots a regiment or two,
Incite a pogrom here, some arson there,
Covet their neighbour's goods — and fleece them bare —
Impoverish more the poor; staff regiments
With well-paid Krauts and mercenary French;
Astonished Europe all but overwhelm
With such a strong and wise, enlightened realm.

Ah, French and Germans! Just you wait your turn!
Soon Tsarist *ukases* your ears will burn;
When on your napes you feel the scourge's blow
And behold your cities in the lurid glow
Of firestorms glinting off sharp Russian swords!
Then, I reckon, you'll be at a loss for words —
When your great fan the Tsar requests to hear ya
Warble your Alexandrines in Siberia!

The Tsar, like a bowling ball, rolled through the ranks
And the jostled pins gave back a clattering "thanks"
To his fair greeting coughing back their cheers,

Wishing him health in turn: "One hundred years!"
Growled the men, like a hundred grumbling bears;
Then came his order. No sooner in the ears
Of his commandant, than again it slips
Out of that mug in turn, and from lips to lips
Bounds down the line to the last N.C.O.
Weapons a-clatter, sudden to-and-fro
Of boots and sabre, bridle, gun and whip;
If you have ever been aboard a ship
As meal-time approaches, and have seen a
Cook supervise the boiling of farina,
How in a giant cauldron sailors pump
Rivers of water, while other tars dump
Baskets of grits, and while the fire roars,
Still others churn the porridge with tin oars —
Or if you've ever had the happy chance
Of visiting the parliament in France
(A larger cauldron, tending to get hotter
When any committee proposes any matter)
And deputies begin their fierce debates
While all of starving Europe, drooling waits
In hopes that — Soon! — they'll be served liberty
— Though clouds of steam are all that one can see —
A pinch of Liberalism, a dash of prayer,
The chamber's nearly brim-full with hot air;
Someone cries "Freedom!" and the chamber roils
And yet — alas — a watched pot never boils.
Then, someone mentions the intents of Kings,
Despots and Tsars, and nations suffering.
The chamber, bored, impatient, cries for Order
Until the Treasurer scurries in, his quarter-
ly report pressed to his side, and starts to wheeze
Percentages, stamp taxes, customs fees;
The whole room shakes with tumult and wild cries
And clouds of clamour darken senate skies —
Outside, nations jubilate, cabinets shake
Aroused: can this be Liberty's earthquake?
Until a voice chagrined calls out, "Relax!

He's only going on about the tax..."
Whoever's seen that bubbling pot of grits
Or that no less seething chamber, surely gets
What sort of bustling chaos was unloosed
When the Tsar's order landed in their midst —
The thwack of arms presented, stomping boots,
The thundering of three hundred drums at once,
A sound not far dissimilar to that crunch
When, on the River Neva, crash ice floes;
The infantry formed up in even rows,
Column on column, wave on wave they come,
At each wave's crest an officer, and a drum,
The Tsar there in the midst, immobile as the sun,
While regiments like planets round him run.
The Tsar then loosed his adjutants, and each
Like bird uncaged, or rabid dog unleashed
Flew here and there with slashing crop and screech;
Cacophony of officers, N.C.O.s,
Pipers and kettle-drums (those drums!) follow.
The infantry, like to an anchor chain
Unwound, extends along the snowy plain;
The squares of cavalry unite, and stand
A solid wall of horse and armoured man.
What sort of martial pirouettes ensued,
When came that squadron's turn to be reviewed,
How like a pack of dogs teased, then unleashed
They charged the infantry, as 'twere a beast
Tied to a baiting-pole, and how the rank
Of infantry defensively then shrank,
Presenting bayonets as a hedgehog
Bristles its needles at a foaming dog;
And how, at last, again were brought to heel
The cavalry, in mid-charge, who then wheeled
And ceded stage to cannon and caisson
Dragged here and there in the best French fashion
(Missteps were clubbed right, in the Russian mode).
Ah, the arrests, the trampling of necks,
The falls from horses all too bravely rode,

The praise the Tsar received (did you expect
Anything else?) Alas, so grand a theme!
Could I describe it, such would be my fame!
And yet my muse, aflight, is just a dud
Descending to the dull prosaic mud
Without a flash, to fizzle on the sod,
And I, like Homer — though gods war! — I nod.

Once every feint and figure'd been exhausted
Of which the Tsar had ever heard or seen
And the distinguished guests sufficiently frosted,
It grew so quiet, you might have heard a pin
Fall — then the great mass of sheepskin, overcoat
And kaftan that had ringed the Platz about
Began to dissipate, each his own way,
And palace scullions bustled, setting tea.

Ambassadors of every foreign land
Who maugre freezing cold and deadly boredom
To please the Tsar are always near at hand
To wax effusive: "Wonderful! Ah! Awesome!"
Were growing hoarse, for having freely spent
(With new ardour) the same old compliments:
"The Tsar's such a magnificent tactician,"
"Each Marshal's worthy of his high commission,"
And "Eyes have never seen such soldiers: brave,
Devoted..." "Ooh!" "Ah!" (yawn) and so they rave...
At last, the ritual to an end is brought
With jeers at Napoleon — "That idiot!"
And each takes out his pocketwatch and sighs
Lest (Blast it!) there should be some damned reprise
Of Charge, Parade, and Wheeling, Caissons Rumbling —
It's late, it's freezing, and the tummy's grumbling!

Yet still the Tsar remained there, sitting tall
On his mount (to the chagrin of all);
Now he dismissed his tired, dun-coloured men
Only to call them back (again and again)

Some twenty times — more than I'd care to mention —
He had them drawn up rigid at attention,
Had them form phalanx-square, and now a fan,
Like an old card sharp, who will deal a hand
To his own self when no one else is there;
Thus played the Tsar at martial solitaire
Until he too grew bored, quickly faced rear
And in a cloud of generals disappeared.
Long stood the troops confused, in the same place
He left them, daring not to About Face
Or march away, until — at last — the drums
And trumpets blared retreat, and they, benumbed
And shivering, two hundred lines, retreat
From training ground back into city street.
How changed they were! Now, they did not resemble
Those rushing Alpine floods that made us tremble
When, over cliff and rock they seemed to break
To settle on this deep and peaceful lake;
No longer like green wavelets do they play
In happy agitation, lapping gay;
Those regiments arrived fresh, white and clean —
These now with mud and dirty snow obscene,
Convulsed with tremors, are tired, cold and wet,
Bedraggled, shambling, steaming with bitter sweat.

Now all are gone: actors and audience.
On the vacant grounds are found but the remnants
Of twenty corpses — this one dressed in white
(Cavalryman), while that one's colors might
Be any — boot and hoof trampled him so
He's buried deep already in the snow.
These men, set up as course-guards for the rows
Of infantry and horse — stood still, and froze;
This one misstepped — "Right face!" — faced left instead:
Struck by his neighbour's rifle, dropped down dead;
All of them, tossed on wagons, that are driven
By police lackeys — the dead, the barely living —
All to be tossed into a common pit,

Tamped down again — and that's the end of it.
One of them had ribs crushed, another one
Was sliced in half by the wheel of a cannon —
When he beheld his blood and guts spurt out
He shrieked loud, until ordered "Shut your mouth!
The Tsar can hear you!" And so used was he
To blind obedience that he died, silently.
The poor tormented man was quickly covered
By someone's greatcoat — his last moans thus smothered;
For should the Tsar, unbreakfasted, behold but
On his still empty stomach such a cold cut,
His appetite would be ruined for the day;
No matter what savouries bedeck his tray
He'd turn his nose up at the choicest meat,
And, cross, he'd stubbornly refuse to eat.

The last man wounded was a thing of wonder:
They stifled, beat, fairly tore him asunder
To keep him quiet — it was all in vain.
He kept on moaning in his searing pain
And cursed the Tsar! Up close the crowds drew
To this last martyr of that day's review:
The steed he'd ridden of a sudden stood
Stock-still — Then came the rushing flood
Of later waves — he was smashed, his rider thrown
Beneath the thundering hooves of bay and roan.
Though beasts are kinder far than human folk
And each horse swerved — alas! — one of them broke
The lad's arm, snapping it in two, quite clean.
The bone poked blinding white against the green
Of his parade doublet; he too grew pale
But fainted not; he raised an angry wail,
With his whole arm gesturing to the skies,
Then to the witnesses, who heard his cries.
What were his words? None say, for fear of spies.
They'd only say, it was some foreign tongue,
"Tsar, Tsaru" declined in some Baltic jargon…
The young recruit — for so the rumour ran —

Was noble-born, a Lithuanian
Torn from his studies, jammed in uniform;
His officer, who held all Poles in scorn,
Gave him on purpose an unbroken steed:
"Let's make the bastard blueblood Polack bleed!"
No more than this did anybody hear,
And then, without a trace, he disappeared.
But one fine day! O, Tsar — that child's name
Will be required of you! And more of the same!
All of those thousands, whom to death you threw
In mine, in camp — these debts will soon come due!

Next day, a dog was heard howling at first light,
And there, on the parade ground, against the white
Background of snow, there hunched a spot of black
Around which the faithful hound turned his tracks.
Some people ran to see, and what they found:
A corpse, missed by those who had cleared the ground,
Half soldier, half peasant, long beard and shaven head,
Half buried in the snow, but wholly dead —
Batman to some forgetful officer,
He sat there guarding his master's warm fur;
Wearing but cap, and soldier's overcoat
He guarded it, and never thought to throw't
Over his own back; left there, his command
To "Wait!" and so he waited, with one hand
Clutching the coat, the other he'd keep warm,
But didn't slide it in his uniform
Until he froze quite through and through, and thus
His own dog found him, and raised this sad ruckus.
The frost sealed fast the lid of his right eye,
His left froze open, as if he'd still yet try
To keep his master's property safe and sound
(He faced, as ordered, still the parade ground)
Awaiting his lord and master! As is right;
"Sit there!" was ordered, and so he sat, all night.
Masters give orders, servants must obey;
And so he'll sit on till the Judgment Day,

Still faithful to his master's voice, though dead —
"Make sure that no one steals that coat!" he said,
And so he did — though by his lord forgot —
Who left, without wasting a second thought!
Was he so careless? Or was he... conniving?
A greenhorn — think they — from the sticks arriving
At the parade ground, not because of posting,
But to show off; of new epaulettes boasting.
Maybe from the review he went a-dining,
Or to some blushing coquette took a shining;
Maybe he sat at cards until he went broke
And, as he lost his purse, forgot his bloke;
Maybe... it all was his conscious design
To leave his servant, and his fur, behind,
As both stank too much of the countryside
And both were somewhat galling to his pride:
Old, out of fashion, what need he for fur
Since in mere doublet rode the Emperor?
Or "At review, and you come dressed like this?
In rags like that? Are you an anarchist?"
Such sneers like that a fop would mortify!
Best leave the rags, and let the peasant die...

Poor, frozen hero! such a death, by God,
Shames your humanity, and but befits a dog.
And your reward? Your master's laugh: "That's rich!
Faithful to death even. An exemplary bitch!"
Poor, frozen man! Why is it my heart bleeds
And my eye tears at this your faithful deed?
My heart is rent for you, poor brother Slav;
Poor nation! — thus I mused beside his grave —
Who know but such heroism: of a slave!

### The Day Before the Petersburg Flood of 1824
### Oleszkiewicz

When worse than Arctic frosts the heavens sear
And suddenly the skies grow livid, smears
Like those that on a corpse that's lain too near
The hearth blotch out, and as it grows too warm
(But not with living heat) there start to swarm
Up from the body wisps that seem like breaths,
But are foul gases of decay and death —
So was it here. Those myriad vapours white,
That fairy-giant city in the heights
Of heaven crumbled and fell to the earth
That gave its sister-phantom city birth;
And there, condensed, those acres-full of steam
Ran through the streets in ever-growing streams
Fed by the melting snows. Before nightfall,
Roads became Stygian marshes, frightful
In mud and rising waters; coach and landau
Shed useless skids and wagon wheels wallowed
Through muck and puddle; so much smoke and fog
No eye discerned the carts along that slogged:
Nothing but carriage lights, that, glowing sallow
Slid like fata morganas over a bog.

Some travellers, young, that evening made their way
Down to the Neva, where at the end of day
They liked to walk, for no *chinovniks* grace
The spot, nor spies, who abhor an open space.
Their easy speech was in a foreign tongue;
Sometimes, one of them hummed a foreign song;
Sometimes they halted — had a look around —
Anyone listening? — No; and on they wound
Their way, humming, to the Neva's verge
Which runs on vastly, like an Alpine gorge,
Until they drew up, where amidst granite walls
The rough-hewn road down to the water falls.
There, far below them, they beheld a man

At river's edge. A lantern in his hand,
He was no spy — here was no secret matter;
Nor ferry-man — none ventured on the water
At this time, nor was he a fisherman
(He'd neither pole nor fishnet in his hand).
He'd nothing but some papers, and that lantern.
They drew up closer, but he didn't turn
An eye in their direction. Then he drew
A rope out of the water, counted through
Each sodden knot, before he jotted down
The number; it seemed he wished to sound
The water's depth. The light reflected thus
From the ice glowed on his mysterious
Scroll, and lit his inclined countenance
Yellow — like clouds when the sun nears the west.
His face: beautiful, noble, and severe.
When he — still rapt in musing on his page —
Heard the group's footsteps suddenly draw near,
He made a hand-sign, asking them to wait,
As if he needed silence, to cogitate.
There was something so odd in that mere gesture
That any odd intent, that they might pester
Him for an explanation died away.
Although they'd drawn up close and had been gay,
Joking and laughing, all of them grew solemn;
None dared to break the silence. Of a sudden,
One looked more closely at his face, his eyes,
And gasped out in a burst of stunned surprise,
"It's him!" "Who?" "Why, that famous Polish dabbler,
The painter — they call him *guślarz* rather,
For long ago he tossed aside his pots
Of paint and now on the kabbalah his thoughts
Are bent, and on Scripture... So the rumour goes
That he holds converse with spirits, and dead souls."
The painter then drew up to his full height
And said — as if to no one but the looming night —
"Who lives to see what morning shall reveal
Shall see — not the last, but the second ordeal:

The Lord will shake the Assyrian throne,
And quake the foundations of Babylon.
And yet, O Lord! Spare these eyes the third trial!"
He spoke, and left the young group standing there;
Lantern in hand, he ascended the stairs,
Among the terraces to disappear.
None understood what they had chanced to hear.
Some stood in silent wonder, others joked
"A *guślarz*!" laughing nervously, "What a bloke!
Cuckoo!" Some moments more they loitered there
Amidst the growing gloom, the cooling air,
Then they went home. Not strolling. At a tear.

One stayed behind. Up those same stairs he ran
To race along the terrace; he saw no man
Then — There! — he glimpsed the lantern from afar,
Winking some versts hence, like an errant star.
Although he hadn't seen his countenance,
Nor clearly caught what of him said his friends,
The timbre of that voice, those dooming words,
Shook him to the core. And so, thus spurred,
He raced with all the speed that he could muster
Through dark and fog, on roads unknown, fast, faster,
Behind the lantern winking now, now hid,
Now — snuffed? — No, there it was, no more it fled;
But stood still, in the centre of an empty square.
The lad ran on, until he drew up where
A pile of stones reared in the open space,
And on one stood the painter, right hand raised
Aloft, head bared, in silence, rigid, tall,
His gaze directed toward the Palace walls,
And there, they seemed fixed on a lone window
And in that window, on a faint light that glowed;
He whispered heaven-wards, as if in prayer,
Then raised his voice, as if no one were there:

"You're not asleep, Tsar! Though the night is deep,
And all your lackeys snore, you're not asleep!

The Lord is merciful: He has not rent
You from your soul, which warns of punishment
Awaiting you. But you would stifle it,
Your conscience, if you might just drowse a bit!
You screw your eyes closed, but they won't obey,
And stare on, waking, as if it were noonday.
Yet even in sleep you've no escape, it seems!
How many times your angel's sent you dreams,
Stronger, more vivid, images — warnings?

"He was not evil born, was once a man —
By faint degrees devolved he to tyrant;
The Lord's angels depart when man rebels;
Thus he drew ever closer to the devils;
The last faint throbs of conscience now he stifles
And beats away forebodings like mere trifles.
Tomorrow again his flatterers will fawn
And raise him on high... till Satan pulls him down.

"His suffering slaves, the lowest of the low,
Will be the first to feel the vengeful blow.
For when the lightning falls among dead matter,
The heights: tree-top and towers, first are shattered.
But among men, the searing punishment
Most frequently first strikes the innocent...

"They fall asleep to liquor, quarreling harridans;
They wake tomorrow — poor lifeless carrions!
Sleep on in peace like stupid animals
Until God's ire, like to a hunter falls
Among you, spooking out of brake and fen
Each beast, unto the deepest, wildest den.

"Hark! — There! — The winds rise, there they raise their heads
Like marine monsters from their Arctic beds;
Of icy mists they've fashioned their swift wings
And from their fetters they unchain the seas;
Hark, hark! — And hear the abyss roar oceanic,

The steeds of icebergs press on, driving panic
Before them: rearing, tearing icy reins.
Their mad destructive rush nothing restrains:
Burst, all but one of their gigantic chains
And soon those links will snap beneath the strain..."

He spoke — and when he saw he wasn't alone,
Blew out the lantern; suddenly, he was gone.
He flashed and disappeared like a foretaste
Of doom impending, which makes the heart race,
Then, before it's comprehended fully — fades.

*The end [of this fragment]*

**To My Muscovite Friends**
*this fragment is dedicated, by the Author*

Do you remember me? Whenever my mind traces
The story of my friends' deaths, jailings and banishments,
I remember all of you, and your foreign faces
Possess, in all my musings, the rights of citizens.

Where are you now? Ryleev, my noble friend, and young,
Whose neck I often clasped, from the Tsar's unjust docket
Was led to the tree of shame, from which he was then hung.
A curse to such people, who murder their own prophets!

That hand, which Bestuzhev extended me in friendship,
A poet's and soldier's hand, torn from both sword and quill
By the same Tsar's order, who bound it to a mine skip,
Chained with Polish hands underground, where it labours still.

Others, it may be, met with punishments worse by far:
By appointments, perhaps, or by a medal disgraced,
Their souls bartered, for aye, to the favour of the Tsar,
Before whose throne they now grovel, prostrate, on their face.

Perhaps you've sold your tongues, with which you extol his deeds,
And with your friends' martyrdom, you fatten your purses.
Perhaps in my own homeland you make my kinsmen bleed,
And in the Tsar's presence, you boast of orphans' curses.

If perchance these songs of mine should pierce the Northern skies,
Flying to you, from lands of freedom, on mournful wing,
And should you hear their call far above the fields of ice,
May they be harbingers of freedom, like cranes, of spring.

You'll recognise my voice: when you knew me, in fetters
Crawling low, like a snake, I fooled the despot with smiles.
But my heart's deep secrets lay bare to you, his betters;
For you was I always dove-like, without any guile.

Now this cup of venom I pour out in bitter flood.
Burning is my speech, and corrosive its every sound.
I distilled this poison from my homeland's tears and blood.
May it burn — not you — but the chains with which you are bound.

And should it so befall, that you complain of my songs,
I'll take it as a dog's barking when, too long resigned
To pinch collar, and the hand that's yanked it for so long,
Bares his teeth at long last — *Come on. Yank it one more time!*

# FOREFATHERS' EVE, PART IV

*The Priest's rectory — The table still uncleared after supper — Priest — Hermit — Children — Two candles on the table — a lamp burning before an icon of the Blessed Virgin Mary — A wall clock striking the hour.*

*I took up the crumbling shrouds that lay in the coffins. I cast off the noble comfort of resignation, just to be able to declare again and again: 'Ah, it was not always thus!' One thousand joys have been tossed into the tomb forever and you stand here alone and count them over! Wretched, needy man! Open not the tattered Book of the Past! ... Are you not sad enough already?*

— *Jean Paul*

PRIEST.
   Up from the table, children! Now
   We've eaten of our daily bread
   It's time to kneel — come, gather round —
   And thank our Father. Bow your heads.
   Today our Church holds festival
   For Christian souls departed hence:
   Fathers and mothers, brothers, all
   Suffer in purging, hopeful torments.
   For them we offer our humble prayer.

   */Opens a book/*

   Here is a fitting text.

CHILDREN.
   "In those days..."

*PRIEST.*
   Shh! Wait! Somebody's knocking. Who's there?

/The Hermit enters, wildly dressed/

CHILDREN.
   Jesus and Mary!

*PRIEST.*
               Who's at the door?

/Confused/

   Who are... Why are you here? What for?

CHILDREN.
   A dead man! Dead! A ghost! A vampire!
   In God's name...! Get away from here!

*PRIEST.*
   Tell us your name. Come. Have no fear.

HERMIT. /Slowly and sadly/
   A dead man... Dead...! You're right, my child.

CHILDREN.
   A dead man! Daddy, don't take his hand!

HERMIT.
   Dead... to the world. Do you understand?
   I am a hermit from the wilds.

*PRIEST.*
   Why do you come so late at night?
   What is your name? Here in the light
   When I look closely at you... You're
   Like someone I knew... years before
   I... Tell me, are you from around here?

HERMIT.
    Ah, yes! In youth, but... it's been years —
    Before I died... Three years ago...
    But why are you so keen to know
    My name, my parentage? When the bell
    Tolls for the dead, the sexton tells
    Each nosey gossip *'Who's it for*?
    Just say a prayer. Move on!' No more...
    That's me — dead to the world. So there!
    Still curious? Why? Just say a prayer.
    My name...

*/Looks at the clock/*

            Too early. Still can't tell.
    I've come a long way. Perhaps from Hell,
    Perhaps from Heaven, I don't know.
    But to this country. Father, show
    Me, if you know it, which way to run!

PRIEST. */Gently, with a smile/*
    The roads of death I'd show no one.

*/Confidentially/*

    We priests are to make crooked paths straight.

HERMIT. */Mournfully/*
    Ah — safe at home — though others stray.
    Whether peace or riot grip the world,
    A nation falls, a lover dies,
    What care you? At your fireplace curled
    While dark sleet freezes shut my eyes!
    You hear the thunder round the skies?
    You hear the swirling winds carouse?

*/Looks around/*

Ah — blest the life in one's own little house!

/Sings/

The loveless life's a happy life,
Of peaceful nights and days sans strife
    In a quiet little house!

/Sings/

Leave, pretty maid, your palace high
And come into my cottage nigh.
I've armfuls of sweet flowers there
And a tender loving heart to share.

You hear the pigeons coo and bill,
The silver murmur of the rill —
For those like us who love so well,
Sufficient is a hermit's cell.

**PRIEST.**
You praise my home and call my hearthside blest —
The maid will have it blazing in a trice.
Sit down and warm yourself. You need a rest.

**HERMIT.**
Ha! 'Warm yourself'! Father, that's good advice.

/Sings, pointing to his breast/

You don't know what a fire's burning here,
Despite the rain, despite the cold,
Always aflame!
At times some ice or snow I'll press
To this my burning, blazing heart:
The snow melts into swirling steam...
Always aflame!

My breast would melt the stoutest ore —
So hot it is — a thousand times more,

*/Pointing at the chimney/*

A million times more!
You don't know what a fire is burning here,
Despite the ice, despite the snow,
Always aflame!

PRIEST. */Aside/*
I say my piece — he says his.
He neither sees, nor aught he hears.

*/To the Hermit/*

The rain's soaked right through all your clothes —
You're trembling like a leaf, when the wind blows!
Whoever you are, you've come quite a way.

HERMIT.
Who am I...? Not yet... I still can't say.
I've come from far — I myself don't understand,
From Heaven? or Hell...? But I've come to this land...
Meanwhile, here's a little admonition.

PRIEST. */Aside/*
I'd better humour him, in his condition...

HERMIT.
Show me... You know the road that leads to death?

PRIEST.
I know the gate, its length and breadth.
But from where you stand, young and strong,
The rode to the graveside's worldly long.

HERMIT. /*Confusedly, sadly, to himself*/
   And yet I've run it, in a single breath!

PRIEST.
   And that's just why you're tired and sick.
   You've got to get your strength back. Food, and cheer...

HERMIT. /*Wildly*/
   And then we'll go?

PRIEST. /*Smiling*/
   I'll just pack our kit.
   All right?

HERMIT. /*Distractedly, with irritation*/
   All right.

PRIEST.
   Children, come here!
   We've got a guest this evening, see?
   Till I return, you keep him company.

CHILD. /*Examines him closely*/
   Please sir, why are you dressed so oddly?
   Just like a bandit! What a sight!
   Or a wild man from a fairy tale.
   Your cloak is patched with odds and ends,
   Look! Rotten sailcloth scraps he mends
   With Chinee silk! And in his hair,
   Grass, leaves, and twigs! So fresh and fair...!
   Have you been rolling in the swale?

/*Noting a knife, which the Hermit hides*/

   What's that you've got there? Let me see!
   Ribbons for sale? A rosary?
   Ha, ha, ha, ha!

My my, you are a sight to see!
Ha, ha, ha, ha!

HERMIT. /*Starting, as if he remembered something*/
O children, it's not right for you to laugh!
Listen, I once knew a girl, when I was half
Your age, as sad and luckless as you see
Me now, broken by the selfsame misery!
She wore just such rags, and in her hair
Such leaves and twigs as now I wear.
When she would come into a town
The whole village would gather round
To laugh at her misfortune.
Jeering, pointing, they'd chase her out
Into the fields. Once, I too joined the rout...
Just once! I mocked her too. Maybe
That's why I've come to share her portion?
Who knows? God in His majesty
Takes the side of misery;
I was so happy, so carefree, then —
Who knew that it would fall to me,
Such a just punishment?

/*Sings*/

The loveless life's a happy life
Of peaceful nights and days sans strife.

/*The Priest enters, with wine and a plate*/

HERMIT.
Father... Sad songs... Do you know any?

PRIEST.
In my long life I've heard too many.
And yet, chin up! Be of good cheer —
After a storm, the heavens always clear...

HERMIT. */Sings/*
>To leave her, O, how hard, how hard!
>To reach her, harder still, by God!
>He who hath ears, well, let him hear!

PRIEST.
>Eat now, my friend. We'll see to that later.

HERMIT.
>A simple song, but you'll not find a greater
>In any romance...

*/Smiling, taking down some books/*

>Father — *La nouvelle Heloise?*
>You know it? And poor Werther's miseries?

*/Sings/*

>So much I've borne, so much endured,
>Perhaps my death will ease the woe.
>If through my love you've been injured,
>With blood I'll square the debt I owe.

*/Takes out the knife/*

PRIEST. */Seizing his wrist/*
>What are you doing...! Have you lost your mind?
>Put that blade down! Grab his hands — Stop!
>Are you a Christian? Such a godless thought!
>Do you know the Gospels?

HERMIT. */Putting the knife away/*
>And you — Do you know pain?
>All right. It's not time for that just yet.

>*/Looks at the clock/*

The clock says nine — and three tapers are lit!

/Sings/

So much I've borne, so much endured,
Perhaps my death will ease the woe.
If through my love you've been injured,
With blood I'll square the debt I owe.

Why must I be with you obsessed?
Why did your glance my heart constrain?
Why chose I you, spurning the rest?
You! To another's ring enchained!

Ah! Had you but heard that, in Goethe's words,
In her voice, as her fingers stroked the keys…!
But you meditate only on godly deserts;
Safe in your priestly calling's pious duties.

/Leafing through the books/

And yet you'll read of secular devotions…?
Such bandit-books breed dangerous emotions!

/Tossing a book aside/

Heavenly tortures of my youth!
Those books wrenched out my wings at the very roots,
Twisting them to upward flight,
Foiling descent, strain howsoever I might!
I dreamt a lover glimpsed only in a dream,
And her I longed for, holding in despite
All earthly creatures, all of the common rout;
I searched, ah! Where did I not seek her out,
That love divine, found not beneath this sun
But only on the sea-foam of my imagination!
Such a fevered desire my heart did twist,
I sought an ideal that did not exist

In these frigid times,
So I flew off to the golden climes
Sung into being by poets and sages,
Goaded by hunger that nothing assuages
Until, after wandering through lands far and near,
I found her — and I found her here!
Oh, just as I was about to cast myself down
And in the filthy stream of luxury to drown,
I found her! Whom I never thought I'd find.
I found her! Just to lose her for all time!

*PRIEST.*

I share in your misfortune, my brother.
But hope always remains, and there are other
Cures... How long have you been ill?

*HERMIT.*

Ill?

*PRIEST.*

How long have you been mourning your loss?

*HERMIT.*

How long? I've given my word. I can't tell.
But someone else can. I've got a friend,
The faithful companion of all my wandering.

*/Looks around/*

How peaceful here inside! How warm!
And out there: winds and thunder, storm...
My comrade's shivering at your door
While we mewl on over old heart-sores.
Good Father, bid him share your hearthside too!

*PRIEST.*

My door has never shut out misery.

*HERMIT.*
    Stay, brother, stay — I'll bring him in myself.

*/The Hermit goes out./*

*CHILDREN.*
    Ha, ha, ha! Daddy, what's up with him?
    He scurries out, he scurries in,
    He wears — and talks! — such jumbled trash!

*PRIEST.*
    Children! Tears follow jeers and laughs!
    The poor man's sick — and maybe worse...

*CHILDREN.*
    What? He's healthy as a horse!

*PRIEST.*
    And so he looks — but his heart's an open wound.

*HERMIT ./Dragging in a fir bough/*

    Come in, brother! Come!

*PRIEST.*
    And his reason's unbound.

*HERMIT.*
    Come in, brother! Don't be afraid, they're friends!

*CHILDREN.*
    Daddy! Look what he's got in his hands!
    That's nothing but a fir-tree bough!

*HERMIT./To the Priest, pointing at the bough/*
    A hermit will make his friends in the deep woods.
    Are you surprised at the figure he cuts?

*PRIEST.*
　　Whose?

*HERMIT*
　　My friend here.

*PRIEST.*
　　What? Your friend — that stick?

*HERMIT.*
　　He's not much to look at, I admit —
　　Remember, he was raised in the woods. Say hello!

*/Raises high the bough/*

*CHILDREN.*
　　What are you doing!? Father! No!
　　Don't strike him, you bandit! Get out of here! Go!

*HERMIT.*
　　A bandit? Yes, little children, you're right.
　　But such as only himself would smite...

*PRIEST.*
　　Brother, get hold of yourself! Why
　　This... fir tree?

*HERMIT.*
　　　　　　　Fir tree? Ah! The learned eye!
　　Father, train it more nearly upon this cypress —
　　This memento of parting — this mark of my distress —

*/Takes up some books/*

　　Here — take up your ancient lore and seek
　　What of cypress, and fir, says your learned Greek.
　　Those lovers blest, their woman's love to share
　　With myrtle from her hand would cinct their hair.

/Pause/

This broken branch — of cypress or of fir —
Sighs yet that last "fare well" I had of her.
I have it from her hand, and keep it still
My fast companion in both good and ill.
Unfeeling, it's kinder than most who sympathise —
He laughs not at my tears, nor yawns at my cries.
He alone remains, of once so many friends!
He knows each secret in my deep heart locked.
If aught of me you wish to comprehend,
Ask him! I'll leave you two alone to talk.

/To the bough/

Tell him how long I've been mourning my loss.
A long time, it has to be. This was
A cypress seedling merely, when I took
It from her hand in parting. Now just look:
I bore it with me, set it in the loam,
Watered it with my tears far from my home —
Just look how it has grown. A sturdy tree,
A thickly leaved sublimity!
The tree I've torn this from already waves
Its weeping braids above my waiting grave —
When from the angry heavens' scorn
My beaten eyes I shall for all time turn.

/Sighs gently/

Ah! Just this colour was her hair —
Like this cypress bark!
Want to see?

/Searches, and pulls something hidden in his breast/

I can't undo these bindings...

*/With ever more effort/*

    So slight a bond — the slim windings
    Of a girl's braid!... Yet no sooner had I lain
    It on my breast, that it grew about me, to constrain
    Like a hairshirt, my chest,
    Sinking into my flesh, rooting in my breast.
    I can barely breathe, so tight this lovelock spins!
    I suffer greatly! Yes, for great are my sins!

PRIEST.
    Yet calm yourself! Soft! Accept these words of peace —
    However great, my child, your sufferings
    Endured in this life, such penitence brings
    Augmented in the next, God's balming grace!

HERMIT.
    Penance? For what? Pray — what might be my sin?
    Pure love? And are its wages eternal death?
    That same God created love, whose creative breath
    Gave life to her delightful graces
    And bound two souls in the embrace
    Of such chains — for all time!
    Before He plucked them from the slope of light
    For them to wither in this fleshly blight
    He bound them fast together — for all time!
    Now, as we're parted by evil hands
    The chain's stretched taut — but such bands
    No one can break! Though force now separates
    Us, stifles our feelings, still we trace
    A perfect circle, as compass-like, we race
    The perimeter of love.

PRIEST.
    What the Lord above
    Hath joined, no man may sunder.
    Your present troubles may be overcome.

*HERMIT.*
    I wonder —
Perhaps when beyond this vile flesh we arise,
When one soul, now rent in two, once more unifies...
For here below all such hopes are dead,
And sundered paths my love and I must tread.
It's always present to me — the hour we were to part:
It was Autumn; I remember the chilly nighttime air,
Just hours before my leaving, as through the park I erred
Seeking in thought, in prayer, something to shield my heart
— Too delicate by nature — some sturdy defence
From the piercing salvos of her final glance.
I wandered aimlessly from tree to tree
On that most lovely night! I still can see,
Fresh sprinkled with late-fallen rain, the lawn,
Shining as if with jewels, with dew, near dawn;
The vales all sunk in mist, like seas of snow;
From this side, lava-like, a burly cloud
Spills in, from that, the pale moon waxes, glows
In paler heavens, the late stars thinning out —
And there above me hangs the eastern star —
I greet him now each day, watching him rise!
Then suddenly, I glimpsed her in surprise:
There — on the path, near the veranda...
All dressed in white, amid the bosky gloom,
She stood, like the column of a tomb!
Then she came running — like the western breeze
With eyes cast down — and never glanced at me!
Her cheek was pale as she drew near,
I bent down, looked askance —
And in her eye I glimpsed a tear.
"In a few hours I'll be far hence!"
I whispered. "Fare well," she. Then — barely heard:
"Forget!" Forget?! How easily uttered, that word!
Command instead, my love, your shadow depart
And no more dog your steps, than this my heart
From you to stray!

"Forget!"
How easy to say!!

*/Sings/*

Stop your sobbing, cease your weeping
As we go our separate ways
For all time...

*/Cuts his singing short/*

... thy memory keeping
Banished I, for all my days!
Mere memories...? In a few hours I start!
I seize her hand, and lay it on my heart

*/Sings/*

More lovely than the very seraphim,
　　The loveliest of all Eve's earthly kin,
Her blue eyes brighter than the sun in May
　　Glancing from still blue lakes its golden ray.

A kiss from her was like nectar divine
　　As lip with lip, like living flames entwine,
As echoed note answered by distant lyre
　　While both in ravished harmony expire.

Heart hastes to winged heart in fleet embrace
　　Trembling the lips, and fevered the face,
Soul melts in soul... Earth and heaven confound
　　This our passion oceanic that over us sounds!

Ah, Father, you can't feel — you, who've never felt
A lover's kiss upon your own lips melt!
Let laymen curse, let youths their madness bawl —
Your heart is hardened against Nature's call.

Once, love! I roamed the regions of the blest —
When first, your lips upon my own did rest!
/Sings/

    A kiss from her was like nectar divine
        As lip with lip, like living flames entwine,
    As echoed note answered by distant lyre
        While both in ravished harmony expire.

/He grabs at a Child and makes to kiss her — she escapes/

PRIEST.
    He's just like you, a man! Why do you flee?

HERMIT.
    Ah, Father — everything shuns misery,
As if the wretched were a ghoul from Hell.
Ah, yes, and she herself fled me as well!
"Farewell!" and off she sped along the path
As if she were a lightning flash.

/To the Children/

    Why was it that she ran away?
Was it something I chanced to say?
Was it I struck her with too bold a glance?
I must remember!

/Thinks hard/

                My mind's awhirl, perchance...
No, no! I see it all as plain as day:
It's all right here — Nothing has gone astray —
I said, two words, only two words, that I...

/With sorrow/

    Father — two words!
"Tomorrow!" and "Goodbye!"

"Farewell!" and from the fir she strips this bough:
"This is," she said,

/He points at the floor/

              "All that remains us now.
Farewell!" and off she sped along the path
As if she were a lightning flash!

PRIEST.
My son, I feel your pain, deeply I do!
And yet, there's thousands more, worse off than you.
At more than one graveside I've shed my tears —
I pray my parents' rest these many years,
Two of my children I've lain in the cold earth,
And she, who shared my better and my worse,
My wife, whom I loved more than I can say!
But what's to do? God gives, God takes away!
God's will be done! Blessed be His holy Name!

HERMIT./Strongly/
Your wife?

PRIEST
      The memory rends my heart in twain!

HERMIT.
Wherever I go, someone's mourning his wife!
It's not my fault! I've never seen your wife!

/Coming to/

Take comfort, blubbering husband, in your woe —
Your helpmeet was dead already, during life!

PRIEST.
What? How?

HERMIT.
      Dead, as soon as they pronounced her "wife!"
Marriage tamps living maidens down below
The earth, cutting them off from kin and friends
And... everybody else. The girl's life ends
As soon as she the stranger's threshold crosses.

PRIEST.
Although your bitter words would mask your loss,
She lives still, your love, I gather from your words?

HERMIT. /With irony/
Alive? And for that we can thank the Lord!
Alive? How? What is it you expect?
I'll kneel, I'll kiss the cross, I give you my word,
She's dead, and never shall she resurrect!

/Pause. then slowly/

For there are different types of death:
There is the common sort, that takes
A thousand souls at every breath,
That snuffs the old and weak, and breaks
The strong and hale, and there's the kind
That took from me, Maryla mine.

/Sings/

There by Niemen's feeder stream
On the blooming meadow green,
A sombre hillock can be seen
With its base enwreathed, entire
Of thorn and bramble and of briar...

/Stops singing/

Ah, and it's a sad sight, fell,
When in full bloom, beauty must

Bid the sunlit world farewell
Crumbling, still green, to the dust!
Look, look! On the white bedsheet, pale
She rests, like clouds on milky skies!
Around her stand, with sob and wail
The mournful priest at her bedside,
And sadder still, the help and maids
And sadder still, the friend in braids
And sadder still, the girl's own mother,
Saddest of all, her broken lover.
Look, see the bloom sink from her lips,
See how the light from her eye slips;
The cheeks, where roses late did bloom
Now wither in the creeping gloom.
Just as a peony will faint
When from the feeding earth it's rent,
Just so her lips fade, livid blue
Against her face's ashen hue.
With pain she lifted up her head
And gazed with eyes that paled in frost,
Then fell again upon the bed
As pale as the communion Host.
Her hands grow icy, and her heart
Now beats, now stills; she's here, she's gone…
That eye, which once shone as the sun…
Look, Father, here, upon this ring —
All that remains me now — a shard
Of memory — See how the stone sparks?
Such flashes did her eyes impart
To all who met them — but the flash
That was her soul? Snuffed out, alas!
No longer through her eyes it shines.
They glow with borrowed light — the kind
That phosphors rotten wood at night
Or lends to dew reflected light
Before it's shaken from the bough
Which then is merely damp, and brown.
With pain she lifted up her head

And gazed with eyes that paled in frost,
Then fell again upon the bed
As pale as the communion Host.
Her hands grow icy, and her heart
Now beats, now stills; she's here, she's gone!

CHILD.
She's dead, the girl? O, what a shame!
I can't help sobbing at your story!
Eternal rest grant her, O Lord!
Don't cry! We'll pray for her, the same
As for all souls in Purgatory.
Was she your sister? Or your friend?

HERMIT.
That's one sort of death, my children.
But there's another kind, far worse,
When one does not die all at once
But piecemeal, slowly — How it hurts!
Two souls together bear the brunt
Of its dart, but only one is killed;
Only in one all hope is stilled;
The other dances free, unscathed.
And she lives on, free, fresh, and gay.
Oh, tears she'll shed, a few — she must!
But then her feelings slowly rust.
At last, her heart crumbles away.
That kind of death would two at once slay,
But only one of them is killed,
Only in one all hope is stilled;
The other dances free, unscathed.
And she lives on, free, fresh, and gay.
That sort of death killed... I won't say who!
But it's much worse than death is, true?
A corpse, who turns his gaze on you...

/The children run away/

And yet she died...! I weep, I wring
My hands, and gossips in a ring
Stretch forth their necks and say "He lies!"
They jerk my arm — "Open your eyes
And see, you madman, she's alive!"

/To the Priest/

Untruths repeated still are lies
Though a thousand times the lie be said.
The heart speaks true, and my heart sighs:
"No hope, no hope! Maryla's dead!"

/Pause/

Of death, a third kind yet remains —
Eternal, as the Gospel teaches.
Woe to the man, whose death brings pains
Eternal; children, will my fate
Be such? So far no man's eye reaches.
And yet my sins are heavy, great!

*PRIEST.*
Against yourself, and against the world
You've sinned more than against the Lord.
Neither for chuckles nor for tears was man
Made, but to serve his fellow man.
The trials you've seen, however great, or
Harsh, are minuscule when you compare
Them to the vastness of the universe.
God's servant will his sorrows bravely bear
Unto the grave the sinner longs for — later,
The latter fool wakes from his pain — to worse.

*HERMIT.* /Astounded/
Father! What tricks are these? What sleight of hand?

/Aside/

Is he a wizard? Is he casting spells?
Or did he eavesdrop on our conversations?

*/To the Priest/*

Those very words fell from her lips as well!
All that you say, I heard from her, verbatim.
That selfsame evening, when we said farewell.

*/With irony/*

A perfect setting for a homily:
Such pretty sentiments! So elevated!
"Fatherland, fame, and learning!" Thus she prated —
Like hail from shingles, her words drummed off me
Until they rattled me asleep.
Though once even I, as the rhyming fad is
Was stirred to sermons too, by brave Militiades:

*/Sings/*

"Upward, o youth!
Until thy flight
Surpass in truth
The sun, whose light
Bathes the entire race of man
From sea to sea, and land to land!"

I meant it then, and might have meant it still
Had she not all ideals in me killed —
With one light breath overturning battlements
Raised for the dwelling places of giants.
Nothing remains now but the tottering walls
That crumble beneath the footfalls
Of butterflies.
And now she tries
To raise castles on eggshells?
To my atlas-career she brought a halt

Transforming me into an ant! The vault
Of heaven, now, she would have me bear?
In vain! Man has but one spark of strength that flames
In youth. Should Minerva blow
Life into his soul, a new Plato
Arises; if the torch is lit by Mars,
A hero bursts forth, who in scarlet wars,
With virtues great, and sometimes, greater crimes,
Towards the shining Pantheon he climbs;
Sceptres are dashed down by a shepherd's rod
And thrones overturned by one imperious nod.

/Pause, then slowly/

And if the spark's lit by a lover's eye
Sometimes it sputters dimly in the heart's gloom
Like a votive lamp in a Roman catacomb.

PRIEST.
O, you unfortunate, misguided youth!
For these laments, which stutter from your breast,
That you're no criminal, I know for truth —
And her beauty, which so your mind torments
Excited in you no mere corporal lust.
So mightily you loved, so true and just
Your feelings: Love her still, though from afar.
Through her, a criminal would virtue find;
And you, virtuous, would turn to crime?
Whatever it be that separates you here,
Love's gravity pulls your star, her star near —
Though unseen to each other in the mist,
The clouds will part, and their two orbits
Will link forever in a heavenly dance
When with this earth, the chains that bind you burst
And you will know each other, as at first.
When eyes washed clean melt in renewed glance.
Sundered below, you'll be as one above;
God pardons all, that has its font in love.

HERMIT.
What? How do you know that? What does this all mean?

/Mimics Priest's voice/

"Her heart as pure as sacred is her cheek!
The chains that bind you here will fall away!"
You know all that — Were you eavesdropping,
Did you pry away
Our secret, hidden in our hearts' depths?
Which to no other friend we dared to speak?
For with one hand upon this bough,
Another on our breast,
We made a solemn vow
Never to speak of these things, unto death!

But once I remember... One time I transferred
By a magical stroke of the thieving brush
Her likeness; but when I showed it to friends —
Not a single one of them was stirred
By the awesome beauty that my heart distends.
Our holy sentiments, to them was mush.
They see with their eyes — how might they glimpse the soul?
Like wolves, or astronomers, they gaze at the skies,
Creeping with compass across the starry pole,
Unable to see with lovers' or poets' eyes...

So do I venerate her lifeless image
That I dare never soil it with my lips.
And when at night by lamp or pale moon's visage
I dress my bed, no piece of clothing slips
From my breast before I shade her view,
Lying thereon this sacred sprig of yew.
As for my friends...! They witness the latreia
With which I serve this icon — and they snort
With laughter! Or they yawn a
Sigh discreet: "You bet she's pretty, sport!"
Or sneer impatiently: "Aw, cut the drama!"

O! That old man and his damned reason. Lord!
Our secret! He's the betrayer!

/Ever more confused/

He gabbed it out in public! Right out loud!
And some kid, or some gossip from the crowd
Came and betrayed it to you, in confession!

/Raving his utmost/

Maybe you wormed it out of me, last session
In the sin-box?

PRIEST.
What's with all this wrangling
Of treasons, confessions, and secrets uncovered?
However knotted your story's yarn, poor lover,
The deft eye won't be long in its untangling!

HERMIT.
That's true — For eyes and ears are always near
To glimpse the candid, the unguarded overhear!
A man keeps his heart's counsel all the day;
At night, in dreams, he gives it all away.
Once, long ago! It so happened to me.
I had just met her. I said nary a word
To anyone, but that night, my mother overheard
What my unconscious lips in dreams confessed.
I'd barely said Good Morning at breakfast,
And she: "Whence this your new-found piety?
All last night long you moaned the Litany
To the Virgin Immaculate!"
I blushed in recognition — and that night
Made sure to close my door
So she might not guess any more.
Now, I'm without a home, without a door
To guard my thoughts from others. Now, as I sleep

Wherever I fall, it's impossible to keep
My inmost thoughts from others' ears —
They may be broadcast for anyone to hear!
Storms burst, and winds blow
Lightnings flash and die —
So many shapes they throw
For any to espy
Before they fade again.
One image only do I see etched
Before my eyes, whether I throw myself prone
Upon the ground and plumb the earth's depths,
There it shines, like the moon
Reflected on the pond's still pane —
I reach for it, it disappears again
But to return; or whether I lift my eye
Into the azure — it hangs there in the sky:
An angel's figure, assumed
Above the clouds, in the heights of heaven.
Then, like an eaglet, above the simoom
On feathery sails she hovers

/He looks aloft/

Still, so still, about to stoop and cover
The prey already fixed by her spear-like gaze;
So still, against the sun's rays
As if netted there herself — entwined
In webs of sky; so above me she shines
Forever!

/Sings/

Whether the earth is baked by the sun
    Or sleeps beneath the cloak of night
I see her, after her I run,
       With her never, yet she's never out of sight!

And when she appears to me — whenever,
If I'm alone in field or in wood,
I struggle to keep silent; would that I might!
My disobedient tongue always rebels
And I must call upon her. Soft, with slight
Tones, yet someone is always near
As I invoke her name, some caitiff hears
And thus this very morning it befell,
Some traitor eavesdropped on me.
Morning it was... I'll describe it. I still can see
Fresh-sprinkled with late-fallen rain, the lawn
Shining as if with jewels, with dew, near dawn,
The vales all sunk in mist, like seas of snow;
In paler heavens, the late stars thinning out —
And there above me hangs the eastern star —
I greet him now each day, watching him rise!
Near the veranda —

*/He starts/*

                    Ha ha! Derailed again. Surprise!
It's not THAT morning I meant to name.
This god-damned romantic fever is to blame!
My head will spin like this as long as I live!

*/Pause, recalls/*

So, morning. Rain is pouring like a sieve,
The cold wind blowing,
I, sobbing, moaning,
Hid my soaking noggin in a bush...

*/Smiles gently/*

And though I chid my whining tongue, Now, hush!
Somebody heard me. Just me wailing?
Or my stupid gob, tattle-taling
Her name out loud?

When there's a desert, you know, there's a crowd.

PRIEST.
 You poor, sick youth!
 What are you saying? Who heard what?

HERMIT. /In all seriousness/

 Who? Well, to tell the truth,
 The little bug that crawled near my nut —
 A lightning bug it was — on the wet leaves.
 Oh, how alike they are to you and me!
 He crawled right close to my rain-sodden head
 (Wanting to cheer me up, I guess) and said:
 "Poor man! What use, this lover's mewling?
 Is it you're fault that you have a soft heart?
 Quit all this crying. Who are you fooling?
 You're trapped, just like I am. This part
 Of me that's always blinking bright
 Shines gaily in the glooms of night.
 Now, I once thought that it would bring me glory,
 But sadly ends each firefly's brief story.
 This cheery spark of mine you see
 Betrays me to my enemy.
 Upon how many brilliant friends of mine
 The evil lizards have already dined?
 Oh, how I wish I could put out this fire
 Yet flame I must — until I shall expire!"

/Pause; points to his heart /

 Yes! Flame I must — until I shall expire!

CHILDREN.
 Gosh, that's a miracle! Did you hear?
 Daddy, can such a thing be true?

/The Priest walks away, wringing his hands/

A lightning bug, if you clap him to your ear,
He'll speak in human voice to you?

*HERMIT.*
Why not? Little one, come here
And on this countertop lay your little ear.
A poor soul begs you for a prayer.
D'you hear him tapping there?

*CHILD.*
Da-da-da-da-da-da- Dad!
He's really tapping, Daddy! Tapping like mad!
It sounds like a watch under a pillow!
Daddy, what can that be?

*HERMIT.*
                Oh, just a little fellow.
You can hardly see him with eyes, or
Lenses — in his past life though, he was a miser.
Little soul, what is your pleasure?
"I beg three Hail Marys, please."
Beg on, you skinflint! You see, I knew him —
This usurer — lived next door to him.
He scratched himself a mound of treasure
But knocked a widow's cottage down
— And her there, begging on her knees,
Her kids all grovelling on the ground! —
He'd never spare shilling or crust
To those in need; o no! He'd trussed
His coins and banknotes tight and fast
And kept them hidden deep; at last
He died, and for his sins he knocks
His timid pleas in his treasure-box.
And so he'll suffer, locked in pain
Until he pays all back again.
He'll get no alms from me!
But if there be

Among you anyone who'd like to say
A prayer for him, well, go on: pray away!

*/Re-enter Priest, with some water in a bowl/*

HERMIT. */Ever more confused/*
Well? Did you hear that demon whine?

PRIEST.
Dear God! What now, this time?

*/Looks around/*

There's no one here!

HERMIT.
Clean out your ear!

*/To a Child/*

Come here, come close, my lad:
Did you not hear him?

CHILD.
               It's true, Dad!
I heard a tiny voice.

HERMIT.
              Well then?

PRIEST.
It's time to go to bed, children.
It's quiet here as a deep, black pool.

HERMIT.
So Nature speaks to a deaf old fool.

*PRIEST.*
    Brother, come, take some water, cool
    Your burning forehead. You'll feel better.

*HERMIT. /Takes some water, washes his face; the clock strikes. After a few chimes, the hermit drops the bowl onto the floor and stares off in front of him, seriously, gloomily/*
    That's ten o'clock

*/A rooster crows/*

    And the first cock.
    Time runs on, life slips by.
    One lamp burns down.

*/A candle on the table goes out/*

    Once midnight sounds...
    Dear God, how cold am I!

*/The Priest stands still, staring at the candle in surprise/*

    A cold wind whistles through the cracks.
    It chills me to the bone!

*/The Hermit moves to the stove/*

    Where am I?

*PRIEST.*
              Among friends! At home!

*HERMIT. /More clear-headedly/*
    I must have set you somewhat aback —
    A stranger, strangely dressed as well!
    Have I been babbling? Please, don't tell
    A soul what you have overheard
    From this poor wanderer — not a word!

I come from far away...
/Looks round; still more clearly/

                              In my youth, once
In the broad daylight I was trounced
By a wingèd bandit

/Smiles/

                                  who robbed me blind
Of all the wealth I once possessed,

Leaving me naked, so I dress
Myself in whatever I chance to find

/Picking off leaves and fixing his clothes, sadly/

To cover my innocence as I might.

PRIEST. /Tears his eyes away from the candle; to the Hermit/
    Calm down, for God's sake!

/To the Children/

                              Who put out that light?

HERMIT.
    Each miracle you'd like to reason out;
    But nature, like man, has mysteries
    Which she hides not only from the vulgar rout,
    But never betrays to wise men or to priests!

PRIEST. /Grabs his hand/
    My son!

HERMIT. /Moved, shocked/
        Son? that voice, like a thunder peal
    Has chased away the clouds that gloomed my mind.

*/Looks around/*

> I see now where I am, and in whose hands!
> My second father! And this, my fatherland!
> I recognise this house! Though changed, I say:
> Your children grown — your hair all flecked with grey!

PRIEST. */Confused, takes the candle, looks closely at the Hermit/*
> You know me? I know... you! No! It can't be!

HERMIT.
> Gustaw.

PRIEST.
> Gustaw! You're Gustaw!

*/Hugs him/*

> Good Lord! Praise the day!
> My student, my son!

GUSTAW. */Embracing him/*
> Father! Press me once more to your heart!
> But then... and soon... I must be on my way.
> And oh! A long road awaits you as well!
> But we'll meet again — there, never more to part.

PRIEST.
> Gustaw! It's really you? So long! And whence?
> Where have you been, my dear friend, these long years?
> You vanished like a stone that disappears
> When tossed into a pond. And then — silence —
> No word from you, no letter, no scrap of news
> From the one star pupil of mine, in whose
> Talents I dared to hope such great success —
> And — nothing! Then, today! So lost — so dressed...

GUSTAW. /Angrily/
　　Old man! And shall I pay you back in kind?
　　Speak out my charge, haul you to an assize?
　　It's you that killed me! Teaching me to read —
　　Both lofty books, and Nature's lovely screed.
　　It's you that made earth hell,

/Mournful smile/

　　　　　　　　　　　　　and paradise!

/Strongly, with contempt/

　　While it's just dirt!

PRIEST.
　　　　　　　　Dear Christ! What's this I hear?
　　You say I killed you? My conscience is clean!
　　I loved you like a son!

GUSTAW.
　　　　　　　　For that alone,
　　Do I forgive you!

PRIEST.
　　　　　　　If you had only known
　　How often I prayed to see you once again...

GUSTAW. /Embraces him/
　　It seems your prayer was answered, my old friend.
　　Let me embrace you one more time, before
　　The second candle gutters...

/Looks at the clock/

　　　　　　　　　　　But now it's late,
　　And such a long, long journey yet awaits!

*PRIEST.*
>Gustaw, my ears are greedy for your news,
>But that can wait. What you need now is rest.
>Tomorrow —

*GUSTAW.*
>                    Thanks, but I can't be your guest.
>Nor could I repay your kindness.

*PRIEST.*
>                    Gustaw, hush!

*GUSTAW.*
>No! Cursed are those who do not pay! They must!
>Reciprocal labour, feelings, one small tear
>In scot symbolic, though the balance be
>Quit by our Father in Heaven! As for me,
>A pilgrim through these lands of memory,
>Where each square ell a tearful tribute exacts,
>Having now wept myself dry in such heart's tax,
>I don't want to incur any further debts!

*/Pause/*

>Not long ago, my wanderings led me back
>To my old homestead — now an empty wrack —
>Wherever the eye fell, ruins and decay:
>Fence-slats and hearth-stones prised up, torn away,
>The yard in weeds and nettles overgrown...
>A cemetery, that was once my home!
>How different this homecoming from those
>When, a young scholar who in triumph goes
>Home at the end of the school year,
>I was greeted by kin ere I even drew near
>The outskirts of my home town! Sisters, brother
>Stopping the horses, pulling me to mother
>Who waits on the front porch to greet me
>With a parental blessing — there to meet me

With old friends crowding round, laughter and cheer...
And now: a desert. No kind soul draws near,
Only a barking dog... Old Blackie! Here, boy!
                              He comes bounding
As fast as age and illness let him, an old friend;
The family pet. Alone he, at the end
Remained of all our servants to defend
The gates unlocked, the empty house... So thin
And undernourished, lame, he but begins
To leap on me in joy, when he falls dead...
I hugged him one last time, lifted my head,
A light glowed in the window. Once inside,
What's going on? In the very room where Mother died
A thief kneels, tearing at the groaning wood,
The floorboards over which her bed once stood,
Looking for — what? I never will find out:
I pounced on him in ire and grabbed his throat,
Throttling him until his eyeballs swelled
Like apples in his face, and then I fell
Down on the floor myself, and sobbed. Near dawn
I heard small feet come shuffling, hobbling on,
Behind a cane — A woman dressed in rags,
Sick, pale, more like a purgatorial sprite
She seemed than living woman. When she caught sight
Of this ghost in the empty house, she sagged
Against the wall in terror, and made the cross
On brow and breast... "Don't be afraid!" I rushed
To reassure her. "God be praised! My dear,
Who are you? And what is it you do here?"
"I'm a poor woman," she sobbed out with tears.
"I served the masters of this house for years —
Good people, they! May they both rest in peace!
Alas, their life was not one full of ease,
For them or their children! Now they've passed, their home
Decays and crumbles slowly to the loam;
They're gone, and their son Gustaw too, must be
Dead by now — All that's left here is me!"

The blood slammed in my heart. I tumbled, floored:
All's gone!

*PRIEST.*
    All save your soul, and the Good Lord!
All passes here below. Happiness, pain...

*GUSTAW.*
    How many memories here, in your home again!
There, with the other children, on the sand
I played, and just beyond — the little glade
Where, searching out birds' nests we often ran.
Beneath our windows slid a little creek
Where on hot summer afternoons we'd bathe,
And in the woods we'd play at hide and seek.
I met Homer and Tasso beneath those trees,
And with King John relieved the Viennese.
At night, beneath a pagan moon of blood
My mates and I fought for the Holy Rood.
Beyond those hills loomed the Teutonic Knights;
Here, I disposed my legions for the fight;
Our wooden swords now Polish damascene:
We rushed into the fray with wild careen,
Thrusting and slashing till on all sides lay
Turbans and Turkish heads snipped in the fray;
"The field is ours!" victoriously we'd cheer
While riderless, the Arab steeds sped clear.
That hill, for us, was where the Muslim tents
Were pitched; thence did we chase them. Then, by chance,
She once materialised there to watch our games —
And gone, like that! were Godfrey, John, St. James,
The prophet's banner, tents, Vienna besieged,
And I, captived, dropped meekly to my knees.
From that day on: Through her, with her, and only She!
With her is tinctured each local memory.
Here did I first her face divine espy;
There did she first address me; she and I
Sat in that copse of trees reading Rousseau;

Here did I frame a bower of sprays, below
Which she might rest protected from the sun;
About these woods would I, enamoured, run
To gather bouquets or to fill a dish
With berries; by these limpid springs we'd fish
For silver carp and rainbow-speckled trout.
And now...

/Weeps/

PRIEST.
    Weep, weep, if you've aught to weep about;
Such recollections gnaw at us, and bring
Regrets, which — alas — can't change anything.

GUSTAW.
    So many years have passed, so much has changed;
This heart's the same, however far I've ranged.
And now I'm back, where was my great delight,
Returned, burned through, in such a wretched plight.
Let's say a child retains a treasured stone
He used to play with, and wherever he roamed,
Kept it, memento-like, through all his years.
Should some kind hand place that stone on his bier,
And from that rock no bitter tear ever fell,
Priest, damn that pebble to the deepest hell!

PRIEST.
    Why should those tears be bitter? Memories
Are mixed with nectar, and they bring relief
To those who feel them rightly; toxic lees
Scald but the tears of the unrepentant thief.

GUSTAW.
    I'll tell you more. Once in this park I erred,
Same time of day, same season, same chilly nighttime air.
And the same dew shone on the bejewelled lawn,
The same pale stars were thinning out near dawn,

And the moon, and the eastern star on high
That I greet each day in the fresh new sky;
The same love burning within, the same care...
All as it always was — but — she's not there!
Something stirred near the bench — my heart leaps to believe —
Can it be her? No. Just the wind in the dead leaves.
That veranda-bench! My hope's cradle and bier.
There we met — there we parted —
                              What I'd gone through here!
Perhaps just yesterday here she retired
To rest... I breathe the same air she respired!
I stop and listen, cast round a futile gaze
And see, above me... only a spider, that sways
Suspended from a leaf by his thin line.
How very slight, the filaments that bind
Him, and myself, to this sublunar world!
I fell back on a tree-trunk. Then, dry, curled,
On the far end of the bench, next to a sheaf
Of blooms and grasses, I saw a leaf,
The other half of this you now espy

*/Holds out a leaf/*

That brought to mind the hour we said goodbye!
My dear old friend! I greeted him with a tear.
Long did we talk, for I was keen to hear
All he could tell me of her new routines:
Does she rise early? Where might she be seen?
What are her interests? What tunes does she play
When she sits at the keyboard? Where does she stray
On her daily walks? To what fountain or rill?
She rests her elbows on what windowsill?
Does she blush — modestly — when she chances to recall
Me? Say — does she remember me at all?
And what do I learn as I thus stick in my nose?

*/Angrily, he strikes his own forehead/*

Oh, woman...!

*/Sings/*

"At first..."

*/Stops; then, to the Children/*

You know the old song? It goes:

At first, I reckon
She thinks of you each second.

CHORUS OF CHILDREN.
Love her so beckons
She thinks on you each second.

GUSTAW.
And then, I say,
She thinks on you each day.

CHORUS OF CHILDREN.
Her heart won't stray:
She thinks on you each day.

GUSTAW.
Then each fortnight
(Out of mind, when out of sight).

CHORUS OF CHILDREN.
Her troth she'll plight
But once every fortnight.

GUSTAW.
And then, my friend
Each month, at month's end.

*CHORUS OF CHILDREN.*
>Her love remains
>But like the moon, it wanes.

*GUSTAW.*
>As water courses through the creek
>So love is borne away;
>Once, yearly, she will fondly speak
>Of you... on Easter Day.

*CHORUS OF CHILDREN.*
>Good girl! At least
>Her love's a moveable feast.

*GUSTAW.*
>And so...

*/Showing the leaf/*

>>She tossed away our love's best token;
>The tie that bound us was so lightly broken.
>She's not allowed, it seems, such memories
>As would recall the times she spent with me.
>I left the park, my own footsteps betrayed me,
>As some unseen force to the manor led me.
>The darkness was banished by a thousand lights;
>Steeds neigh, carts crunch the gravel, a festive night.
>I steal up to the wall and raise my eyes:
>Above the sill, through crystal panes I size
>The hall up — all the sparkling tables laid
>With food and drink — I listen — somebody said
>"A toast!" I caught the name — don't ask me whose!
>A voice I know called out "Long may she live!"
>One thousand voices raised the toast anew
>Then — how can I remember this, and still live? —
>A priest called out his blessing upon two...

*/Stares at the door/*

A smiling voice says "thanks," and I know who
That voice belongs to — her, I think —
But I can't see for sure, through the small chink
Of space between the mirror and the door —
But fury choked me, and I saw no more
As I fell lifeless — so thought I at the time —

/Pause/

But life I lost not, I merely lost my mind!

PRIEST.
Poor wretch, to seek out self-inflicted pain!

GUSTAW.
A corpse stretched out next to the wedding feast
I lay, the grass bedewed with tears of gall —
A paradox of agony and tenderness,
Just as the sun arose bloody in the east,
So did I rise — around me all was calm —
I realised, the wedding night was past!
Lightning-fast, age-long, that moment of gloom!
I expect another such on the Day of Doom!

/Pause, slowly/

Then the angel of death led me out of the garden!

PRIEST.
Why tear open scars which have already hardened?
My son — it's an old nugget, sure — but still:
When sentence is passed and there's no hope of pardon,
It's best to recognise the Good Lord's will.

GUSTAW. /Sadly/
Oh no! God spun for us a common thread.
The self-same star shone above our infant bed;
Identical, though brought up differently,

So near in carriage and in age were we;
The same attractions, our distastes the same,
Our thoughts alike, in two hearts burned one flame.
So perfectly matched were we, what wonder
That God knit the weft...

*/With greatest passion/*

...that you tore asunder!

*/More strongly, angrily/*

Woman! You thing of fluff! You flighty revel!
Compared with yours, an angel's beauty pales.
But your soul, ah! is blacker than a...
Good God! And yet for gold you prove so frail?
The world's renown, that you so hotly follow
Is but a bubble: shiny, light... and hollow!
Oh, may whatever you touch now turn to gold!
Wherever you turn your heart, your face,
Kiss, love, embrace gold! glittering, cold!
Had I an equal say in our fates
And God should offer me such a girl
Whose beauty never had been seen before,
The type that set the ancient Greeks to war,
More gorgeous than the angelic ranks that swirl
About His throne, in dreams, in poets' lies,
More gorgeous even than you! I'd still despise
Her for your sake!
If as a dowry, all the gold
Of fabled river Tagus were told
Into a sack, and with it also given
The kingdom of Heaven,
I'd spurn it for your sake!
She'd not even get a second look from me,
Were all these riches offered me, scot-free
For just a fraction of the time
I'd spent on you in vain —

Not for a year, or half a year,
Not for a single caress of mine!

Such an offer I'd disdain
Could I but have you here!

/Roughly/

But you, with heart now frigid, and indifferent brow
Pronounced the fatal sentence,
Enkindled the inferno foul
That melted our sweet chains, and howls
A hell eternal between you and me
For my eternal torments!
You murdered me, seductress! But you shall pay —
Heaven hotly pursues those who betray,
And I... I will not be unavenged;
Traitors, beware! I cry revenge!

/Pulls out a stiletto, with fierce irony/

Here's a nice present for the toffs!
Their blood will be the toast I quaff...
You female degenerate!
I'll twist that bridal spray around your throat
And bear you off to Hell, my rightful loot
And plunder...

/Pauses, reflects/

       What? Kill her? How I prate on!
For that I'd have to be blacker than Satan!
Iron, away!

/Puts away the stiletto/

       Let her own memory gore
Her heart like a stiletto, to the core!

I'll go, but I'll go without a knife;
I'll go myself to cast on her my eye —
To the hall where the leeches glisten with gold,
To the dais, where they recline as man and wife!
This leaf on my brow, clothes tattered
                                  and spattered with mould,
I'll walk right up to the dais where they recline...
See how they rise, flustered, and raise wine
To me in clumsy toast, offer a chair,
Yet I say nothing, standing there.
Feet stumble through the stunned quadrille;
They mumble: "Come, complete the square..."
While I, with leaf on heart, stock still
Say nothing, standing there.
Then she, with her angelic grace
Approaches: "Welcome guest! Please, what's your name?
Whence do you come?" Mutely, I stand there just the same
As always; I merely stand and stare —
Ha, ha! A venomous, viper's glare
To blind her, strike her petrified!
Like smoke, my stare wafts deep inside
Her brain, seeping through her eyelids white
There to brood forever,
Staining each waking thought, and at night
Waking her in fever.

/*More slowly and tenderly*/

And she so delicate, so lightly bruised,
Like meadow-fluff in Spring
That from the stalk each whispered breeze can wring,
Or fall through the light burden of the dews.
She'd stir at each slight movement of my heart,
At each rough word of mine her tears would start;
Her gaiety by my cloudy brow was doused,
So tightly were our two kindred souls espoused.
What one would think, the other guessed;
Were two beings ever more perplexed

With "I" and "Thou?" Each other's looking-glass
Where, in unfeigned innocence there basked
Our virgin hearts. No sooner shot
Emotion to my eye, than it was caught
By hers and nested in her heart;
No sooner there, but it would start
Its way back into mine.
Dear God, I loved her! Can I now design
To terrify her, and her heart to churn
Between the sharp jaws of Hell's sleepless worm?
And what are her transgressions?
That she seduced me with ambiguous terms?
That her smiles tempted out of me love's passion?
Were her looks false, intending to deceive?
What vows did she break? What promises unweave?
Did I have any hope to claim her, ever?
No, No! I but deceived myself. She, never!
I brewed the poison that eructs my fever.
What for, these ravings? Have I any right
To dream of her — a wretch like me — however slight?
Where is my virtue? My great deeds? My fame?
I've none, I've nothing, as no longer have I
This one love of my life. Did I ever try
To win her hand, my passion to requit?
I was not bold above friendship. That was it —
I only wanted her near
Even as kin with kin — a sister dear
To a brother — God's my witness — Had I her thus,
Then was I satisfied: the two of us
Together chastely, only for to say
"I see her, saw her, will see her today
And each tomorrow,"
Morning and noon and evening to bid
Her first Good Morning, next to her to sit —
No space between for sorrow!

/Pause/

Vain, vain this uprush.
With unsleeping eyes and venomous darts
A swarm patrols the gulf between our hearts;
They buzz "Be off!" And off I must...
To die!

/With sorrow/

People of stone! You cannot guess
How painful is the hermit's death!
As he lies dying, his expiring gaze
A foreign world — he so alone! — surveys,
With no kind hand to close his snuffed-out eyes
Nor bear his body to the muddy sleep
Wherein he will await the Last Assize;
No friendly hand a clutch of dust will spread
In pity, or tamp down that final bed;
No one will weep!
I only I could visit you in dreams;
If at the memory of my distress
You'd — one day only — pin upon your dress
A mourning-band; if those bright beams
Would mist, and shed one passing tear above me,
As you sigh — furtively — "God, how he loved me!"

/With wild irony/

You puppy! Stop your yapping. Snivelling girl!
Shall I, like Fortune's bastard, expire sobbing?
The heavens have given me a proper drubbing:
They've torn all things from me — my entire world.
But they can't snatch the remnants of my pride!
Alive, I never begged tittle or jot;
I shan't beg pity now that I have died!

/Determined/

Do what you wish! You're lord of your own will —

Forget...! I shall forget her!

/*Confused*/

                                        Have I not?
Her face... Ever more blurry... Quite erased!
Swallowed entire into the eternal deeps.
How I disdain my raving!
Yet still I sigh! Can it be her I'm craving?
Can I not forget her in the very grave?
I see her clearly! And there, upon her face —
Tears! Tears for me! Dear God! She truly weeps!

/*Mournfully*/

Weep, sweetheart, weep! Your Gustaw is dying!

/*With determination*/

Here we go then, Gustaw — Play the man!

/*Lifts again the stiletto*/
/*Mournfully*/

Fear not, my darling, for he has no fear!
He takes from you nothing that you hold dear.
I leave you all, by testament and right —
This life, this world, all pleasure and delight...

/*Fiercely*/

And your...! All... Nothing I ask in return!
Not even one single tear wasted on me!

/*To the Priest, who enters with Servants*/

Listen, you...! Should you ever chance to see

/*With ever more violence*/

A certain girl... a woman... superhumanly fair
And should she inquire
How it was I died? Don't say from despair;
Tell her my blood surged with a happy fire,
That I was always gay, never chanced
To reminisce of lovers lost; I drank,
Gambled at cards and always broke the bank;
That every night to early morn I'd dance,
Heart always carefree, never moody or rankled
With vain regrets; that, dancing...

/Stamps his foot/

                                        I turned my ankle —

That's how I died!

/Stabs himself/

PRIEST.
                    Jesus my Lord the Christ!

/Grabs Gustaw's hand. Gustaw remains standing, the clock strikes/

GUSTAW. /Struggling with death, looks at the clock/
    The chain rattles, and eleven strikes!

PRIEST.
    Gustaw!

/The rooster crows a second time/

GUSTAW.
              The second sign.
    Time runs on, life is spent,

/Clock stops chiming, the second candle burns down/

    Guttered, the second candle —
    My pain is at an end!

*/Pulls out the stiletto, puts it away/*

PRIEST.
    What can we do?! Dear God! Is it too late?
    He stuck it in, up to the very handle!
    His madness drove him to his fate!

GUSTAW. */With a cold smile/*
    So why does he not fall?

PRIEST. */Seizes his hand/*
    O crime! Dear Lord, forgive him all —

GUSTAW.
    A crime like this one can't commit
    Just any day — collect your wits
    And fear not. Thus the criminal
    But reenacts his scene of pain
    Didactically — but to explain.

PRIEST.
    How? What? What's going on?

GUSTAW.
    Spells, smoke and mirrors — sleights of hand.

PRIEST.
    My legs are trembling, my hair stands on end —
    In the Name of the Father and the Son...

GUSTAW. */Looks at the clock/*
    Two hours have struck, of love and of despair.
    Now comes the third hour; the hour of... beware —

PRIEST. */Trying to sit Gustaw down/*
    Sit down, lie down — give that wicked blade here.
    Let me bind that wound —

*GUSTAW.*
                              No, Father, have no fear.
   Until the Last Trump that blade will be sheathed.
   And that wound? A trifle. Do I not breathe?

*PRIEST.*
   As God is my witness, I know not what —

*GUSTAW.*
                                      Charms,
   Magic perhaps? You know, there are such arms,
   Costly ones, that slit the very soul
   Although they seem to leave the body whole.
   By such a weapon was I run through twice.

*/Pause, he smiles/*

   Such weapons here are wielded by a woman's eyes,

*/Gloomily/*

   And after death, by a sinner's vain regrets!

*PRIEST.*
   And may God give all penitent souls rest!
   Why stand you so stiffly? And stare to one side?
   Your eyes...! My God! Covered with cloudy scales —
   Your pulse has stopped; your hands are cold as rime —
   What does this mean?

*GUSTAW.*
                      Of that, some other time.
   Hear now what's led me across the great divide.
   When I arrived here, when I stepped inside,
   You and your children were offering prayers
   For those who wander the Purgatorial vales...

PRIEST. /*Grabbing a crucifix*/
   Yes, yes! We'll finish them —

GUSTAW.
                        All right, but first, confess:
   You believe in Hell, Purgatory, and the rest?

PRIEST.
   I believe in everything the Good Lord preaches
   In His Gospel, and our Mother the Church teaches.

GUSTAW.
   And in the old rites? Do you still believe
   What your grandfather did? Forefathers' Eve?

PRIEST.
   That ritual was once a pagan feast.
   The Church enables, nay commands, her priest
   To enlighten her folk, and stamp out superstition.

GUSTAW. /*Pointing to the ground*/
   And I, Father, am entrusted with a mission
   By others to convince you to relent.
   Return us our Dziady! The Judge Omnipotent
   Rates one true tear of pity shed here below
   More than seas of mourning poured out just for show —
   Paid keeners and horses beribboned in black.
   When a sincere hand sets on a gravestone one,
   Just one, votive lamp, it gleams like the sun
   In the eternal realm — I tell you truly —
   More than thousands set there out of irksome duty.
   When simple folk bring offerings of honey,
   Milk and some poppyseed on that hallowed night,
   Far better will that ease a poor soul's plight
   Than modish funeral breakfasts, that stink of money.

*PRIEST.*
　　For sure. And yet those midnight gatherings
　　In chapels and caves are ripe with pagan things,
　　White magic, heretical rituals
　　And superstition. Then the folk, chock-full
　　Of fables, unenlightened, will believe
　　In ghosts and wizards. Ha! Forefathers' Eve!

*GUSTAW.*
　　You don't believe in spirits?

*/Ironically/*

　　　　　　　　　　A soulless world?
　　It lives, but as a skeleton, that's whirled
　　On its dottering career by hidden springs?


　　Or like a clock wound up, whose pendulum swings
　　It on its way in dull perpetual motion?

*/Smiles/*

　　But of Who wound it, do you have a notion?
　　Of cogs and of wheels reason may ably teach,
　　But the key, and the Hand that turns it, are beyond your reach!
　　If your eyes could shed their muddy scales,
　　You'd see, not only, this grand sailing vessel
　　You journey in, but thousands of riggers in the sails.

*/The Children enter. To them/*

　　Children, come close to the counter here.

*/To the counter/*

　　Little soul, what do you need?

*VOICE FROM THE COUNTER.*
                              I beg three prayers.

*PRIEST.* /*Terrified*/
  Glory to God on high…! He speaks! A wraith!
  And the Word became flesh! Run! The sacristan!
  Wake him up…! And the people…!

*GUSTAW.*
                    Shame on you, man!
  What's happened to your reason? And your faith?
  Who fears the Lord need not fear anything.

*PRIEST.*
  What is it that you need… Ah! a goblin! You —

*GUSTAW.*
  I? I need nothing. But so many do!

/*Captures a moth fluttering round a candle*/

  These moths you see, that swarm around a lamp
  Were, in life, of the obscurantist camp.
  They blocked, whenever they could, progress in learning,
  Now, after death, for darkness ever yearning,
  Their damned souls are constrained towards the light —
  A torment irresistible, their fright
  And their compulsion! See that pied-
  Winged butterfly? Before that splendour died
  He was some kinglet, earl, or wealthy count
  Whose wings when spread wide
  Cast withering shadows about
  Nation or city or countryside.
  That smaller, black one — see him? — Look —
  Was a dull witted scourge of books;
  A censor, buzzing from leaf to leaf,
  Befouling sheaf on printed sheaf
  Of beauty, with his all-puissant pen,

*Non licet!* here, and here again,
Mixing the sweetest pollen
With the venom of his sting;
The seeds of knowledge thus fallen
Trod by every creeping thing...
That other buzzing swarm of midges there
That nervously flit through the burly air
Were proud bootlickers, the very worst of them
Who ever wielded a lying pen.
The mindless rout of stomachs! Ever set
To wreak destruction on dry clattering wing
Like flights of locusts in the spring,
Scathing the fields
Of mature or tender yields
Wherever their petty god
Who stuffed their bellies, should nod.
For such as these, my children fair —
It's not worth the pain of the briefest prayer.
Others there are more worthy your concern,
Among them your own pupils, your own friends,
Whom you inspired to seek out lofty ends,
Stoking an inborn fire that brighter burned
For your breath. Now I'm finished with my duty.
I've squeezed my whole life into three brief hours,
For your benefit, and with the Heavenly Power's
Concession. Now let your suit be
For them, not me, as you offer up your Mass.
Nothing more than your remembrance do I ask.
On earth, my sin met retribution fair —
Now, is it penance, or reward, my share?
For he who, still on earth, has tasted Heaven,
Whose soul to her predestined half was given,
Who every earthly limit soared above,
Heart and soul losing himself in her he loved,
Thinking her thoughts alone, breathing her breath,
Retains not his identity after death,
But to his one and only love sealed fast
Becomes the shadow that she casts.

If, during life, his mistress was a saint,
He shares her heavenly glory.
If she were spattered by sin's gore, he
Sinks into hell marked by the self-same taint.
I'm fortunate in that God indentured me
To her, an angel. For both her and me
The future's bright. Meanwhile, a shade, I range
Beside her, the diapason of pain
And ecstasy; when she recalls me, sighs,
And drops a tear discreetly from her eyes,
I near her lips; I gently part her hair;
I mix my substance with the fragrant air
She breathes; I become one with her! And then,
Heaven!
But oh...! Only those who love, who part and yearn
Will understand the envy with which I burn
When...
Still must there pass by many a long season
Thus, before she's called to the embrace
Of Him Who made her. Then, keeping her pace,
I too shall steal into the Blessed Regions.

/The clock strikes/

Heed well the wisdom you've been given,
The daughter of the Lord's own breath:
Who during life has tasted Heaven
Won't get there quickly, after death.

CHORUS.
Such is the wisdom we've been given,
The daughter of the Lord's own breath:
Who during life has tasted Heaven
Won't get there quickly, after death.

# THE POET'S EXPLANATORY NOTES TO PART III

[*Translator's note: Mickiewicz provided explanatory notes only for Part III.*]

The Russian words *chin* and *chinovnik,* as used here, have a significance only understandable to Lithuanians. In Russia, in order to exist as anything other than a peasant or a merchant, in other words, in order to possess the privilege of not being subject to punishment by flogging, one must enter the civil service and be enrolled in an official *class* or *chin.* There are fourteen such classes; one must serve several years in one, before being able to move into another. *Chinovniks* are subject to various examinations, similar to the formalities still to be found in the Mandarin hierarchy in China – and it was thus that the word, so it seems, was introduced to Russia by the Mongols. Peter I so understood the meaning of the term, and went on to develop the entire system in a truly Chinese spirit. Often, the *chinovnik* is not an official, but only an aspirant to the office for which he has a right to hope. Each class or *chin* has its equivalent in military rank, and thus: a doctor of philosophy or medicine is enrolled in the eighth class with the rank of major (*collegiate assessor*); the "Freulein" or waiting maid in the employ of the imperial household holds the rank of captain; a bishop or archpriest is a general. Between *chinovniks* of higher and lower ranks there exists the same sort of submissiveness, and the same rigour in observing it, as obtains in the army.

*And heard at night the bell that terrifies / The post-chaise*

A terrifying sound, as it might bode the arrival of the Feldjäger, a type of imperial gendarme especially charged with hunting out persons under government suspicion. They usually ride about in post-chaises known as *kibitki,* which are wooden carts without amortisation or metal parts; they are thin, flat, and higher in the front than in the rear. Byron speaks of these carts in his *Don Juan.* The Feldjäger usually arrives at night, tears the suspect out of his home, and never tells anyone where he is taking him. The *kibitka* is equipped with a bell, like a postman's wagon. No one, unless he has spent some time in Lithuania, is capable of imagining the terror which grips the entire house, whenever such a bell sounds at the gate.

*The devil sits in muck. Go ask him why.*
This particular devil haunts the area around Pinsk, which is famed for its muddy surroundings.

*One fresh breeze / Would knock him dizzy to his knees.*
Prisoners, who have spent a long time incarcerated, often experience a feeling of inebriation when they first emerge into the fresh air.

*Tears at harvest homes bring bad luck.*
The Lithuanian proverb deals with the so-called *inkrutowiny*, celebrated by the people when one moves into a new home. It is hosted by the owner when he takes possession of the new house.

*It's clear as any ukase from senate session!*
Russian senatorial decrees (ukases) have become proverbial for their murkiness. This is especially true of judicial ukases, or sentencings, which are usually so elaborately drawn up that they can be explained in different, contrary fashions, which necessitates a second trial. This is in the interest of the senatorial chancelleries, which reap enormous profits from trials.

*Collegiate Registrar (to Sovietnik).*
The *kolleski regestrator* or collegiate registrar belongs to one of the lowest *chins*. Sovietniks, or advisors, are of different types and species, such as: honorary, collegiate, secret, and practical advisors. A certain Russian wit liked to say that a Practical Secret Advisor is a triple falsehood, because he doesn't advise, knows nothing of any secrets, and is the most impractical of all God's creations. Once, this same wit overheard some people speaking of a certain *chinovnik* as a good man. "Call him a good boy, rather," he interrupted. "How can a *chinovnik* be called a man while he is still just a registrar? In Russia, to be considered a man, one has to be a State Advisor at the very least."

*They make us come dance at balls.*
In Russia, an official invitation to a ball is a command, especially if the ball in question is given to celebrate the birthday, name-day, wedding,

etc., of the Tsar, any other member of the ruling family, or even of some important official. In such a case, a person under suspicion, or one who is out of favour, exposes himself to no trifling danger, should he not accept the invitation and attend. It has happened in Russia that family members of those imprisoned or sentenced to the gallows have attended court balls. In Lithuania, at the same time that Field Marshal Ivan Dibitsch was moving against the Poles, and General Matvei Chrapowitzky was stifling uprisings and incarcerating those involved in them, these same men issued public invitations to the Polish population to attend victory celebrations and balls. Such balls are later described in the official newspapers as voluntary effusions of the limitless adoration in which the best and most merciful of monarchs is held by his subject peoples.

*None other than old Yermolov.*
Many people in Russia are convinced that the Tsar is able to send a *kibitka* to arrest any crowned head of Europe. Of course, we don't really know what sort of answer a Feldjäger would receive, were he sent out on such a mission. What is true is that Novosiltsov was fond of saying that "There will never be peace in Europe, until we impose such order throughout the continent, that one of our Feldjägers might perform in Paris and Istanbul the same duties he carries out in Vilnius, and with the same ease." Because of the great popularity of his name, the deposition of General Yermolov from the government of Georgia was universally seen as something more significant than any victory over any European kinglet. One ought not to be surprised at such opinions. We recall that during the combined Russian-Prussian siege of Danzig, His Royal Highness the Prince of Württemberg sent word to General Rapp, who was commanding the French garrison in the city, that a Russian general is equal in rank to any King, and might well bear such a title, if such were the wish of the Tsar (I cite General Rapp's journal).

*Treasures were poured out in a golden flood.*
So said Theodoric, the King of the Ostrogoths, upon beholding the Coliseum in Rome for the first time.

*The clock shows midday's already grown old; / The sun is now descending in the west.*

In wintertime, dusk falls around three o'clock in the afternoon in Petersburg.

*Always so close, yet when drawn near – it flies.*
The smoke ascending in wintertime over northern cities sometimes resolves itself into fantastic shapes similar to the *mirages* which deceive sailors on the high seas, and travellers over the desert sands of Arabia. The *mirage* now seems to be a city, now a village, now a lake or an oasis; the shapes it forms are quite realistic, but it is all only an illusion. They are unreal, and continue to recede before the traveller who tries to approach them, until they finally disappear.

*Torn from the ocean's wave and northern Finn.*
The Finns, known among the Russians as Chuchontsy or Chuchny, once lived along the banks of the muddy River Neva, where Petersburg was later founded.

*From distant lands, and the sea's bosom ripped.*
The story of the foundation and erection of Petersburg may be found in the works of many historians. It is well known that of the inhabitants of the area, some were chased from their homes, and others were impressed into the labours of construction, so that more than one hundred thousand perished during the building. Granite and marble were sent for from distant lands beyond the sea.

*Gathered [...] in one Peaceful Flock.*
Those denominations that split from the Catholic Church enjoy special protection in Russia. This is because, first of all, the faithful of these confessions often and easily convert to the Greek faith, following the example of many a German princess and prince; second, because the pastors of these sects constitute the strongest support of despotism, convincing their congregations to a blind obedience to civil authority, even in questions of faith, which Catholics refer to the Magisterium. It is also well known that, at the command of the Prussian King, the Augsburg and Genevan denominations united to form one Church.

*Thick smoking crowds, as if they're walking chimneys.*
The steam that arises from people's mouths during the bitterest cold forms columns, sometimes several ells in height.

*The Second Tsaritsa built this monument.*
Thus is written on the statue of Peter: *Petro primo Catharina secunda.*

*To humbly fall here, at her imperial throne.*
This line, literally *To fall here at Her feet imperial*, is translated from the verses of a Russian poet, whose name I cannot now recall.

*His road ends surely, at immortality!*
These are faithful descriptions of both the colossal equine statue of Peter, carved by Falconet, and the equine statue of Marcus Aurelius, which today stands on the Capitol at Rome.

*Guardsmen's chargers / Can be had for the price of a mere three souls.*
Russian cavalry horses are beautiful, and expensive. It's not unheard of to pay several thousand francs for one guardsman's horse. A grown man, of statutory size, can be bought for one thousand. During the famine in Belarus, a woman could be bought in Petersburg for two hundred francs. With shame I admit that certain Polish landholders in Belarus provided such goods for sale.

*Like a tarantula, when someone blows / A puff of air at her arachnid nose.*
Tarantulas, large, poisonous spiders, are native to the southern steppes of Russia and Poland.

*Beribboned, like mediaeval fools they ride.*
There exist around sixty Russian Orders (taking into account the various classes), so-called imperial cyphers and "buckles" indicating length of service. It is not unusual to see twenty honorary badges adorning one uniform.

*They neither waste nor wane.*
One royal official actually did put an end to his life, and for the simple reason that at an official court celebration he was directed to a lower place than his rank deserved. He was a true Vatel amongst *chinovniks.*

*His metronome's the whip.*
Cf. the portrait of the Tsarevich Aleksandr which hangs in the Hermitage in Petersburg. The English painter George Dawe has pictured him as a child, in a hussar's uniform, with whip in hand.

*Oleszkiewicz*
Józef Oleszkiewicz, a painter well known in Petersburg for his virtues, deep learning and mystical prophecies. Cf. his obituary in Petersburg newspapers from 1830.

# BIBLIOGRAPHY

**Primary Source Used for the Translation.**
MICKIEWICZ, Adam. *Dzieła poetyckie,* ed. S. Pigoń. Vol. III, *Utwory dramatyczne.* Warszawa: Czytelnik, 1983.

**Secondary Sources Referenced in the Introduction.**
ANONYMOUS. "Obituary — Adam Mickiewicz," in *The Gentleman's Review* (May, 1856), 45:537-540, p. 538a.

BOROWY, Wacław. *O poezji Mickiewicza.* Lublin: Towarzystwo Naukowe KUL, 1958.

CAMUS, Albert. *Actuelles III: chroniques algériennes 1939-1958.* Paris: Gallimard, 1994.

DZIEWULSKA, Małgorzata. *Artyści i pielgrzymi.* Wrocław: Wydawnictwo Dolnośląskie, 1995.

EVKDOKIMOV, Paul. *Prawosławie.* Warszawa: PAX, 1964.

FIUT, Aleksander, et. al. *Kompleks Konwicki: materiały z sesji naukowej zorganizowanej w dniach 27-29 października 2009 roku przez Wydział Zarządzania i Komunikacji Społecznej UJ oraz Wydział Polonistyki UJ.* Kraków: Universitas, 2010.

GŁĘBICKA-GIZA, Barbara. "'DOLINA ISSY', 'LAWA' i 'KRONIKA WYPADKÓW MIŁOSNYCH'. O autorskiej twórczości TADEUSZA KONWICKIEGO," in *Kwartalnik Filmowy* 44 (2002), 104.

GÓRSKI, Konrad Górski, *Racjonalizm i mistyka w Improwizacji Konrada*. Warszawa: [s.n.], 1922.

GROCHOWSKI, Piotr. *Dziady. Rzecz o wędrownych żebrakach i ich pieśniach*. Toruń: Wydawnictwo Naukowe Uniwersytetu Mikołaja Kopernika, 2009.

HULME, T. E. "Searchers After Reality: Haldane," in *New Age*, 19 August 1909, pp. 315-316.

KOROPECKYJ, Roman. *The Politics of Revitalization: Adam Mickiewicz between* Forefathers' Eve, Part 3 *and* Pan Tadeusz. Boulder: East European Monographs, 2001.

KOSIŃSKI, Dariusz, and LIMANOWSKI, Mieczysław. *Polski teatr przemiany*. Wrocław: Instytut im. Jerzego Grotowskiego, 2007.

KRASZEWSKI, Charles S. "Revenant Spirits in Slovak Folk Narrative Poems," *Kosmas*, XX (2007) 2:1-27.

KRASZEWSKI, Charles S. Romantic Hero and Contemporary Anti-Hero in Polish and Czech Literature: Great Souls and Grey Men. Lewiston/Queenston/Lampeter: The Edwin Mellen Press, 1997.

KURLANSKY, Mark. *1968: The Year that Rocked the World*. New York: Random House, 2005.

LUKAS, Katarzyna. "Der romantische Protagonist als Träger des katholischen Weltbildes. Über den IV. Teil des dramatischen Fragments Dziady von Adam Mickiewicz in deutschsprachigen Übersetzungen." *Studia Germanica Posnaniensia* XXX (2006): 5-33.

MICKIEWICZ, Adam Mickiewicz, *Dziady. Nowe wydanie zupełne*. Wrocław: H. Skutsch, 1864.

MIŁOSZ, Czesław. *The History of Polish Literature.* Berkeley: University of California Press, 1983.

OLSZEWSKA, Kinga. *Wanderers Across Language: Exile in Irish and Polish Literature of the Twentieth Century.* Oxford: Legenda, 2007.

PIGOŃ, Stanisław. *Formowanie* Dziadów części drugiej. Warszawa: Państwowy Instytut Wydawniczy, 1967.

POUND, Ezra. *ABC of Reading.* New York: New Directions, 1960.

POUND, Ezra. *The Spirit of Romance.* New York: New Directions, 2005.

PRAZ, Mario. *The Romantic Agony.* Oxford: Oxford University Press, 1970.

PRZYBOŚ, Julian Przyboś. *Czytając Mickiewicza.* Warszawa: Rytm, 1998.

ROMANSKA, Magda. *The Post-traumatic Theatre of Grotowski and Kantor: History and Holocaust in Akropolis and The Dead Class.* London: Anthem Press, 2012.

RYMKIEWICZ, Jarosław Marek. *Żmut.* Warszawa: Czytelnik, 1991.

SALATA, Kris. "O Homem Interior e sua Ação: Jerzy Grotowski e a herança de Adam Mickiewicz e do romantismo polonês." P*, *Revista Brasileira de Estudos da Presença* 3.1 (2013): 39-70.

STARZEC, Helena ed., et al. *Romantyzm: Literatura polska dla klasy II liceum ogólnokształcącego oraz techników i liceów zawodowych.* Warszawa: Wydawnictwo Szkolne i Pedagogiczne, 1974.

STEFANOWSKA, Zofia. *Próba zdrowego rozumu.* Warszawa: Państwowy Instytut Wydawniczy, 1976.

STOCK, Noel. *The Life of Ezra Pound.* New York: Avon, 1970.

SZELWACH, Grzegorz. *Listy Adama Mickiewicza (Lata 1817-1833).* New York: PIASA Books, 2006.

TARNOWSKI, Stanisław. *Historya literatury polskiej. Tom V: Wiek XIX, 1831-1850.* Kraków: Spółka wydawnicza polska, 1905.

WALC, Jan. *Architekt Arki.* Chotomów: Verba, 1991.

WITKOWSKA, Alina. *Literatura romantyzmu.* Warszawa: Państwowy Instytut Wydawniczy, 1987.

## ABOUT THE TRANSLATOR

**Charles S. Kraszewski** (b. 1962) is a poet, translator and literary critic. He has published three volumes of original verse: *Beast* (Alexandria, 2013), *Diet of Nails* (Boston, 2013) and *Chanameed* (Atlanta, 2015). Among his critical works is *Irresolute Heresiarch: Catholicism, Gnosticism and Paganism in the Poetry of Czesław Miłosz* (Newcastle-on-Tyne, 2012); many of his verse translations are collected in the volume *Rossetti's Armadillo* (Newcastle-on-Tyne, 2014). This translation of Adam Mickiewicz's *Forefathers' Eve* is the first complete verse translation of the cycle published in English. It has been exploited in its entirety by the Teatr Polski in Wrocław, and partially set to music by Arturas Bumšteinas in his contemporary orchestral work *Different Trains* (2014).

# CONTENTS

INTRODUCTION . . . . . . . . . . . . . . . . 5

FOREFATHERS' EVE, PART I . . . . . . . . . . . . . 127

FOREFATHERS' EVE, PART II . . . . . . . . . . . 145

FOREFATHERS' EVE, PART III . . . . . . . . . . . 171

FOREFATHERS' EVE, PASSAGES . . . . . . . . . . . 309

FOREFATHERS' EVE, PART IV . . . . . . . . . . . 345

THE POET'S EXPLANATORY NOTES TO PART III . . . . . 403

BIBLIOGRAPHY . . . . . . . . . . . . . . . . 409

ABOUT THE TRANSLATOR . . . . . . . . . . . . 413

Dear Reader,

Thank you for purchasing this book.

We at Glagoslav Publications are glad to welcome you, and hope that you find our books to be a source of knowledge and inspiration. We want to show the beauty and depth of the Slavic region to everyone looking to expand their horizon and learn something new about different cultures and different people, and we believe that with this book we have managed to do just that.

Now that you've gotten to know us, we want to get to know you. We value communication with our readers and want to hear from you! We offer several options:

– Join our Book Club on Goodreads, Library Thing and Shelfari, and receive special offers and information about our giveaways;

– Share your opinion about our books on Amazon, Barnes & Noble, Waterstones and other bookstores;

– Join us on Facebook and Twitter for updates on our publications and news about our authors;

– Visit our site www.glagoslav.com to check out our Catalogue and subscribe to our Newsletter.

Glagoslav Publications is getting ready to release a new collection and planning some interesting surprises — stay with us to find out more!

Glagoslav Publications<br>
Office 36, 88-90 Hatton Garden<br>
EC1N 8PN London, UK<br>
Tel: + 44 (0) 20 32 86 99 82<br>
Email: contact@glagoslav.com

Glagoslav Publications Catalogue

- The Time of Women by Elena Chizhova
- Sin by Zakhar Prilepin
- Hardly Ever Otherwise by Maria Matios
- Khatyn by Ales Adamovich
- Christened with Crosses by Eduard Kochergin
- The Vital Needs of the Dead by Igor Sakhnovsky
- A Poet and Bin Laden by Hamid Ismailov
- Kobzar by Taras Shevchenko
- White Shanghai by Elvira Baryakina
- The Stone Bridge by Alexander Terekhov
- King Stakh's Wild Hunt by Uladzimir Karatkevich
- Depeche Mode by Serhii Zhadan
- Herstories, An Anthology of New Ukrainian Women Prose Writers
- The Battle of the Sexes Russian Style by Nadezhda Ptushkina
- A Book Without Photographs by Sergey Shargunov
- Sankya by Zakhar Prilepin
- Wolf Messing by Tatiana Lungin
- Good Stalin by Victor Erofeyev
- Solar Plexus by Rustam Ibragimbekov
- Don't Call me a Victim! by Dina Yafasova
- A History of Belarus by Lubov Bazan
- Children's Fashion of the Russian Empire by Alexander Vasiliev
- Boris Yeltsin - The Decade that Shook the World by Boris Minaev
- A Man Of Change - A study of the political life of Boris Yeltsin
- Gnedich by Maria Rybakova
- Marina Tsvetaeva - The Essential Poetry
- Multiple Personalities by Tatyana Shcherbina
- The Investigator by Margarita Khemlin
- Leo Tolstoy – Flight from paradise by Pavel Basinsky
- Moscow in the 1930 by Natalia Gromova
- Prisoner by Anna Nemzer
- Alpine Ballad by Vasil Bykau
- The Complete Correspondence of Hryhory
- The Tale of Aypi by Ak Welsapar
- Selected Poems by Lydia Grigorieva
- The Fantastic Worlds of Yuri Vynnychuk
- The Garden of Divine Songs and Collected Poetry of Hryhory Skovoroda
- Adventures in the Slavic Kitchen: A Book of Essays with Recipes

More coming soon…

www.ingramcontent.com/pod-product-compliance
Lightning Source LLC
Chambersburg PA
CBHW031054080526
44587CB00011B/678